Literary Research: Strategies and Sources
Series Editors: Peggy Keeran & Jennifer Bowers

Every literary age presents scholars with both predictable and unique research challenges. This series fills a gap in the field of reference literature by featuring research strategies and by recommending the best tools for conducting specialized period and national literary research. Emphasizing research methodology, each series volume takes into account the unique challenges inherent in conducting research of that specific literary period and outlines the best practices for researching within it. Volumes place the research process within the period's historical context and use a narrative structure to analyze and compare print and electronic reference sources. Following an introduction to online searching, chapters typically will cover these types of resources: general literary reference materials; library catalogs; print and online bibliographies, indexes, and annual reviews; scholarly journals; contemporary reviews; period journals and newspapers; microform and digital collections; manuscripts and archives; and Web resources. Additional or alternative chapters may be included to highlight a particular research problem or to examine other pertinent period or national literary resources.

1. *Literary Research and the British Romantic Era* by Peggy Keeran and Jennifer Bowers, 2005.
2. *Literary Research and the Era of American Nationalism and Romanticism* by Angela Courtney, 2008.
3. *Literary Research and American Modernism* by Robert N. Matuozzi and Elizabeth B. Lindsay, 2008.
4. *Literary Research and the American Realism and Naturalism Period* by Linda L. Stein and Peter J. Lehu, 2009.
5. *Literary Research and Irish Literature* by J. Greg Matthews, 2009.

Literary Research and Irish Literature

Strategies and Sources

J. Greg Matthews

Literary Research: Strategies and Sources, No. 5

THE SCARECROW PRESS, INC.
Lanham, Maryland • Toronto • Plymouth, UK
2009

SCARECROW PRESS, INC.

Published in the United States of America
by Scarecrow Press, Inc.
A wholly owned subsidary of
The Rowman & Littlefield Publishing Group, Inc.
4501 Forbes Boulevard, Suite 200, Lanham, Maryland 20706
www.scarecrowpress.com

Estover Road
Plymouth PL6 7PY
United Kingdom

British Library Cataloguing in Publication Information Available

Library of Congress Cataloging-in-Publication Data

Matthews, J. Greg, 1968–
    Literary research and Irish literature : strategies and sources / J. Greg Matthews.
        p. cm. — (Literary research: strategies and sources ; no. 5)
    Includes bibliographical references and indexes.
    ISBN-13: 978-0-8108-6366-8 (pbk. : alk. paper)
    ISBN-10: 0-8108-6366-9 (pbk. : alk. paper)
    ISBN-13: 978-0-8108-6367-5 (ebook)
    ISBN-10: 0-8108-6367-7 (ebook)
    1. English literature—Irish authors—Research—Methodology. 2. Irish literature—
Research—Methodology. 3. Ireland—Literatures—Research—Methodology.
4. English literature—Irish authors—Information resources. 5. Irish literature—
Information resources. 6. Ireland—Literatures—Information resources. I. Title.
PR8711.M38 2009
820.9'9415072—dc22   2008029230

⊗™ The paper used in this publication meets the minimum requirements of American
National Standard for Information Sciences—Permanence of Paper for Printed Library
Materials, ANSI/NISO Z39.48-1992.
Manufactured in the United States of America.

Contents

Acknowledgments

Thanks to Martin Dillon at Scarecrow Press for his flexibility and for clarifying the finer points of the publishing process. Thanks also to Kellie Hagan, production editor, for helping to get this project onto the bookshelves.

Peggy Keeran and Jennifer Bowers deserve grateful recognition for their work as series editors as well as for the generous encouragement, patience, and guidance they have extended from beginning to end. Their expert input, particularly regarding reference resources and narrative continuity, vastly improved the present effort, and their enthusiasm sustained the project from its inception to its publication.

Several Washington State University Libraries colleagues, past and present, require mention here. First, thanks to all who asked how things were going from time to time. Thanks, too, to Amanda Cain for putting in an early good word. Former Dean of Libraries Ginny Steel supported this endeavor with her characteristic kindness, confidence, and leadership. Thanks to Head of Cataloging Lihong Zhu, Interim Dean of Libraries Cindy Kaag, and the WSU Provost's Office for supporting a special leave request. Lihong also deserves gratitude for her good cheer and for promoting scholarship in the Cataloging Department, where I am lucky to work with funny and gifted people. Thanks to Doug Lambeth, Glen Ames, Suzanne James-Bacon, and Susan Ferguson for their persistent good humor, and thanks to Daryl Herbison for years of insightful conversation and friendship. Thanks also to Bob Matuozzi for his encouragement to submit a proposal for this series and for sharing wisdom he gained co-authoring another volume in this series. Finally, Beth Lindsay made this project possible. From forwarding the call for proposals to making suggestions for final edits, her contributions to the project have been essential and inestimable.

Thanks to the members of the DMBz Wargames Club, especially the Painting Night regulars. Their curiosity about this endeavor was heartening, and their relentless, good-natured shenanigans continue to offer laughter and perspective.

Other close friends and family played crucial roles in this process as well. Thanks to Rick, Anna, Aric, and Jack Fehrenbacher and Al, Nik, Cole, and Sam Wildey, who have offered years of ceaseless friendship, support, and encouragement. Richard Tyson kept in touch no matter where in the world he happened to be. His gifts for conversation and zeal for learning are inspirational. To the friend who has known me longer than any other, Rachel Ruggeri, I owe inexpressible gratitude. She and her family have always treated me as one of their own, and their support has been unconditional. Likewise, Doug and Bobbie Matthews and Amy Gonzalez, my dad, mom, and sister, have always lovingly fostered my ambitions and hopes. Their excitement for this book has given me more than a few incentives to finish it.

Jackson Q. Matthews, an extraordinary person and talented librarian, deserves thanks every day for her remarkable selflessness and reasonableness. She is always eager to help, and her creative and optimistic influence assures that this book contains at least a few good ideas.

Finally, I would like to thank two extraordinary teachers and mentors, Professor John F. Desmond and Professor Irvin Y. Hashimoto. Lessons they taught and the decency with which they conducted themselves in and out of the classroom continue to impress, delight, and instruct almost twenty years later. With thanks, I respectfully dedicate this book to them.

The errors, omissions, and limitations present in this volume are my own.

Introduction

Approaching the study of a literary age or a national literature presents scholars with both predictable and unique research challenges. Librarians work with literary scholars to anticipate these challenges by helping them to locate and use standard and specialized reference tools for the purpose of identifying viable primary and secondary sources that can add value to research projects. The goal of this volume, along with others published in the *Literary Research: Sources and Strategies* series, is to describe some of the best practices for researching Irish literature and to address some of the challenges scholars may face working in such a vast and evolving subject area. Scholars who possess a working knowledge of standard resources and who have been trained to employ reliable research practices are equipped to solve questions that can be resolved by routine procedures as well as more esoteric issues that may require consultation with librarians. In addition to learning effective research skills, this book aims to provide information that places the research process into larger scholarly and historical contexts by taking into account how the changing critical settings in which Irish literature has been defined, discussed, and published influence and complicate today's research environment.

This guide focuses on Irish literature, which presents intriguing challenges to both scholars and librarians. On a fundamental level, the issue of defining what Irish literature is remains open to debate. Given the potentially broad historical, political, and cultural parameters within which to broach the topic, the present volume treats authors and works that many scholars may reject as not Irish, as well as representative Anglo-Irish literature and writers. In addition, Irish Gaelic authors, works, and resources are also covered, as are foreign-language literature originating in Ireland, such as Latin works produced during the Middle Ages. This book seeks to be inclusive in the interests of avoiding arbitrary limitations as well as to raise and consider some of the compelling issues that Irish literary scholars may face.

Attempting a survey of the reference material available to the researcher of Irish literature reveals that some areas have and continue to receive widespread critical attention while other matters remain underrepresented in the scholarly record. Works devoted to the lives and works of Yeats, Joyce, and Beckett, for example, far outnumber those treating influential writers such as Lady Gregory, Edna O'Brien, and Medbh McGuckian. Likewise, canonical Anglo-Irish writers, Jonathan Swift, Maria Edgeworth, Oscar Wilde, and Bernard Shaw among them, have been widely studied, while their Irish connections are subject to continuing critical scrutiny. By and large, research on male authors and their work is more readily available than criticism concerned with women writers, a situation that is common in most literary research contexts. As a result, researchers of canonical figures will find overwhelming amounts of scholarship published on well-known authors, including websites devoted to their works and academic studies about their lives, relationships, and the times in which they lived. On the other hand, information about lesser-known and women authors may be limited to essays and remarks published in general works or studies narrowly devoted to a particular group of writers or a specific time period. An obvious conclusion to draw from such evidence is that it is easier to find information about widely studied authors and works than it is to locate criticism about writers and works considered minor. In turn, this research environment corresponds to certain historical and cultural values that have shaped the ways researchers have approached, thought about, and commented upon Irish literature.

While a keyword search for "Yeats" in the *MLA International Bibliography* will retrieve hundreds of records, a search for Deirdre Madden or Dorothy Nelson will result in less than ten hits each. How does a scholar identify relevant materials when finding too many or too few citations? Beyond *MLAIB* and the library catalog, what other sources exist to help the researcher locate as much viable information as possible? Which resources help identify authors, works, scholarly journals, periodicals, newspapers, and essays relevant to the study of Irish literature? When indexes are not available, what techniques can scholars use to find articles by topic within periodicals and newspapers? How can researchers identify pertinent manuscript and archival collections? What were the reputations of various authors during their lifetimes, and how has critical reception and understanding of their work changed through the years? Which journals and magazines have and continue to review their writing and what are the potential biases (e.g., literary, political, social) of these publications? Who are the audiences of these sources? How can scholars delineate the cultural and political influences that permit or discourage particular types of literary output? How can researchers gain an understanding of contemporary views of particular literary genres and forms, such as stream-of-consciousness fiction and Modernist poetry, during the times in which these types of literature flourished or were widely practiced and published? Finally, how do issues such as these affect Irish literary research? These are only a few of the questions addressed in this guide.

As previously stated, this book's scope is wide. It attempts to discuss the primary and secondary research resources available, and specifically directs advice to the scholar of Irish literature. While this volume provides clues for identifying relevant items, the materials treated in its pages vary in quality and application, and so illustrate the disparate and inchoate character of the field itself. The sources discussed include: general research guides; union library catalogs; print and online bibliographies; manuscripts and archives; microfilm and digitization projects; scholarly journals, periodicals, and newspapers; contemporary and current reviews; and electronic texts, journals, and Web resources. Some of these resources address topics and subjects that may exceed authors, works, and themes relevant to Irish literary studies, while others specifically deal with Irish literature. Each chapter addresses examples of both kinds of research tools, and offers insights on how researchers can best use them to extract relevant information. When applicable, chapters examine how the creation, storage, and retrieval of electronic information have enriched literary research in general, as well as scholarly work in Irish literature.

Although concerned with covering scholarly resources, research methodology is the central concept of this guide. Indeed, sound searching skills are crucial to the success of scholars in search of relevant materials. Without them, researchers can waste valuable time and effort designated for reading and integrating research materials into a scholarly work simply figuring out how to use a reference tool. This volume emphasizes the processes that enable scholars to become effective researchers. In addition, it covers search strategies as well as the evaluation and comparison of sources to better serve scholars who may be familiar with one or two basic electronic resources, but who do not often take full advantage of these sources, or even realize that there may be more appropriate resources available for their purposes. Chapters examine core and specialized print and electronic research tools and standard search techniques, go over strengths and weaknesses of each, and suggest how various tools relate to one another.

Though organized and written as a narrative intended to provide overall coherence to the research process, readers can also use this book as a descriptive guide to recommended reference tools. Of course, by the time this work is published, new resources will surely be available to scholars of Irish literature. Still, researchers who avail themselves of and apply knowledge of various Irish literary contexts, the reference sources used to access them, and the search techniques to make the research process as effective and rewarding as possible, will succeed in the use of their chosen tools as well as build a sturdy foundation of primary and secondary evidence upon which to support their research.

Chapter One

Basics of Online Searching

One of the cornerstones of solid research is a strong understanding of online searching fundamentals. We live in an era in which more and more information is available online, and the gulf between credible, critically researched and organized information and online data posted to the Internet without attribution, source, or citation widens day by day. Complicating this volatile research scenario is the design and function of Internet search engines and research databases, resources which sometimes appear similar but offer services unique from one another and sometimes yield widely divergent results for researchers. Increasingly, researchers—those with experience as well as novices—assume that search strategies that work well in Internet search engines are equally successful in online research databases. Yet, many search engines and databases process commands in different ways, in addition to providing diverse kinds of information for the researcher. Fortunately, mastering practical search strategies will enable the scholar of Irish literature to search consistently across various online resources, both online research databases as well as Internet resources. This chapter describes basic online search strategies and shows how to use them in a variety of online research platforms.

STEP 1: WRITE A RESEARCH
QUESTION AS A TOPIC SENTENCE

Before beginning to conduct online research, writing down a research question as a topic sentence will help the researcher define core ideas and concepts relevant to her research project. These ideas and concepts will then provide the basis for developing search strategies for credible scholarly sources. If one is interested in researching Yeats' influence on American poetry, for example, a possible topic sentence might read: "I want to explore the influence of Yeats' poetry on American poetry." Main concepts here are *influence, Yeats' poetry* and *American poetry*. You may be interested in a broader topic, such as "The figure of the mother in 20th century Irish literature." Here, *mother*, *20th century*, and *Irish literature* are main concepts.

STEP 2: BRAINSTORM KEYWORDS

A researcher can use the main concepts identified in a topic sentence to think of additional keywords that will be useful in a search for relevant resources. Keywords suggest other ways to think about and describe a topic, as well as provide the researcher with other search terms in the event that preliminary searches are unsuccessful. In the topic sentence about Yeats' poetry, for example, *influence* is an idea that may be too vague as a keyword. On the other hand, *Yeats' poetry* can be qualified by terms such as *Yeats' early* or *late poetry*, and *American poetry* can be narrowed by terms such as *postmodern* and *symbolist American poetry*. While the second topic sentence is wider in scope, thinking of keywords related to the core ideas further expands the selection of search terms. In addition to *mother*, for example, one could consider *motherhood* and *mothers and children* as related keywords. Likewise, *20th century Irish literature* might also appear as *modern Irish literature* in the catalog. *Irish literature* easily suggests many forms and genres: *Irish fiction, Irish drama, Irish poetry*, and *the Irish novel*, not to mention *Irish mythology* and *Irish folklore*. Generally, asking what a topic sentence means—Yeats' early or late poetry? The figure of the mother in what kinds of Irish literary work(s)?— is an excellent way to generate keywords for searching.

Once a researcher has a list of keywords, she can create a table of concepts that will help her visualize the brainstorming process. In table 1.1, topic sentence concepts appear at the top of the table and related terms are listed underneath.

Table 1.1.   Possible keywords for searching topic "The figure of the mother in 20th century Irish literature."

Concept #1	Concept #2	Concept #3
mother	Irish literature	modern
motherhood	Irish fiction	20th century
mothers and children	Irish drama	contemporary
	Irish poetry	postmodern

STEP 3: STRUCTURE OF ELECTRONIC RECORDS: MARC RECORDS IN ONLINE CATALOGS

As suggested above, the scholar of Irish literature has many online research tools at her disposal. Search engines, for example, retrieve information from databases by means of criteria that identify and extract records that seem relevant based on search terms, which commonly consist of titles, creators, or keywords. Step 4 will focus on search strategies. The present section explores some of the intricacies of database record structure, specifically MARC record structure, to illustrate the logical connections between search strategies and search results.

One of the fundamental tools of scholarship is the online library catalog. Online catalogs, commonly referred to as OPACs (Online Public Access Catalogs), combine features of search engines and databases and allow researchers to retrieve information about resources such as books, journals, and electronic resources, and sometimes provide access to resources themselves, such as digitized materials and electronic journals. The formal term for an OPAC record is the MARC (MAchine Readable Cataloging) record, a standard cataloging data format developed by the Library of Congress in the 1960s. Because MARC is a standard format, libraries are able to contract with a variety of commercial library software vendors, such as SirsiDynix and Innovative Interfaces, to integrate library data for cataloging, organization, and access through a Web-based interface. Using this integrated software, library professionals catalog materials by creating descriptions of them in MARC format. MARC coding allows the software to organize data in MARC records into indexes. Finally, these indexes provide access to data cataloged in a MARC record by means of a Web-based interface. This interface is the front end of the catalog that library patrons see and use when they search for resources. Generally, library catalog interfaces provide several search options that correspond to indexes based on MARC data, such as author, title, subject, and keyword searches, as well as indexes that allow patrons to search exclusively for specific kinds of materials, such as DVDs or periodicals. To illustrate how indexes available from the search interface of a library catalog correspond to MARC data, we will examine two cataloging records. The first record describes a periodical, the second a book.

MARC records are hierarchical in nature. MARC cataloging divides each part of the bibliographic record into fields and subfields. Individual fields are assigned three-digit numeric tags that the search engine uses to retrieve records from a specific index. Libraries decide which indexes they will provide for patrons and then create these indexes based on MARC fields with their integrated software. If a library, for example, decides to create an index that will allow patrons to search for only periodicals by title, then MARC tag 222, which identifies bibliographic records as periodical records, may be included in the search criteria for a periodical title index. Figure 1.1 highlights some of the features of a MARC record that describes a periodical, *Éire-Ireland*. If a library owns a title and has decided to include MARC field 222 in its periodical title index, then a researcher conducting a periodical title search for a particular journal will find a record describing it in the catalog.

Figure 1.2 is a modified MARC record for Margot Gayle Backus' book *The Gothic Family Romance: Heterosexuality, Child Sacrifice, and the Anglo-Irish Colonial Order* and illustrates other MARC fields that libraries can use as criteria for search indexes. Tag 245, for example, specifies the MARC field for monograph titles. If a library owns this book and creates a title index that includes the 245 field, patrons searching for this book by title will find a record for it in the library catalog. The library can create search indexes based on other fields in this record as well. The 100 tag indicates the author, while the 020 tag designates the International Standard Book Number (ISBN). The 260 field describes where the book was published, by whom, and when, and the 650 fields contain Library of Congress subject headings. Libraries can create indexes based on each one of these MARC tags, which allow researchers to search catalogs specifically by author, ISBN, publisher, or subject. Such narrow searches are most useful in the advanced stages of the research process. When starting a research project, however, keyword searches are the most flexible, and allow library users to search multiple MARC tags in combination. For example, a library could include 100, 245, 260, and 650 tags in a keyword searching index, which would enable one to search for *backus*, *anglo-irish*, and *duke university press* simultaneously in the author, title, publisher, and subject fields.

```
001   1567683
010   sn 87012955 |z78002498
210 0 Éire-Irel. |b (St.Paul)
222 0 Éire-Ireland |b(St. Paul)
245 00 Éire-Ireland: |ba journal of Irish studies.
260   St. Paul, |b Irish American Cultural Institute.
362 0 v. 1-  spring 1965/66-
710 2 Irish American Cultural Institute.
```

Figure 1.1.   Modified MARC record for *Éire-Ireland*, with tag 222 highlighted. Source: Washington State University Libraries, Griffin catalog.

```
001   41049488
010   99020689
020   082232380X (cloth : alk. paper)
020   0822324148 (paper : alk. paper)
043   e-ie---
049   NTEA
050 00 PR8807.F25|bB33 1999
082 00 823.009/355|221
100 1  Backus, Margot Gayle,|d1961-
245 14 The Gothic family romance :|bheterosexuality, child sacrifice, and the Anglo-Irish
       colonial order /|cMargot Gayle Backus.
260    Durham [N.C.] :|bDuke University Press,|c1999.
300    xi, 291 p. ;|c24 cm.
440  0 Post-contemporary interventions.
504    Includes bibliographical references (p. [267]-277) and index.
650  0 English fiction|xIrish authors|xHistory and criticism.
650  0 Family in literature.
650  0 Psychological fiction, English|xHistory and criticism.
650  0 Domestic fiction, English|xHistory and criticism.
650  0 Capitalism and literature|zIreland|xHistory.
650  0 Repression (Psychology) in literature.
650  0 Gothic revival (Literature)|zIreland.
650  0 Parent and child in literature.
650  0 Heterosexuality in literature.
650  0 Imperialism in literature.
650  0 British|zIreland|xHistory.
650  0 Colonies in literature.
```

Figure 1.2. Modified *MARC* record for *The Gothic Family Romance: Heterosexuality, Child Sacrifice, and the Anglo-Irish Colonial Order*, with tags 100, 245, 260, and 650s highlighted. Source: Washington State University Libraries, Griffin catalog.

This brief discussion of MARC records highlights the mechanics of record location and retrieval during an OPAC search. By understanding how search engines use indexes to match a researcher's search terms with data tagged in MARC records, it becomes easier to use established search strategies to retrieve relevant sources. It is not necessary to remember the specifics of MARC coding in order to use the catalog. After all, most OPAC interfaces do not show MARC tags in front-end record displays. Still, understanding how search engines retrieve records informs the researcher's ability to choose the most effective search strategies in various research scenarios.

STEP 4: CREATING SEARCH STRATEGIES

Field Searching

The previous section summarizes how libraries create different indexes designed to search for fields in a MARC record. For example, indexes common in many library catalogs allow patrons to search for specific authors and titles. Searching a catalog by means of these specific indexes is called *field searching*, which enables researchers to focus on a particular piece of information contained in the record. For example, the 260 field in figure 1.2 features three pieces of information—the place of publication, the publisher, and year of publication—all of which are searchable. While search engines vary from one library to another, the MARC record is a standard format used in most library catalogs, and almost any MARC field, including author, title, subject, publication type, publication date, or language, is searchable. Most field searches are necessarily narrow in scope and limit the search to specific parts of a record. Searching by *keyword*, on the other hand, allows one to search several fields at once. Many library catalogs provide keyword searching as a default searching option because it has the potential to retrieve almost any piece of information contained in a record. Not all library search engines are set up to retrieve the same information, however, so search results may vary between catalogs for the same search.

Boolean Searches

Just as MARC records are standard components of virtually all online catalogs, most searchable online databases use some form of Boolean logic to facilitate the retrieval of relevant information during keyword searches. Yet databases that use strict Boolean operators to retrieve records often fail to return any results during typical keyword searches consisting of a string of terms. Understanding how Boolean operators work will help explain this phenomenon, as well as strengthen your own searching skills.

George Boole, a nineteenth-century British philosopher and mathematician, is the namesake of Boolean logic and Boolean operators. Boolean logic describes the relationships and operations between sets, and has subsequently provided the foundation for modern computer design as well as for data retrieval. Essentially, Boolean operators define relationships between concepts. Online databases typically use three operators for searching: *and*, *or*, and *not*. Above, Step 2 already touched on the idea of Boolean logic and operators to narrow, broaden, or exclude concepts from searches. A more detailed discussion of Boolean concepts follows.

Boolean Operator "And"

And narrows the search. Table 1.1 in Step 2 shows how the term *and* narrows a search. Here, *and* connects separate concepts of the topic described by keywords:

*mother **and** Irish literature **and** modern*

If a researcher typed this string of keywords connected by Boolean operators into an online bibliographic database requiring Boolean logic, she would receive a list of records containing all of these terms. Boolean searches are often illustrated as diagrams to show how concepts are combined with operators. Figure 1.3 provides an example.

The three concepts overlap in the shaded area of the diagram. This shaded portion represents what the search engine attempts to locate and retrieve from the database: the nexus where three separate concepts connect. All three concepts, expressed in the search as keywords connected by operators, must occur in a single record in order for the search to retrieve a record relevant to the search.

Figure 1.4 is an example of a record retrieved from the *MLA International Bibliography* (*MLAIB*) database using the above keyword search. Keywords are in bold and in italics to indicate where the search engine located the keywords: in the source and subject fields.

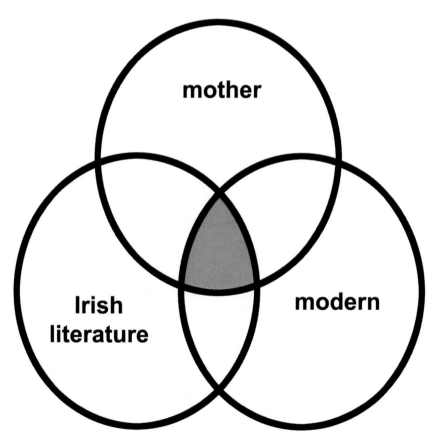

Figure 1.3.   Boolean *and* search.

Herren, Graley. "Splitting Images: Samuel Beckett's Nacht und Träume." *Modern Drama*, 43:2 (2000 Summer), pp. 182-91.

Subject Terms:	*Irish literature*; 1900-1999; Beckett, Samuel (1906-1989): Nacht und Träume; drama; treatment of desire; *mother*; Christian iconography; relationship to Veronica, Saint; theories of Kuryluk, Ewa (1946-); Veronica and Her Cloth (1991).
	French literature; 1900-1999; Beckett, Samuel (1906-1989); Nacht und Träume; drama; treatment of desire; *mother*; Christian iconography; relationship to Veronica, Saint; theories of Kuryluk, Ewa (1946-); Veronica and Her Cloth (1991).
Language:	English

Figure 1.4.   Modified record retrieved from *MLAIB* using Boolean *and* to combine separate concepts. Source: *MLAIB*, via InfoTrac.

Boolean Operator "Or"

Or broadens the search. In table 1.1, each concept has several related keywords. If a researcher connects those keywords to each other with the operator *or*, all of them will be searched simultaneously:

Irish fiction **or** *Irish drama* **or** *Irish poetry*

A library catalog that uses Boolean operators will retrieve all records in which any one of these terms appears during a keyword search. Figure 1.5 illustrates this idea.

Boolean Operator "Not"

Not excludes unwanted concepts from the search. Researchers sometimes find that concepts irrelevant to their topic keep appearing in search results. During a search for *colonial*, for example, the search engine returns several records describing sources about *post-colonial* themes. Boolean logic allows one to exclude unwanted topics by means of the *not* operator.

colonial **not** *post-colonial*

Separating *colonial* from the modifier *post* will eliminate from the search citations that include the concept *post-colonial*. *Not* can be a problematic operator, however. While it efficiently excludes records that contain unwanted concepts, it can also block potentially relevant records from database searches, such as a book that covers both colonial and post-colonial literatures.

Figure 1.5. Boolean *or* search.

Truncation/Wildcards

Most databases utilize several symbols to allow researchers to customize searches in various ways. Many search engines, for example, allow users to find the stems of keywords with variant endings by means of truncation symbols such as *, #, !, or ?. Truncation and wildcard options are not necessarily consistent between databases. Fortunately, help menus and advanced searching documentation in most databases describe which truncation symbols can be used and for what purposes. A truncation symbol commonly used in many search engines and databases is the asterisk (*). If a researcher truncates the concept *mother** in the *MLAIB*, for example, she will retrieve records that include concepts such as *mothers*, *motherhood*, *mothering* and *mother-daughter relations*.

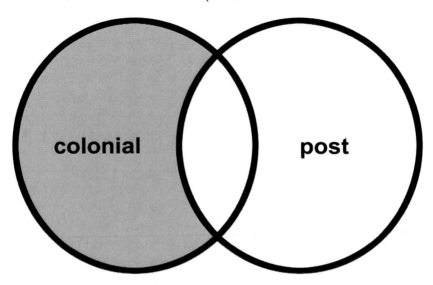

Figure 1.6.   Boolean *not* search.

Truncating search terms is a useful but limited searching strategy. Terms that are too truncated retrieve many unwanted search results. Truncating *modern* to *mod**, for example, retrieves an impressive list of concepts, including *modern*, *modernism*, and *modesty*. The longer term *modern** is a more effectively truncated search term because it limits results to records that include *modern*, *modernism*, and *modernity* as relevant concepts.

Wildcard symbols are basically truncation symbols that can be used within a search term to find singular and plural forms of words. Inputting *wom?n* into a search engine, for example, will retrieve records containing *woman*, *women*, and *womyn*. Again, the help features in most databases will explain truncation and wildcard symbols and how to use them.

Nesting

Nesting is a search strategy that combines complex Boolean operator and truncation searches. In a nested search, similar concepts are grouped together with parentheses. Nested search terms cue the database to search first for content within parentheses, followed by a search for remaining terms in the search string, from left to right. Because this strategy prioritizes concepts for the search engine, nesting provides more sophisticated searching options for the scholar. For example, using keywords from Concept #2 in table 1.1, a researcher can conduct the following searches separately:

mother **and** modern* **and** Irish fiction*
mother **and** modern* **and** Irish drama*
mother **and** modern* **and** Irish poetry*

Nesting, on the other hand, allows one to group together keywords listed under a single concept:

mother **and** modern* **and** (Irish fiction **or** Irish drama **or** Irish poetry)*

Because they eliminate duplicate results, nested searches provide a more efficient alternative to the individual searches listed above.

Phrase Searching/Proximity Operators

Previous sections in this chapter have touched on the idea that search engines and databases are separate technologies that work together to fulfill searches. This section explores this idea in more depth, and in so doing, addresses some complex searching issues. It is important to emphasize the idea that search engines determine how to retrieve the content of a database. It is also important to emphasize that the structure of a record in a database determines whether or not the record can be retrieved by means of the search terms entered by a researcher. Searching for sources about the author W. B. Yeats, also known as William Butler Yeats, illustrates how search engines interact with databases, as well as how search terms interact with database records. *Yeats, W. B. (William Butler), 1865*–1939 is the Library of Congress subject heading for this author. The rest of this section reviews how entering different searches for this author will affect the list of results retrieved.

When a phrase represents a research concept, researchers can consult help screens to see if a database allows or recommends phrase or proximity searching for record retrieval. Some search engines require searchers to place quotation marks around a phrase in order to prompt the system to retrieve terms that occur next to each other: "*Irish troubles*," for example. Other search engines require proximity operators to retrieve adjacent terms: *Irish w troubles*.

The *WorldCat* database, discussed at greater length in chapter 3, uses the *FirstSearch* interface as its search engine. To repeat the opening point of this section, *WorldCat* and *FirstSearch* are separate technologies that work together to fulfill searches. Basically, *WorldCat* provides content in the form of database records, and *FirstSearch* searches for and retrieves records relevant to a search. *FirstSearch* is a versatile search engine that allows researchers to use either proximity operators or quotation marks in search phrases. If

phrases are not distinguished by means of either proximity operators or quotation marks, the search engine conducts a keyword search by default, and automatically connects the words in the search phrase with the Boolean operator *and* to retrieve records containing the search terms (table 1.2 below).

While the *FirstSearch* search engine allows researchers to use quotation
marks in phrase searches ("william yeats," for example), phrase searching is
not always effective. Using proximity operators, on the other hand, provides
for more flexible relationships between search terms. As a result, proximity
searches are often more successful than phrase searches. The *FirstSearch*
search engine uses the following proximity operators in the *WorldCat* database:

w   *with*—operator used to indicate required word order; *wn* (in which *n*
       refers to number) indicates the number of words between the words
       searched: *william w2 yeats*.
n   *near*—operator used to indicate flexible word order; *nn* (in which *n*
       again refers to a number) indicates the number of words between the
       words searched: *william n2 yeats*.

Table 1.2 shows results the *FirstSearch* search engine retrieves from *World-
Cat* based on various search strategies.

• The last search for *william yeats* returns the largest set of results because
  the *FirstSearch* search engine separately searches the terms in the database.
  This search strategy often yields records that are "false drops," records in
  which both search terms occur but do not refer to William Yeats. This
  search, for example, retrieved a record describing the book *Friends and the
  Vietnam War: Papers and Presentations from a Pendle Hill Conference,
  Bryn Mawr College, Pennsylvania, July 16–20, 1998*, which includes contributions from William A. Eagles and Liz Yeats.

Table 1.2.   Search strategies and records retrieved by *FirstSearch* in *WorldCat*

Search Strategy	Retrieves	Number of Results
"william yeats"	william yeats	21
william w2 yeats	william yeats william butler yeats	2101
william n2 yeats	william yeats william butler yeats yeats, w. b. (william butler)	2382
william yeats	william and yeats	7932

- The first search for *"william yeats"* returns the smallest set of results because it restricts the search engine to records in which the names occur next to each other in that specific order.
- The second search for *william w2 yeats* enables the search engine to retrieve records that include both *William Yeats* and *William Butler Yeats*, but excludes records in which the author's last name precedes other parts of the name. So records that only contain the Library of Congress subject heading *Yeats, W. B. (William Butler)* are excluded from this search.
- Of the four search strategies summarized above, the third search for *william n2 yeats* is the most flexible because it prompts the search engine to retrieve records in which the author's first and last names occur in any order, whether the last name proceeds the first or vice versa. Also, the middle name may or may not occur in any of the records retrieved. While false drops are possible when using the *n* proximity indicator in a search, this strategy does allow for flexible yet focused searching.

Subject versus Keyword Searches

Among both experienced and novice researchers, "subject" and "keyword" are often used interchangeably to describe any term employed in searching. Subject headings, however, are very different from keywords. Namely, *subject headings* or *descriptors* refer to controlled terms or controlled vocabulary used to describe sources that share common topics. *Keywords*, on the other hand, refer to search terms devised by researchers to locate resources relevant to their interests. Subject headings allow for the standardization of information in database records, while keywords allow researchers to see whether or not, as well as how and where, their search terms occur in database records.

Conducting keyword searches is an effective way to discover subject headings. Once a researcher has found relevant citations, she can review records to see which subject headings have been used to describe her sources. The previous section mentions Library of Congress subject headings, which are the most widely used subject headings in library catalogs. Subject headings established by the Library of Congress are also used in other databases such as *WorldCat*. The printed lists of the *Library of Congress Subject Headings*, also commonly referred to as the *LCSH*, are available as a multi-volume set in the reference departments of most academic libraries, which the Library of Congress revises and updates almost annually.

According to the latest edition of the *LCSH*, the Library of Congress subject heading for the Irish author William Yeats is *Yeats, W. B. (William Butler), 1865–1939*. This heading appears in records that describe sources which have William Yeats as a core subject. LC subject headings are very useful research tools because they provide library catalogs and many databases with standardized search terms and vocabulary. This standardization also enables researchers to refine search terms and retrieve relevant resources more efficiently. For example, if a scholar has been trying to find resources about mother figures in Irish literature by means of keyword searches, the task becomes simpler when the search engine retrieves a record with relevant subject headings. Figure 1.7 is an example of a library catalog record for the book *The Importance of Being Paradoxical: Maternal Presence in the Works of Oscar Wilde* by Patrick M. Horan, which was retrieved with a keyword search for *mother* and irish* and literature**.

Library of Congress subject headings are in bold to highlight additional terms that one can search as keywords: *Mothers, Motherhood in literature*, and *Authors, Irish - - Mothers*. While it is difficult to point to a single subject heading as the most relevant to this search, these subject headings can be combined with others to create relevant subjects for searching. *Authors, Irish -- Mothers*, for example, is a potentially viable subject search relevant to the research topic. In addition, most Web-based library catalogs actively link subject headings to other records. Users simply click on a subject heading to access a list of records that contain the same subject heading from the collection.

As previously mentioned, library catalogs are not the only databases that use controlled terms and vocabulary. Not all databases use the same controlled language, however. Many databases create unique thesauri for assigning subject headings. The *MLAIB* is a notable example of a database that has its own subject thesaurus (see the "subject terms" in figure 1.4 above). Whenever a researcher finds a relevant citation in a database, it is useful to notice which subject terms or descriptors that database uses to describe a topic. If

Author	Horan, Patrick M., 1958-
Title	**The importance of being paradoxical : maternal presence in the works of Oscar Wilde / Patrick M. Horan.**
	Imprint Madison, NJ : Fairleigh Dickinson University Press ; London ; Cranbury, NJ : Associated University Presses, c1997.
Description	144 p. ; 24 cm.
Subject	Wilde, Oscar, 1854-1900 -- Characters -- **Mothers**.
	Wilde, Oscar, 1854-1900 -- Family.
	Wilde, Lady, 1826-1896 -- Family.
	Motherhood in **literature**.
	Authors, **Irish** -- **Mothers**.
	Paradox in **literature**.
	Mothers in **literature**.

Figure 1.7.   Modified catalog record with Library of Congress subject headings used to describe *The Importance of Being Paradoxical*. Source: Washington State University Libraries, Griffin catalog.

the subject headings accurately describe the topic, then the researcher can focus on these terms and continue subject searching in the database. While subject headings relevant in one database may be less useful in other databases, relevant subject headings from a variety of sources can always be searched as keywords in multiple databases.

Relevancy Searching

Search engines display results in a number of ways: alphabetically by author or title, by publication date, or by relevancy ranking. Relevancy ranking varies from one search engine to another, but all search engines rank relevancy by means of a formula that organizes results based upon selected criteria. Basically, search engines rank and display results according to criteria that place the most relevant results at the beginning of the list. Relevancy criteria include:

- the presence of all or some keywords in a record
- the number of occurrences of the words searched (results are ranked higher the more frequently the search terms appear in the record)
- the proximity of search terms to each other (the closer words are to each other, the higher the result is ranked)
- the location of the terms within a record (search terms present in a primary field such as title or subject/descriptor, in an abstract, or near the beginning of a document)

Users can often choose to activate or deactivate relevancy searching, especially in subscription-based search engines. Database help screens describe whether or not relevancy ranking is the default display mode, as well as how to active or deactivate this option in a database. While relevancy searching is a familiar method of information retrieval, especially using Internet search engines such as *Google*, its usefulness as a reliable research strategy is debatable because it emphasizes quantity of results over quality of results. While relevancy searching usually returns large sets of results, these results are not necessarily relevant to the research project, especially when results feature only one keyword that has been frequently searched or located in the primary fields of a number of records.

Limiting/Modifying Searches

Limiting or modifying searches allows researchers to sort a set of search results according to specific characteristics. In many library catalogs and databases, the option to limit results appears as a link within the search results display screen. Users can typically narrow their searches by language, material type (e.g., book, serial, DVD, CD, electronic, dissertation), year(s), publisher, place of publication, or location within a library system. *Google* searchers can limit to a specific domain, such as *.com*, *.org*, or *.edu*.

STEP 5: DATABASES VERSUS SEARCH ENGINES

Having brainstormed terms and acquired a working knowledge of Boolean logic and truncation, a researcher possesses the tools to develop and refine an online search strategy. Again, a fundamental point to remember about online searching is that databases contain content, and the interfaces used to access databases provide search engines. The Modern Language Association (MLA), for example, creates the content of the *MLAIB* database (discussed in chapter 4). Several search engine vendors, such as *EBSCOhost*, *Gale*, *OCLC*, and *SilverPlatter*, have created search engines such as *FirstSearch* and *InfoTrac* to access this content. Some libraries offer users more than one search engine for searching individual databases, but each search engine is unique. Table 1.3 lists some literary research databases and the search engines that provide access to them.

Search engines possess different capabilities and functions, and it is not always obvious how any given search engine conducts a database search. Database help screens and FAQs describe how search engines retrieve content and how to customize searches. As they review this information, researchers might ask themselves some helpful questions:

Table 1.3   Databases and search engines.

DATABASE Contains Content	SEARCH ENGINE Provides Access to Content
MLAIB	EBSCO FirstSearch (OCLC) InfoTrac (Gale) CSA
WorldCat English Short Title Catalogue Poole's Index to Periodical Literature	FirstSearch (OCLC) Eureka (RLG) Paratext C19
ABELL	Chadwyck-Healy/Proquest

- Does the search engine require the Boolean operator *and* to connect separate concepts?
- Does the search engine require Boolean operators to be typed in uppercase characters?
- Does the search engine allow for truncation? What is the truncation symbol?
- What internal wildcard symbol does the search engine use?
- Does the search engine require quotation marks for phrase searching? Are proximity operators required?
- Does the search engine allow users to limit searches by language, material type, date of publication, or location?
- How does the search engine display results? By author? Title? Date?
- Does the search engine display results by relevance? If so, what are the ranking criteria?

It is helpful to keep in mind that databases are dynamic, evolving resources; database vendors continuously update content. Search engines also evolve over time, and researchers can keep current with a search engine's capabilities by reviewing database help screens from time to time. For example, a few years ago, *FirstSearch* did not allow the use of quotation marks to indicate phrase searching. Since that time, phrase searching with quotation marks has become a feature of the *FirstSearch* search engine.

In addition to constant changes, most research databases and search engines are available only to patrons of libraries and organizations that subscribe to them. If a library subscribes to a particular database, users have access to it. For this reason, following chapters provide the URLs for vendors of online subscription databases rather than URLs to databases, most of which are useless to non-subscribers. When possible, a link to the vendor description of a database has been included. In all other cases, a link to the vendor's main webpage has been provided. Typically, there are several ways to find descriptions of databases from a vendor's homepage: searching for the database by title in the search box, if provided; using an alphabetical list of products, if available; accessing links to information about electronic or digital products; or accessing links for academic products. To see which vendors provide access to *MLAIB*, for example, see the MLA website (http://www.mla.org/bib_electronic).

STEP 6: UNDERSTANDING *GOOGLE* SEARCHES

In contrast to the academic databases available through library catalogs or subscription services described above, *Google* has outstripped all competitors to become the search engine of choice for searching resources freely available on the World Wide Web. It is a powerful tool that provides users with a simple, elegant searching interface and unmatched speed and breadth of searchable resources, and it shares many features with the subscription databases. For example, *Google* retrieves very large sets of results, which it ranks by relevance, which in turn is based on criteria derived from other *Google* searches: results are ranked higher in relevance based on how frequently certain terms are used to search, the quality of links to resources that contain the terms searched, and the proximity of terms within the search results. *Google* also allows searchers to use Boolean *OR* and *AND* operators, when entered in upper case characters, as well as phrase searching with quotation marks. Traditional truncation is not a searching option in *Google*, but a technology called "stemming" automatically searches for words similar to a user's search terms based on stem or root words. So a person searching Google with the phrase "Irish modernists," which contains the stem "modern," may also receive resource descriptions mentioning "modern Irish poetry" or "Irish modernism."

Google also incorporates a number of unique features to facilitate quick, broad searches. *Stop words*, for example, are common words or terms (such as articles and prepositions) that *Google* strips from search terms to hasten the retrieval process. But the search engine allows users to search for these words by preceding them with the "+" symbol. A popular example of this search is +to +be +or +not +to +be, which retrieves records in which all of these terms are present, but not necessarily in order. A search for "to be or not to be," on the other hand, retrieves the results that contain the entire phrase. Finally, there are many websites that cover these and other strategies for effectively searching *Google*, including the *Google* help pages (http://www.google.com/help/basics.html). Websites created and maintained by major research university libraries, such as those at the University of Michigan and the University of California, Berkeley, are also excellent resources for online searching ideas and strategies.

While *Google* and most other general Web search engines cannot search the research databases available through library catalogs or subscription services, *Google* has made inroads into searching for academic resources with *Google Scholar*, which provides access to scholarly literature and academic library catalogs, and *Google Book Search*, which allows full-text access to monographs held by academic institutions and digitized for Web access. Even in this rapidly evolving information landscape, however, the Irish literary scholar will still find most of her relevant resources in library catalogs and online databases. *Google* and other tools supplement these research tools.

CONCLUSION

This chapter has introduced and discussed several search techniques and strategies that are applicable in various online research platforms: library catalogs, subscription databases, and search engines used to search the World Wide Web. This information provides the foundation for the rest of this book, and subsequent chapters may revisit specific parts of this chapter or assume a level of knowledge about the search strategies and techniques described here. Researchers should continue to familiarize themselves with the search techniques explained in this chapter, including the use of Boolean operators and truncation, as well as the differences between keyword searching, subject/descriptor searching, phrase searching, and proximity searching. It is also important to recognize how databases differ from search engines, and to understand how these differences may affect searching across a number of online resources.

Chapter Two

General Literary Reference Resources

The resources described in this chapter serve as starting points for research into authors, works, and subjects relevant to Irish literary study. General literary reference resources include biographical works, literary and textual companions, dictionaries, encyclopedias, and research guides, works that typically list and discuss the resources essential for exploring a literary topic. These sources provide useful background information, as well as general overviews that help shape a topic question or the initial stages of a research project. Many of the print and online materials annotated in this chapter cover broad categories, such as "English literary studies" or "British writers," which may seem too general or even irrelevant to Irish literature research. Yet many of these resources contain chapters and sections devoted specifically to Irish literature, authors, and subjects. More and more resources are published each year that treat Irish literature as a subject distinct from British or English literature, but many of these newer, more specific resources have not replaced existing standard tools, such as Harner's *Literary Research Guide* or the *Oxford Dictionary of National Biography*.

RESEARCH GUIDES

Harner, James L. *Literary Research Guide: An Annotated Listing of Reference Sources in English Literary Studies*. 4th ed. New York: Modern Language Association, 2002.
———. *Literary Research Guide*, 22 May 2005, at www.english.tamu.edu/index.php?id=924/ (accessed 31 March 2008).
Marcuse, Michael J. *A Reference Guide for English Studies*. Berkeley: University of California Press, 1990.

Harner's *Literary Research Guide* and Marcuse's *A Reference Guide for English Studies* are widely used literary research guides familiar to English literature students and scholars, and both describe standard literary research sources. Harner's guide devotes a section to Irish literature, as well as to Scottish and Welsh literatures. Marcuse also features an Anglo-Irish literature and Irish Studies section, which lists descriptive citations to works relevant to the study of Irish literature, but in the main his guide is most useful as a supplement to Harner's evaluative study.

Commonly referred to as "Harner," the **Literary Research Guide** is the primary handbook for literary studies in the United States. Intended for advanced undergraduates, graduate students, and scholars, this guide introduces principal resources relevant to conducting literary research and describes their virtues as well as their drawbacks. As such, it is an excellent starting point for a research project, as well as a useful tool for identifying additional resources needed during the research process. More than 1,200 annotated entries evaluate selected print and electronic resources. Entries are organized into chapters by general resource type (e.g., reference books, literary handbooks, dictionaries, encyclopedias, bibliographies, library catalogs, manuscripts, dissertations and theses, and Internet resources, biographical sources, and periodicals), genres, national literatures (e.g., English, Irish, Scottish, Welsh, American), other literatures in English, foreign-language literatures, comparative literature, and literature-related topics and sources. The "Irish Literature" section focuses mainly on general reference works to the exclusion of works devoted to specific authors and literary eras, while sections on British and American literature include citations to resources covering specific time periods.

In addition to Harner's chapter on Irish literature, which describes sources solely dedicated to the subject, Irish literature scholars are encouraged to review the sections "English Literature," "Serial Bibliographies, Indexes, and Abstracts," and "Guides to Dissertations and Theses" for additional relevant resources. As it stands, the "Irish Literature" section provides a rich cross-section of reference works, and covers the following resources: histories and surveys; handbooks, dictionaries, encyclopedias; bibliographies; guides to primary works; guides to scholarship and criticism; language guides; biographical dictionaries; periodicals; background reading; and genres (e.g., fiction, drama and theater, and poetry). Many of the resources Harner evaluates are also described in this research guide. Harner's work, however, addresses many titles that lay beyond the scope of this work and that are potentially useful supplements to the resources addressed in the present volume. Scholars may find the citations to genre-specific resources and background readings especially useful.

Entries in the *Literary Research Guide* follow a standard format. Each begins with a complete citation to the source and mentions, when applicable, reprints and supplements, as well as standard Library of Congress and Dewey call numbers. The annotation outlines the source's scope and arrangement, evaluates its strengths and limitations as a research tool, compares it with similar works, and describes indexing. In addition, annotations frequently list selected reviews and conclude with "see also" references to other relevant sections and works within the *Guide*. Three indexes round out the *Guide*'s contents. An index of names lists authors, editors, compilers, translators, and revisers mentioned in citations or annotations. Names of literary authors, however, are excluded. A title index documents current, former, and variant book, essay, and periodical titles. Subjects are separately indexed with types of reference works. Harner posted on his website until May 2005 the revisions and additions to the fifth edition of the *Literary Research Guide*, which was published in 2008. Here, scholars will find annotations to at least one significant new Irish literature reference, Tom Clyde's *Irish Literary Magazines: An Outline History and Descriptive Bibliography* (Dublin: Irish Academic Press, 2003), as well as revisions of annotations appearing in the fourth print edition of the *Guide*.

Similar in scope to the *Literary Research Guide*, Marcuse's *A Reference Guide for English Studies* evaluates English language and literature reference works published through 1985, though limited coverage of selected sources extends through 1990. Marcuse arranges entries into twenty-four sections: general works; libraries; retrospective and current national bibliography; serial publications; miscellany (e.g., dissertations, microforms, reviews, film adaptations); history and ancillae to historical study; biography and biographical references; archives and manuscripts; language, linguistics, and philology; literary materials and contexts (e.g., folklore, proverbs, symbols); literature (e.g., comparative literature, foreign literatures, women and literature); English literature (including Scottish, Anglo-Irish, Anglo-Welsh, and Commonwealth literatures); medieval; Renaissance and early seventeenth century; Restoration and eighteenth century; nineteenth century; twentieth century; American literature; poetry and versification; theater, drama, and film; prose fiction and nonfiction; rhetoric and composition; bibliography; and English as a profession. In his preface, Marcuse advises users of the guide to begin by consulting the subject index instead of the table of contents, as works relevant to their areas of interest may be listed in unexpected sections.

Generally, sections feature annotated entries describing standard reference sources such as research guides and reviews, bibliographies, encyclopedias, dictionaries, companions, literary histories, and chronologies. Scholarly journals and frequently recommended works about specialized fields of study may also be represented, though without annotation. As in Harner, entries contain citations, specify editions cited, and note standard Library of Congress call numbers. Annotations outline a work's publication history (i.e., number of editions, former titles, names affiliated with publication), purpose, scope, organization, strengths and limitations, and sometimes include "see also" notes and cross-references to related resources such as supplements and other works by the same author(s). A sub-section devoted to "Anglo-Irish literature and Irish studies" appears in the "English literature" section. While some of the works cited here overlap with titles in Harner, Marcuse's annotations often reveal different insights regarding evaluated resources. In addition, *A Reference Guide for English Studies* cites several scholarly journals and forty-seven frequently recommended works relevant to Irish literary studies. Several of the entries for Irish literary studies periodicals provide cross-references to other sections within this guide, including M-60, "Guides to Individual Authors." Organized alphabetically by author, this section lists journals, newsletters, bibliographies, handbooks, editions, concordances, and biographies devoted to canonical Irish authors. Though comparatively modest in range, this section provides information on sources relevant to the study of Joyce, Shaw, Swift, and Yeats. Thorough indexes of authors/compilers/ contributors/editors, titles, and subjects and authors-as-subjects conclude *A Reference Guide for English Studies*.

While a useful complementary resource to Harner, Marcuse's guide possesses its own excellences. Namely, it includes author-specific reference works and cites frequently recommended resources. Though this guide only covers resources published before 1990, scholars can search their library catalog, *WorldCat*, *MLAIB*, and *ABELL* for more recent resources to supplement its contents.

GENERAL IRISH LITERATURE
ENCYCLOPEDIAS AND COMPANIONS

Cleary, Joe, and Claire Connolly. *The Cambridge Companion to Modern Irish Culture*. Cambridge Companions to Culture. Cambridge: Cambridge University Press, 2004. cco.cambridge.org.
McMahon, Seán, and Jo O'Donoghue. *The Mercier Companion to Irish Literature*. Cork: Mercier Press, 1998.
Weekes, Ann Owens. *Unveiling Treasures: The Attic Guide to the Published Works of Irish Women Literary Writers: Drama, Fiction, Poetry*. Dublin: Attic Press, 1993.
Welch, Robert, and Bruce Stewart. *The Oxford Companion to Irish Literature*. Oxford: Clarendon Press, 1996.

Welch, Robert. *The Concise Oxford Companion to Irish Literature.* Oxford: Oxford University Press, 2000. www.oxfordreference.com/views/BOOK %5FSEARCH.html?book=t55&subject=s13.

As reference tools, companions and encyclopedias share a few structural and organizational characteristics. Both consist of entries, which vary in length and detail depending on the scope of the work, that describe figures, works, themes, concepts, issues, and events relevant to a particular subject. Many literary encyclopedias and companions are organized according to time period, such as the eighteenth century or modern era. While many of these resources, especially those devoted to English or British literature written and published during a certain century, cover authors, works, literary movements, and subjects relevant to the study of Irish literature, the companions and encyclopedias outlined in this section specifically address Irish literary figures, history, and scholarship, and either exhibit a broad scope covering a wide range of related subjects or explore a selected topic in more detail. Generally, encyclopedias contain alphabetically arranged entries ranging from a paragraph to several pages in length. Authored and signed by scholars in the field, encyclopedia entries typically feature factual narratives on topics, cross-references to related entries, and brief bibliographies of selected secondary sources. Many encyclopedias include a general index, as well as other supplementary material such as chronologies, illustrations, subject bibliographies, and lists of entries grouped by themes. Oxford University Press publishes companions to numerous disciplines that follow this encyclopedic format (e.g., *Oxford Companion to Irish History*, *Oxford Companion to Twentieth Century Poetry in English*). While the Oxford companions emphasize breadth of coverage and narrative brevity, other companions examine a subject in more scholarly depth, usually containing fewer but lengthier essays of critical scope that range from ten to twenty-five pages. Frequently arranged thematically, these essays conclude with lists of references and suggested sources for further reading. Also referred to as handbooks or guides, companions may feature one or more indexes, chronologies, thematic lists, and supplementary bibliographies. *The Cambridge Companion to Modern Irish Culture* and similar reference books exemplify this type of resource. Despite differences in scope and level of detail, each title described in this section presents information about authors, works, themes, and historical and social context relevant to the study of Irish literature.

A standard source for Irish literary study, ***The Oxford Companion to Irish Literature*** aims for comprehensive treatment of a vast subject: two thousand years of Irish literary expression. Entries vary in length and address authors and works; literary movements and genres; branches of learning; types and cycles of tales; annals and manuscripts; historical events and figures; religion;

translation; mythology and folklore; Celtic culture and archaeology; Irish languages; Irish writing in other languages; and influential non-Irish writers. Detailed cross-references and "see" notes direct readers to other relevant entries and secondary sources. A brief chronology outlining historical events between 6000 B.C.E. to 1994 C.E., a bibliography of selected titles, and two maps of literary interest supplement the primary contents. Notable for its coverage of literary movements, groups, and institutions, as well as connections between historical events and figures and their influence on Irish literary history, this companion serves as a useful, self-contained supplement for the serious student of Irish literature. Though over 150 scholars contributed to and are listed in the front matter of the volume, entries appear without attribution, a textual feature that may frustrate readers who wish to connect descriptions and their authors for further research. In 2000, Oxford published an abridged version of this book under the title *The Concise Oxford Companion to Irish Literature*. Though some lengthy descriptions from the earlier edition have been condensed, this edition adds 140 new entries highlighting authors and works, and is available online at subscribing libraries.

In general, companions and encyclopedias emphasize quick access to and utility of contents. **The Mercier Companion to Irish Literature** exemplifies this kind of functionality in its unadorned simplicity. Basically a selective, alphabetical list of Irish authors, literary works, places, institutions, and events, this companion highlights well-known topics relevant to Irish literary study. Contents cover Irish literature from the seventh to twenty-first centuries and mainly represent figures and works commonly considered significant and influential. Though entries include cross-references, no other supplementary materials (e.g., indexes, bibliographies, or chronologies) accompany the text. Entry narratives suggest a thorough reader's knowledge and enthusiasm for the subjects addressed, especially the entries about writers and their works. Some topics overlap those included in *The Oxford Companion to Irish Literature* and *The Concise Oxford Companion to Irish Literature*, yet contemporary Irish fiction writers born during the late twentieth century, such as Deirdre Madden and Colm Tóibín, are particularly well represented, documented, and cross-referenced in this brief, informal guide. This resource is recommended to scholars seeking a well-written, thoughtful, and concise overview of Irish authors and their works.

Thematic encyclopedias and companions can serve a dual purpose for researchers. As the term suggests, such resources focus on a specific area of critical attention or interest, and so provide access to information concentrated on a chosen topic. On the other hand, such resources may treat a narrow frame of reference in very general terms in order to provide the broadest coverage possible on a particular subject of interest. Weekes' **Unveiling Trea-**

sures: The Attic Guide to the Published Works of Irish Women Literary Writers: Drama, Fiction, Poetry is a fitting example of just such a reference source. Unlike the other resources discussed in this section, the *Attic Guide* represents the scholarly work of a single author/compiler. This guide alphabetically lists women authors, familiar and obscure (e.g., Maeve Binchy and Elinor Mary Sweetman), popular and literary (e.g., Polly Devlin and Kate O'Brien), writing in various genres from the eighteenth century to the present day. In her introduction, Weekes emphasizes collection rather than evaluation as the principal intention of this book, and outlines her expansive and inclusive selection criteria: "The designation 'Irish' is not limited to women born in Ireland to Irish parents, but to women who identify themselves or their work with Ireland" (Weekes 1993, 5). In a sense, then, the authors discussed have selected themselves for inclusion by their self-articulated connections to Ireland and Irish heritage through their work. As a result, this resource possesses a critical credibility that suits its thematic scope, as well as its utility as a reference source containing information about writers who may not appear in similar Irish literary sources emphasizing figures commonly treated as canonical, such as Yeats, Joyce, O'Connor, and O'Faoláin. Entries vary in length from a few lines to several pages and consist of information summarizing place of birth and education, and dates of birth and death, as appropriate. Descriptions follow and tend to focus on how, when, and why selected authors began to write, as well as brief critical discussions of and quotes from creative works. Entries conclude with lists of primary works and citations. While entries are not cross-referenced, an index of names includes "see" references to pseudonyms, personal titles, and Gaelic and Anglicized versions of authors' names (e.g., "Bheasach, Brídín. *see* Holmes, Marie").

In addition to sources devoted to the subject, literature scholars can also discover relevant information in resources more general or interdisciplinary in scope. *The Cambridge Companion to Modern Irish Culture*, for example, is an authoritative, comprehensive introduction to historical and social influences on modern Irish culture. Unlike the other guides outlined in this section, entries are not alphabetically arranged. Instead, this volume consists of eighteen critical essays divided between two parts. Individual scholars who have published widely in their fields of expertise author each entry. Part 1, "Cultural Politics," addresses politics, language, religion, social movements, and historical events that continue to have a pervasive influence on Irish culture. Part 2, "Cultural Practices and Cultural Forms," focuses on Irish arts and leisure. Scholars of Irish literature may find chapters "Modernism and the Irish Revival," "Poetry in Ireland," "Irish Prose Fiction," and "Irish Theatre" of particular relevance, though all entries provide for compelling contextual reading into Irish cultural matters. Illustrations, a chronology, a map, and a general index supplement the text. Each entry concludes with notes and a list of recommended titles for further reading. The chronology presents a thorough comparison of "Irish cultural and intellectual events," major events in "Irish history," "International cultural and intellectual events," and significant events in "International history" occurring in any given year between 1789 and 2000 that shows fascinating connections between Irish and American literary production, for example, among other compelling correspondences. In general, *The Cambridge Companion to Modern Irish Culture* exemplifies a scholarly resource designed for critical study. In contrast to the other resources described in this section, it is not a source of ready reference. On the other hand, it is an academically substantive and credible treatment of a broad topic especially well-suited to advanced research into modern Irish literature. Conveniently, Cambridge Companions are available online at subscribing institutions.

GENRE IRISH LITERATURE
ENCYCLOPEDIAS AND COMPANIONS

Campbell, Matthew. *The Cambridge Companion to Contemporary Irish Poetry*. Cambridge Companions to Literature. Cambridge: Cambridge University Press, 2003. cco.cambridge.org.
Foster, John Wilson. *The Cambridge Companion to the Irish Novel*. Cambridge Companions to Literature. Cambridge: Cambridge University Press, 2006. cco.cambridge.org.
Richards, Shaun. *The Cambridge Companion to Twentieth-Century Irish Drama*. Cambridge Companions to Literature. Cambridge: Cambridge University Press, 2004. cco.cambridge.org.
Schrank, Bernice, and William W. Demastes. *Irish Playwrights, 1880–1995: A Research and Production Sourcebook*. Westport, CT: Greenwood Press, 1997.

The reference sources described in this section focus on Irish literature produced in different genres. Like the general Irish literature encyclopedias and companions previously outlined, these resources may treat authors and works representing several centuries of Irish literary history. Others limit coverage to specific eras and time periods. Genre-specific works provide scholars with critical overviews of authors writing and works produced in a particular literary form, often within a specific timeframe. In addition to suggesting compelling connections between authors and their works, such companions and encyclopedias are great sources of bibliographies, citations, and suggestions for further reading relevant to further study within a genre.

Covering over three hundred years of the varied and complex history of the Irish novel, ***The Cambridge Companion to the Irish Novel*** explores authors and works of fiction in a format similar to that of *The Cambridge Companion to Modern Irish Culture*. Arranged according to a broadly chronological framework, fourteen scholarly essays provide historical, social, and political contexts for several Irish novelists and their work. Topics include: the eighteenth-century Irish novel; nationalism and the Irish novel; colonialism in the Irish novel; Irish Gothic; religion and Irish fiction; Irish modernism; Irish regionalism and realism; the Irish-language novel; Irish women novelists; the post-modern Irish novel; twentieth-century Irish fiction; the novel and the Troubles; and contemporary Irish fiction. Generally, contributors to this companion address these topics in respect to readings of specific authors and texts, and each chapter concludes with a list of recommended reading. A chronology and index supplement this volume, which contributes new insights and perspectives regarding the historical, literary, and cultural forces that have shaped the development of the Irish novel over time.

Among all other literary genres, poetry arguably represents some of the most significant Irish literary achievements. Though Irish poetic traditions extend far into the past, ***The Cambridge Companion to Contemporary Irish Poetry*** examines Irish poetry produced since 1949. Fourteen chapters explore relatively broad subjects, such as modernization and modernism, the anti-pastoral aesthetic, the personal and public responsibilities of the poet, Irish-language poetry, and poetry and nationalism, all in the context of individual poets' work. Contributors also compare the cultural and historical backgrounds of contemporary Irish poetry with other modern national literatures. Because this companion treats fifty years of literary output, it provides a concentrated critical review of this dynamic period of poetic activity. As a result, contemporary Irish poetry seems to possess a vitality and momentum that may not be as noticeable in a resource such as *The Cambridge Companion to the Irish Novel*, which covers three centuries of writing. Chapters conclude with citations to recommended further reading, and a chronology outlines events significant to the history of contemporary Irish poetry. A general index supplements this scholarly resource.

In many ways, positive awareness of Irish culture began to arise in the theaters and literary circles of Dublin as Ireland's social and political conditions began to shift during the first half of the twentieth century. ***The Cambridge Companion to Twentieth-Century Irish Drama*** documents, among other literary matters, the development of the Irish Literary Revival, its precedents, and its ongoing influences. Broader in scope than *The Cambridge Companion to Contemporary Irish Poetry*, this companion features nineteen scholarly essays on nineteenth-century Irish melodrama, the major figures of the Revival, significant women playwrights, modern Irish dramatists and their work, and Irish history plays. Like the other Cambridge companions outlined in this chapter, *The Cambridge Companion to Twentieth-Century Irish Drama* includes a chronology and general index to aid readers who wish to browse the authors, works, events, themes, and subjects covered. Suggestions for further reading conclude each chapter. In general, the essays in this collection examine the political contexts of Irish drama written and produced throughout the twentieth century.

Similar in scope to *The Cambridge Companion to Twentieth-Century Irish Drama*, Schrank and Demastes' ***Irish Playwrights, 1880–1995: A Research and Production Sourcebook*** offers scholars a closer critical look at the creation of the Abbey Theatre and the playwrights closely associated with its organization and development, Lady Gregory and W. B. Yeats chief among them. Outlining the history of Irish drama from the late nineteenth century to 1995, this resource describes the lives and works of thirty-two playwrights. Entries are arranged alphabetically and include profiles of notable literary figures such as George Bernard Shaw, John Millington Synge, Oscar Wilde, Sean O'Casey, and Samuel Beckett, as well as contemporary playwrights such as Frank McGuinness and Christina Reid. Entries include: brief author biographies; production histories for major works and summaries of how they were critically received by contemporaries; critical assessments of playwrights' careers; bibliographies of primary and secondary works; and lists of locations of unpublished and archival sources. A general, selected bibliography concludes the volume.

BIOGRAPHICAL SOURCES

Brady, Anne, and Brian Talbot Cleeve. *A Biographical Dictionary of Irish Writers*. New York: St. Martin's Press, 1985.
Cleeve, Brian Talbot. *Dictionary of Irish Writers*. Cork: Mercier Press, 1967.
Dictionary of Literary Biography. Detroit, MI: Gale Research Co., 1978.
Gonzalez, Alexander G. *Irish Women Writers: An A-to-Z Guide*. Westport, CT: Greenwood Press, 2006.
———. *Modern Irish Writers: A Bio-Critical Sourcebook*. Westport, CT: Greenwood Press, 1997.
Matthew, H. C. G., and Brian Howard Harrison. *Oxford Dictionary of National Biography: In Association with the British Academy: From the Earliest Times to the Year 2000*. Oxford: Oxford University Press, 2004.
———. *Oxford Dictionary of National Biography*. Oxford: Oxford University Press, 2004. www.oxforddnb.com/.

Several of the sources already outlined in this chapter contain biographical information concerning Irish authors and literary figures, though biography is not their primary focus. This section, however, describes reference resources biographical in scope, some of which are devoted specifically to Irish writers. Others address Irish literary figures in the context of British biography. These resources serve as useful supplements to the general and genre companions and encyclopedias previously reviewed, as well as potential sources of information on Irish authors and literary figures not represented in other works.

The *Oxford Dictionary of National Biography* (*ODNB*) contains over fifty thousand biographical entries about people who have played influential roles in the history of the British Isles from the fourth century B.C.E. through the twentieth century. The *ODNB* revises and replaces a standard reference work begun in 1882, the *Dictionary of National Biography* (*DNB*), and features rewritten or revised entries for the 38,607 subjects covered in the original version of the *DNB* (1885–1900) and its supplements (1901–1996), as well as over sixteen thousand new biographies, to provide total coverage for 54,922 individuals. Over four hundred entries address significant families or groups. In addition to expanding coverage of all periods and professions, the *ODNB* fleshes out previously neglected subjects, especially women, rulers of Roman Britain, pre-revolutionary Americans, twentieth-century figures, and representatives from business and labor industries (viii). Despite these welcomed changes, the *ODNB* retains the selection criteria of its predecessor to include only subjects who have been deceased since December 31, 2000, while the online version features entries of subjects deceased since 2004. Though the *ODNB* considerably expands the contents of the *DNB*, the older version is an especially useful resource for scholars researching changes in a person's critical reputation and reception, as well as exploring how critical values and biases evolve over time. Comparing the contemporary *DNB* biography of Oscar Wilde published in 1901, for example, with the most recent *ODNB* print and online entries reveals compelling differences, particularly in respect to acknowledgement and discussion of Wilde's sexuality. Researchers who only have access to the original *Dictionary of National Biography* can consult Harner for an overview of its strengths and limitations.

Arranged alphabetically, entries provide a general overview of an individual's "activities, character, and significance" (v) and, when possible, an assessment of the subject's posthumous reputation. Factual details in each entry may include full birth name and name changes throughout life; dates and places of birth, baptism, marriage(s), death, and burial; information about parents', siblings', spouses', and noteworthy family members' names, life dates, and occupations; and education histories. Entries vary in length from a few paragraphs to scholarly essays organized by chronological and topical headings, though a majority of entries do not feature headings. Headings in the entry for James Joyce illustrate the range of coverage typically devoted to canonical figures in the *ODNB*: "Childhood and schooling"; "University years and intellectual development, 1899–1902"; "Paris and back"; "The beginnings of *A Portrait of the Artist as a Young Man* and *Dubliners*"; "Nora and 'exile'"; "Dubliners in Trieste, Rome, and Dublin"; "A published writer, 1907–1914"; "The war years, 1914–1918"; "From the *Portrait* to *Ulysses*"; "Publication of *Ulysses*"; *Work in Progress* begins"; "Crisis and consolidation, 1928–1939"; "*Finnegans Wake*"; "Last years, 1939–1941"; "The Joyce archive"; and "Critical and cultural heritage." Other figures, such as George Moore, receive a more condensed treatment: "Informal education in Paris"; "First novels"; "The works of the 1890s"; and "*Hail and Farewell* and last writings." Contributors sign each essay, and revised entries also note original authors. While entries conclude with lists of primary and secondary sources consulted by contributors, significant publications produced by subjects are discussed within the essays themselves. Finally, when such information is available, entries provide references to paper, film, and sound archives; artists and galleries responsible for portrait likenesses; and details concerning the wealth of subjects at death. Over ten thousand black-and-white images from the National Portrait Gallery supplement the *ODNB* with visual references relevant to subjects, including portraits, coins, seals, effigies, and iconographic imagery. Published as a separate volume, the *Index to Contributors* lists authors who either composed new material or revised previous essays for this resource, and specifies which articles they contributed.

In addition to the print version of the *Oxford Dictionary of National Biography*, Oxford University Press publishes a subscription-based online version of this standard resource that provides access to the complete texts of the *ODNB*, the original *DNB*, and new contents updated three times a year. While the default "Quick Search" feature permits keyword searching, the advanced "People" search option enables scholars to search for subjects by name, fields of interest (e.g., art, literature, religion and belief, scholarship and research), sex, dates spanning a subject's life or a period of significant activity, places and life events (e.g., birth, baptism, education, burial), religious affiliation and denomination, and by text (keywords) appearing throughout an article. By means of these fields, researchers have the potential to compile subsets of Irish literary figures organized according to specific search limits. In both quick and advanced name search options, users may input names in regular ("James Mangan") or reverse order ("Mangan, James"), though this latter option requires a comma between surnames and first names in order to retrieve results. Other search options permit keyword and phrase searching within reference material (e.g., sources, archives, and likenesses) appended to subject essays, by contributor, or for images by artist and date.

Though the essays in the online edition of the *ODNB* are identical to those in the print reference, online texts have been enhanced with hyperlinks to other relevant articles about related or affiliated figures. The article for W. B. Yeats, for example, includes links to essays about Jack Butler Yeats, Maud Gonne, Augusta Gregory, and Francis Stuart, as well as links to an earlier version (published in 2004) of the current article and the original *Dictionary of National Biography* essay on Yeats (published in 1949) preserved in the *DNB* archive. Some entries provide links to additional online entries on subjects published in resources such as the *National Portrait Gallery*, *National Register of Archives*, and *Royal Historical Society Bibliography*. In addition, the *ODNB* allows scholars to search thematic groupings of biographical subjects (e.g., Nobel prize-winners in the *Oxford DNB*, heads of government in Ireland, 1919–2003, high-kings of Ireland, c. 452–1172) or features on historical developments and events, such as women in high politics, 1700–2000, and a survey of significant figures in British law ("Lives of the law").

The *ODNB* is an excellent source for biographical information on selected, deceased Irish literary figures, especially well-known authors. The citations to secondary sources, archives, and image resources that conclude each entry are particularly useful in respect to further research on authors who may not have been as rigorously documented in other literary reference works. On the other hand, scholars seeking biographical information for a wider range of Irish literary persons may require a resource focused on Irish writers. *A Biographical Dictionary of Irish Writers* fulfills this need. A revised edition of the three-volume reference published as the *Dictionary of Irish Writers*, this resource contains brief biographical sketches of over 1,800 Irish writers from the fourth to twentieth centuries, including the seventh-century hagiographer Adamnán, the tenth-century annalist Dubhdalethe, and the eighteenth-century poet Máire Ní Laoghaire. Authors represented include writers of short and long fiction and non-fiction, poets, playwrights, translators, journalists, historians, hagiographers, and academics. Divided into two parts, "Writers in English" and "Writers in Irish and Latin," respectively, alphabetically arranged entries vary in length from a few sentences to several paragraphs and outline salient facts about writers' lives: dates and locations of birth and death; birth and married names; education and degrees; memberships and affiliations; and significant events and relationships. Though entries typically mention selected primary works by each subject, citations to secondary sources are limited to anthologies, collections, and series in which an author's principal works appear. In addition to the sheer breadth of biographical information available in *A Biographical Dictionary of Irish Writers*, scholars have access to separate entries for authors writing in both English and Irish, which often provide comparative information about writers' literary reputations and regard among different critical and cultural circles.

Presenting critical biographies supplemented by bibliographical information, ***Modern Irish Writers: A Bio-Critical Sourcebook*** contains seventy-
seven alphabetically organized essays on prominent twentieth-century Irish
literary figures contributed by Irish literature scholars and teachers. Entries
are divided into sections that outline a subject's biography, major works and
themes, and critical reception. Bibliographies of selected works by and studies of the author follow main entries. In addition, a main bibliography covering the entire volume provides citations to literary histories, general Irish literature criticism, and secondary works on Irish fiction, drama, and poetry. A
general index lists authors and subjects; page numbers printed in bold indicate where readers can locate the main entry on an author of interest. Gonzalez's "Introduction" is an excellent evaluative overview of widely available
reference works and secondary sources relevant to the study of modern Irish
literature. ***Irish Women Writers: An A-to-Z Guide***, also edited by Gonzalez,
is a useful companion volume to *Modern Irish Writers*, as well as a premier
reference for biographical and bibliographical information for a range of Irish
women writers. Following essentially the same format as *Modern Irish Writers*, this work covers seventy-five twentieth-century Irish women novelists,
poets, and playwrights who represent a spectrum of critical attention and
opinion. One of the great virtues of this work is its treatment of several Irish
authors such as Biddy Jenkinson and Eithne Strong who, until recently, have
remained relatively unknown outside Ireland. Entries include brief biographies, discussions of major works and themes, and summaries of subjects'
critical reception. Selected bibliographies of primary and secondary sources
conclude each entry, while a selected bibliography and general index supplement the volume's contents.

The ***Dictionary of Literary Biography*** (*DLB*) is an ongoing, multi-volume
series (currently over three hundred and thirty volumes). Each volume addresses authors working in a specific genre, representing a national literature,
and/or writing during a particular literary period. Although international in
scope and covering writers from antiquity to the present, the *DLB* primarily
emphasizes British and American literary authors and subjects. Several recent
volumes in the series focus on Irish literary topics, while older titles contain
information relevant to Irish literary study, but present it in the context of
British literature. Other older volumes ostensibly devoted to British subjects
also cover Irish prose writers, poets, playwrights, and novelists from the seventeenth to twentieth centuries. Volume 13, entitled *British Dramatists Since
World War II*, for example, includes entries on Samuel Beckett, Brendan Be-
han, Brian Friel, and Hugh Leonard. Researchers using older *DLB* titles to
identify information on Irish authors can browse tables of contents to verify
entries on Irish subjects. Volumes relevant to Irish literary study published

and updated during the last ten years include: *British and Irish Dramatists Since World War II* (second, third, and fourth series; volumes 233, 245, and 310, respectively); *Twenty-First Century British and Irish Novelists* (volume 267); *British and Irish Novelists Since 1960* (volume 271); and *British and Irish Short-Fiction Writers, 1945–2000* (volume 319).

Entry format is consistent throughout each volume in the *DLB*. Author entries are signed by contributors and begin with birth and death dates, note cross-references to entries in other *DLB* volumes, and list the subject's publications, including books, works in collections, and contributions to periodicals and other types of literature. The main body of the essay details the author's life and literary career through critical discussions of selected works that fit the volume's thematic focus. Articles also assess the author's influence and critical reputation. Photographic portraits of authors and images of book covers, title pages, and manuscript leaves often illustrate entries. Author essays conclude with citations to some or all of the following bibliographic resources: interviews, bibliographies, biographies, selected critical studies, and manuscript/archival repositories. Some volumes feature special appendixes that offer critical contexts and interpretive texture to organizational themes. For example, *British and Irish Dramatists Since World War II* (fourth series) contains two appendixes that reprint significant interviews and essays concerning British theatre of the seventies: "Playwriting for the Seventies: Old Theatres, New Audiences, and the Politics of Revolution," which originally appeared in *Theatre Quarterly* (v. 6, no. 24 (Winter 1976–1977)), and "British Theatre: the Past and the New Breed," originally published in *The Guardian* (6 July 2002). All volumes include selective lists of books for further reading pertinent to the designated theme, as well as a cumulative index that permits researchers to identify in preceding volumes all relevant entries regarding a subject. The latest volume of the *DLB* always contains the most current version of the cumulative index.

In addition to its ongoing publication in print, an online version of the *Dictionary of Literary Biography* is also available by subscription from Gale. Subscribing libraries may purchase online access to the *DLB* on its own or as part of the *Literature Resource Center* (http://www.gale.com/LitRC/). The online *DLB* provides access to over ten thousand articles published in the print edition. Users can search the full text of an author essay by keyword, or conduct field searches by author as subject, title of work, year of birth or death, nationality, subject or genre, and essay topic. Additional fields permit searching by subject ethnicity and gender, as well as searching by and browsing of individual *DLB* volume titles. Online articles are almost identical to print versions, though they sometimes follow slightly different arrangements and do not feature illustrations. On the other hand, online essays provide hyperlinks to other *DLB* essays about subject authors and a greater selection of access points that facilitate searching for topics and authors mentioned within the full text of all the entries.

CHRONOLOGIES

Cahalan, James M. *Modern Irish Literature and Culture: A Chronology*. New York: G. K. Hall, 1993.

Cox, Michael. *The Oxford Chronology of English Literature*. Oxford: Oxford University Press, 2002.

Kelly, John. *A W. B. Yeats Chronology*. Houndmills, Basingstoke, Hampshire: Palgrave Macmillan, 2003.

Many literary reference books and research resources discussed in this chapter feature chronologies of differing lengths and exhibiting varying levels of detail, from simple lists of dates and events to comparative evaluations of significant literary moments and eras in national literatures. For most scholarly tasks, these supplementary timelines provide researchers with valuable historical context for literary study. Detailed chronologies are available for scholars seeking quick access to more comprehensive treatments of intellectual and artistic movements, publishing trends, and authorial output. This section reviews a brief selection of literary chronologies pertinent to the study of Irish literature.

Perhaps the definitive chronological reference for printed literature in English, ***The Oxford Chronology of English Literature*** spans the years from 1474 to 2000 and provides a list of "significant *and* representative" (xiii) books arranged by year of imprint or publication. Published in two volumes, contents cover over four thousand authors and more than thirty thousand works. In general, the *Chronology* emphasizes creative works: poetry, drama, short stories, and novels. However, selected non-fiction (e.g., biographies, letters, criticism), historical and literary scholarship, and reference works, such as the *Encyclopedia Britannica*, are also discussed, and summaries of works considered of high cultural value share space on the page with mention of popular works. Canonical and lesser-known literary figures are represented, including women and working-class writers, as well as Irish, Scottish, and Welsh authors writing in English. Arranged alphabetically by the author's last name, entries for each year provide basic biographical details (e.g., dates of birth and death, pseudonyms) and document the title of the work, title-page matter, imprint information, and notes which cover, when fitting, serialization details, collaborators and illustrators, dates of succeeding editions, contextual information, and cross-references to related titles. The second volume of the *Chronology* consists of separate indexes organized by author, title, and translated authors.

The *Chronology* is primarily useful as a comprehensive guide for pinpointing when certain works were published and specific authors were active, as well as identifying writers working during the same or a similar time period. It does not provide historical contexts for printed literature, and its coverage of Irish literature is necessarily selective and limited to works published in English. With coverage that begins in 1601 and ends in 1992, Calahan's *Modern Irish Literature and Culture: A Chronology* lacks the temporal range of *The Oxford Chronology of English Literature*, yet it focuses on the historical contexts of Irish literature. In addition, it covers Irish Gaelic literature and significant moments in the publication, translation, and transmission of Irish Gaelic works. Structured as a year-by-year chronology, entries for each year are alphabetically organized into categories. Categories are not consistent from year to year, however, and have been selected to highlight individuals, groups, achievements, events, movements, and trends relevant to a particular year. The entry for 1932, for example, the year in which Éamon de Valera was elected the first *Taoiseach* (prime minister) of the newly independent Irish Free State, features the comparatively civil and sober categories architecture, cultural institutions, drama, fiction, and prose non-fiction. In contrast, the 1899 entry includes architecture, drama, fiction, Irish language and literature, literary criticism, periodicals, and poetry, headings that fittingly highlight the year during which the Irish Text Society was founded, the nationalist newspaper the *United Irishman* went into circulation, and Yeats published *The Wind among the Reeds*, which contained poems such as "The Song of Wandering Aengus" and "The Cap and Bells" that have since become definitive artistic documents of the time. Descriptions of major historical events are listed at the beginning of some years, without headings and before other categories, to establish historical frameworks for the literary and cultural information that follows. Primary works are discussed under appropriate category headings, and brief citations to secondary sources appear in some entries. Calahan's chronology concludes with a list of secondary works cited, as well as a general index. The front matter to this volume consists of an excellent bibliographical introduction in which the author directs readers to other reference resources, and a chapter titled "Biographical Sketches of Recurrent Figures," which outlines dates, events, and works associated with influential Irish literary and historical figures.

As suggested in the descriptions of some of the resources covered in this chapter, chronologies devoted to groups or individuals often supplement reference resources. Usually, these chronologies are brief and supply background material to support a source's primary contents. Calahan's work is only one example of a comprehensive, book-length chronology organized around a theme. Kelly's *A W. B. Yeats Chronology* extends the themed chronology concept to focus on the details of a single author's life. A title in Palgrave Macmillan's *Author Chronologies* series, this volume outlines significant moments in Yeats' personal history with a view toward revealing as many dimensions of the man's existence as possible. Yeats' engagement with creative and cultural processes and currents are frequently detailed on a daily basis and, in a few entries, the day and even the approximate time or hour at which something significant transpired has been noted. A list of abbreviations for recurring persons, institutions, and works cited proceeds the chronology proper, while a general index to names, titles, and subjects concludes this thorough resource. Kelly's work evinces the notion that authors whose lives have been well-documented and whose work has been widely read, criticized, and preserved may be examined on this level. Chronologies of such scope and depth require a vast body of primary and secondary material to compile. The *Author Chronologies* series currently features several volumes devoted to Irish writers, among them Beckett, Joyce, and Shaw, all of whom have been subjects of rigorous critical scrutiny over the years.

INDIVIDUAL AUTHOR SOURCES

Ackerley, Chris, and S. E. Gontarski. *The Grove Companion to Samuel Beckett: A Reader's Guide to His Works, Life, and Thought*. New York: Grove Press, 2004.
Fargnoli, A. Nicholas. *James Joyce: A Literary Reference*. New York: Carroll & Graf, 2003.
McCready, Sam. *A William Butler Yeats Encyclopedia*. Westport, CT: Greenwood Press, 1997.

As the example of *A W. B. Yeats Chronology* suggests, individual author sources may be most readily available for canonical and well-known writers and literary figures. Finding comprehensive resources devoted to authors who have not received as much scholarly attention, including women and minority writers, may be more challenging for Irish literary researchers. Related to Kelly's aforementioned chronology in terms of subject and scope, McCready's *A William Butler Yeats Encyclopedia* approaches the life and work of this seminal Irish cultural figure from several biographical and critical angles. People, places, and topics contributing to a more thorough historical and interpretative understanding of Yeats are described, though the author avers that entries cover basic information existing in other resources (xii). Even so, the selection and arrangement of items reflect one scholar's view of what information about Yeats needs to be made available to other critics and researchers in a single reference volume. Beginning with a brief chronology, alphabetical entries detail individuals, groups, locations, works, folklore, myths, and symbols pertinent to scholarly study of Yeats' life and work. Some entries include cross-references printed in bold and references to other information sources. A selected bibliography of secondary and primary resources and a general index of names, titles, and subjects conclude the volume. Literary allusions and references in Yeats' drama and poetry, as well as inspirational artistic, historical, and mythological figures, are particularly well-documented in this resource.

James Joyce: A Literary Reference departs from the standard format of reference books that focus on secondary information and sources devoted to individual authors. This title collects chronologically arranged selections from sources by and about Joyce's life and work to illustrate the evolution of this influential author's complex and intriguing literary career. Contents include excerpts from book reviews, reminiscences, and correspondence that reveal the contemporary responses to Joyce's publications. The opinions represented run the gamut from glowing praise to derision and disgust. Frequently, the editor prefaces entries with descriptive passages summarizing the historical and cultural contexts underlying the selections that follow, and a generous selection of black-and-white reproductions of drawings, photographs, portraits, and facsimiles illustrate this volume's contents. *James Joyce: A Literary Reference* is a useful compendium especially of contemporary book reviews and critical opinions of his work by fellow artists, including Gertrude Stein, Bernard Shaw, Ezra Pound, and T. S. Eliot. Images of the author's family, friends, and boyhood haunts and significant locations mentioned in his fiction complement scholarly consideration of his work, while photographs of covers and title pages of different editions of his books chronicle the evolution of book design and the growth of the Joyce publishing industry throughout the twentieth century. A descriptive chronology, separate bibliographies of primary and secondary sources, and a general index complete the contents of this unique reference work.

The Grove Companion to Samuel Beckett: A Reader's Guide to His Works, Life, and Thought is a comprehensive companion for Beckett readers and scholars. An immanently readable guide compiled by noted Beckett scholars, this reference work demonstrates considerable knowledge of and enthusiasm for the subject, and provides coverage of biographical details and critical concepts relevant to the study of this literary figure renowned for his aversion to celebrity and recognition. Constructed as a cross-referenced A-to-Z list, this resource details relationships, events, and reminiscences that have contributed, directly or indirectly, to Beckett's drama, poetry, and prose. Cross-references appear in bold-face type within entries, and a narrative chronology and bibliography of primary and secondary works frame the substantive contents. Entries display considerable wit and appreciation for Beckett's complex craft. The item devoted to "Dickens, Charles," for example, traces the echo of a single phrase, "flaws of wind," borrowed from the Victorian novelist's *Little Dorritt*, throughout several of Beckett's works (139). In 2006, an identical version of this guide intended for a British readership was published by London-based Faber & Faber as *The Faber Companion to Samuel Beckett: A Reader's Guide to His Works, Life, and Thought*.

CONCLUSION

Usually, scholars consult the general reference resources discussed in this chapter as initial and supplementary research tools. Such sources can serve a number of scholarly ends, depending on the scope and focus of individual works. Some highlight selected resources suited for investigation of a literary topic, while others provide factual information about authors and other literary figures and events (e.g., birth, death, and publication dates). Other reference resources introduce researchers to authors, texts, genres, themes, and historical contexts relevant to the study of Irish literature. Scholars familiar with the layout and kinds of information available in different general reference source categories will be better equipped to select the most useful resource for specific research problems or needs.

Chapter Three

Library Catalogs

Library catalogs are fundamental, essential resources for researchers. There are several kinds of catalogs, all of which share some features and yet differ in crucial ways. In addition to the library catalogs familiar to most users of academic libraries, this chapter also focuses on related resources, including union catalogs, national library catalogs, and cooperative union catalogs, specifically those maintained by OCLC.

While online public access catalogs, commonly referred to as OPACs, are research tools familiar to most contemporary scholars, they are a comparatively recent development in the world of library services and access. OPACs succeed the traditional card catalogs that once served as the primary source of bibliographic maintenance and control, as well as collection access, in most public and academic libraries. While the transition from print catalogs to OPACs has been comparatively swift over the last twenty-five years, the migration of data in print card catalogs to electronic databases has not been as quick or complete. Though most libraries now make their collections available electronically, some items, especially older materials, may not appear in the OPAC. Other print and electronic resources such as finding aids, discussed in chapter 9, are usually available to supplement the gaps in a library's OPAC. This chapter, however, discusses how to conduct comprehensive searches in online catalogs for the purpose of finding relevant research materials.

The transition from traditional print to online catalogs yields many advantages to the researcher. Namely, online catalogs provide users with access points utilized in traditional catalogs, such as authors, titles, and subjects, as well as the capability to search these same access points as keywords. As described in chapter 1, online catalogs often allow for keyword searching of other useful access points such as publisher, series, contents, and notes fields. Some online catalogs offer yet more searching options, including searches by periodical title, ISBN/ISSN, Library of Congress call number, Dewey call number, local call number, or government document number. Researchers can also limit searches by publication date, language, format, and location. In addition, online catalogs frequently include printing, downloading, emailing, and citation formatting options for researchers documenting their work according to a particular bibliographic style such as *MLA* or *Chicago*.

As chapter 1 indicates, the design and function of online resources varies from library to library. Still, records in online catalogs are created according to specific standards and rules observed by most libraries. Catalogers, the library professionals who create bibliographic records, base their work on the Anglo-American cataloging rules, use controlled vocabulary to describe who creates an item and what it is about, and then incorporate this information in records formatted to conform to the MARC (MAchine Readable Cataloging) format.

Catalogers in most English-speaking countries generally use the detailed guidelines outlined in the second edition of the *Anglo-American Cataloging Rules*, revised in 2002 (*AACR2R*), to describe an item's physical and publication information in a format that is consistent with the bibliographical description of other items in a catalog. They also use a controlled vocabulary consisting of words and phrases selected and created by an organization such as the Library of Congress to standardize the language used for bibliographic and content description among cataloging records. Controlled vocabulary includes subject and authority headings. Subject headings are standardized words and phrases used to describe content. Authority headings, on the other hand, are standardized versions of personal or corporate names used to describe an item's creator(s) or biographical subjects, as well as standardized titles created to distinguish the titles of series or works from one another. While most academic and public libraries in the United States use subject and authority headings controlled by the Library of Congress, some specialized libraries use other controlled vocabularies. Small public libraries and school media centers, for example, may utilize Sears headings, which are more general and less technical than Library of Congress headings. In contrast, hospital and medical research libraries often use specialized, highly specific medical subject headings (MeSH) controlled by the National Library of Medicine. After the cataloger describes and assigns subject headings to an item according to the AACR2R and LCSH standards, respectively, he enters this information into specific MARC record fields. Once in MARC format, users can read this bibliographic information on a computer screen and online networks can electronically exchange it. Because this information is standardized, libraries can potentially share bibliographic data with a greater variety of users, including scholars, publishers, and each other, as well as on a wider global scale, if the technology is available to access this information.

Standardized cataloging records provide researchers with consistent information across a range of library catalogs. Libraries in the United States and Britain catalog primary access points—author, title, and subject headings—in similar ways, which allows scholars to work with familiar online researching platforms in different institutions. Generally, the names of authors and other creators, as well as the names and titles of institutions and places such as the Abbey Theatre and the Aran Islands, are described with the same authority headings in most catalogs. Exceptions to this standard do exist, especially in respect to older materials cataloged before the creation or revision of current authority headings. Likewise, items cataloged in the United States usually feature consistent subject headings, but records for resources cataloged elsewhere may exhibit variations of these headings and other cataloging data. While information in catalog records may be similar from one catalog to another, each library organizes its catalog in potentially different ways. Skilled researchers can identify which fields are indexed in a catalog by looking at sample searches described in help screens or by requesting assistance from a reference librarian. In addition, catalog help screens describe which fields are indexed for keyword searching, as well as whether or not the catalog software allows for Boolean, phrase, or proximity keyword searching.

While chapter 1 provides useful overviews of search techniques and technologies, the present chapter describes search strategies intended to facilitate successful searching in library catalogs. Because catalogs differ from one institution to the next, the examples that follow serve as generalized guidelines that may require modifications based on the indexing and searching capabilities of a particular catalog.

AUTHOR SEARCHES AND EVALUATING RESULTS

Searching for works by authors of Irish literature obviously begins with an author field search in a library catalog. For the purposes of the present volume, "works" has several definitions. Works, for example, refers to published or unpublished writings of an individual or several authors. Similarly, a work can refer to the product of a literary effort, such as an essay, letter, novel, play, poem, or a collection of these items. Searching for works by canonical authors is straightforward, and typically requires the researcher to follow the Western convention of inputting the author's last name followed by the first name (e.g., *heaney, seamus*; *o'brien, edna*).

More than one author can share the same name, a fact that may become evident in the results list returned for a simple author search. In such an instance, a researcher can use knowledge of her subject to differentiate between authors with similar names. For example, a simple search for *joyce, james* may yield multiple results, some of which may be irrelevant to the researcher. Each author heading, however, may be distinguished by additional information such as dates of birth and/or death, and middle initials or names. So the Irish literature scholar familiar with James Joyce's life and times will select the heading "Joyce, James, 1882–1941" from the list of headings returned. Alternatively, a researcher can conduct a title search for a specific work by the author of interest to discover the authoritative name heading used in the catalog: a title search for *pomes penyeach*, for example, will also retrieve the authoritative heading for James Joyce. Headings for authors with titles and authors writing under pseudonyms may look a little different from typical author headings. The heading for Yeats' collaborator Lady Isabella Augusta Gregory, for example, does not include her first or middle names or initials: "Gregory, Lady, 1852–1932." Likewise, the influential poet and painter George Russell has separate headings for his pseudonym ("AE, 1867–1935") as well as his full name: "Russell, George William, 1867–1935."

As previously mentioned, records for older works or editions of works by a researcher's author of interest may not appear in the catalog with a Library of Congress authority heading, especially in respect to authors who wrote and published before the second half of the twentieth century. Works by women, minority, and non-canonical authors, in particular, may be inconsistently cataloged under various names. Researchers attempting to compile a comprehensive list of titles by an author can conduct both specific and general name searches to yield the most results.

As described above, searching for works by well-known, canonical authors is a fairly straightforward process. Researchers can also use the same techniques to find works by less well-known or minor authors. Because works by such authors may not be widely published or widely available in separate editions, they may have to be searched in other ways. Anthologies containing works by several authors, for example, are excellent resources for the researcher seeking works by lesser-known or non-canonical authors. Conducting a keyword search for *anthology and women and Irish* will return records for collected works by Irish women writers, such as the *The Field Day Anthology of Irish Writing: Irish Women's Writing and Traditions*. In addition to *anthology*, useful keywords are *sources* and *literary collections*.

If an author's name appears in the contents field or as a subject heading in a catalog record, then a researcher will find anthologies and other sources that contain works by that author in a keyword search. For example, in some cat-

Title	**Mad & bad fairies**
Publisher	[Dublin : Attic Press, c1987]
Description	60 p. : ill. ; 22 cm
Series	Fairytales for feminists ; 3
L.c. subject	English fiction -- Irish authors
	Ireland -- Social life and customs -- Fiction
	English fiction -- Women authors
	Fairy tales -- Ireland
	Feminism -- Ireland -- Fiction
Note	Cover title
Contents	The fate of Aoife and the children of Aobh / Mary Dorcey -- Alice in Thunderland / Maeve Kelly -- Ophelia's tale / Clairr O'Connor -- Thumbelina and the life wing fairy / Joni Crone -- Some day my prince will come / Róisín Sheerin -- The frog prince / Anne Cooper -- The witch-hunt / Máirín Johnston -- The story of Emer / Joni Crone -- An Irish fairy tale / Frances Molloy -- Dick Whittington and her cat / Annie Killean
Other title	Mad and bad fairies
ISBN	094621140X (pbk.) :
LCCN	87183663 //r944
LC CALL NO.	PR8876.2.W65 M33 1987
Dewey call #	823/.01/089287 19

Figure 3.1. Modified catalog record for *Mad & Bad Fairies*. Source: Orbis Cascade Alliance, Summit union catalog.

alogs the keyword search *frances molloy* returns a record for the anthology *Mad & Bad Fairies*, which contains her short story "An Irish Fairy Tale" (see figure 3.1). Conducting an author search for *molloy, frances* may retrieve a record for her novel *No Mate for the Magpie*, but will exclude the record for the previous title, which includes Molloy's name only in the contents note.

Another useful way to search for works by authors of interest, especially lesser-known authors, is to conduct inverted phrase keyword searches for an author's name (e.g., *molloy frances*). Inverted phrase keyword searches often retrieve results that do not appear in author keyword searches because they pick up occurrences of names in other catalog record fields such as subject headings and contents notes. Keyword searches for regular and inverted author names yield different results, including irrelevant titles. Still, both are viable research strategies, especially for the Irish literature scholar seeking hard-to-find texts published in literary collections and anthologies organized around a theme.

After conducting an author search, a researcher evaluates her results to choose which sources are most relevant to her research project. Depending on the size and scope of a library's collection, the results of an author search may contain a variety of editions, reprints, and formats representing the work of a single writer. Different editions and formats possess characteristics and strengths that affect the usability of and access to these materials. For example, works by Irish authors of the eighteenth and nineteenth centuries may be available in various media, including microform, electronic, and print. Historical texts are easily reproduced on microfilm, but this media is notoriously fragile and requires special equipment (and sometimes special training) to use. Chapter 8, "Microform and Digital Collections," addresses these issues in more detail. Electronic resources are dynamic but often non-standardized in respect to usability and design; examples include digitized manuscripts, hyperlinked data, and texts restricted for use by specific users or within particular organizations. Print resources for the researcher may include original editions of a work, manuscript facsimiles, and modern popular or critical editions that include scholarly commentary and contextual material of varying quality.

Several criteria for evaluating texts can help a researcher select what type of format and edition best fulfills her research needs. Are the publisher and editors considered credible and authoritative by other scholars in the field? How current or relevant is the publication date? Where is the place of publication? Answering these questions can assist in determining which edition of a work is the latest scholarly edition or simply a reprint of a trade publication. On the other hand, researchers intending to use older primary documents will most often have restricted access to these materials in the special collections departments of major research libraries. Chapter 9, "Manuscripts and Archives," covers how to work with manuscripts and other archival materials.

TITLE SEARCHES

Title searches retrieve lists of all copies of a specific work owned by a library, results which require the same critical scrutiny of edition, publisher, and format required of author search results. A particular concern for Irish literature scholars searching for Gaelic titles is inconsistent cataloging of Gaelic-language materials. The number of catalogers who possess a solid working knowledge of Gaelic is very small, so records for Gaelic titles are sometimes cataloged in ways that do not work well with the title indexes in most online catalogs. Typically, catalogers input title fields in MARC records according to rules that allow catalog title indexes to ignore initial articles (a, an, the) during a title search. By eliminating such common and frequent terms from a search query, the search engine can more quickly retrieve relevant results. Unfamiliar Gaelic articles (a', an, am, an t-, na, na h-), on the other hand, sometimes appear in MARC records as searchable words in title fields. These errors result in ineffective searches for Gaelic language titles, such as Aisling Ni Dhonnchadha's study of Irish fiction, *An Gearrscéal sa Ghaeilge, 1898–1940*. Fortunately, cooperative cataloging has improved cataloging practices in all languages. Far more common is the appearance of several variants of a single title in a catalog, especially in respect to older titles. Works that have been widely studied and that have come to be considered canonical are typically published in several formats: facsimiles, scholarly editions, or as anthologized works. Each format may have variant titles for the same work. For example, a title search for James Joyce's *A Portrait of the Artist as a Young Man* retrieves dozens of records featuring this title. Joyce is not the author of all the works represented in the list, however. Other titles belong to works about Joyce's novel, and include critical and interpretive texts as well as video recordings of screen adaptations of the book. Careful browsing of such a title list reveals several resources that may have relevance for the scholar, including: critical editions (e.g., *A Portrait of the Artist as a Young Man: Complete, Authoritative Text with Biographical, Historical, and Cultural Contexts, Critical History, and Essays from Contemporary Critical Perspectives*, edited by R. Brandon Kershner); facsimile editions (e.g., *A Portrait of the Artist as a Young Man: A Facsimile of the Final Holograph Manuscript*, prefaced and arranged by Hans Walter Gabler); and related works (e.g., *Stephen Hero: A Part of the First Draft of A Portrait of the Artist as a Young Man*, edited from the manuscript in the Harvard College Library by Theodore Spencer).

A review of records for different versions of *A Portrait of the Artist as a Young Man* may disclose that different editions are further described in notes as "definitive," "authoritative," or "[based on] the definitive text." The Viking critical library edition, published in 1968, for example, may differ in significant ways from the critical edition published by Bedford/St. Martin's in 2006. Using the criteria for evaluating resources outlined in the previous section on author searches, the researcher can decide which critical edition is most appropriate for his project. In addition, reviewing the notes fields in bibliographical records can guide scholars to resources that best fulfill their research needs because they often contain important information that may not appear in a list of brief citations retrieved by a title search.

While title searches are effective at retrieving lists of separately published versions of a title, they do not always locate records for titles published with other works in anthologies and literary collections. Researchers can broaden their searches for specific works by conducting keyword searches for titles of interest. This strategy is a useful way to find shorter works, such as stories, plays, and poems that may be published together with other works by different authors. A keyword search for *synge and playboy of the western world*, for instance, retrieves several titles that include the entire text of John Millington Synge's play, in addition to dramatic or critical texts by other authors.

Title searches are useful for identifying virtually any kind of resource in a variety of media: journals, series, archival materials, government documents, maps, databases, and video and sound recordings. Title searches for Irish literature and culture journals such as *The Irish Digest* and *Éire-Ireland: A Journal of Irish Studies* will retrieve records that reveal the scope of a library's subscription to a journal title, whether or not the title has been cancelled, superseded by or merged with another title, and information on how users can access the title, whether in print, electronic, or microform versions. Title searches for a series such as *Costerus*, on the other hand, will retrieve records for individual volumes cataloged under unique titles that have been issued as separate parts of a single series publication. As mentioned in chapter 1, some library catalogs feature indexes that allow for periodical title and series title searches. As with author keyword searches, title keyword searches work only if the title keywords appear in the contents fields of a bibliographical record and are indexed by the library's catalog database.

SUBJECT SEARCHES

Researchers conduct subject searches to find items about particular topics, themes, historical eras and events, authors, literary works, literary characters, genres, and other access points. Keyword searches and subject heading searches are the two most common strategies researchers use to find items about subjects. As discussed in the sections on author and title searches, depending on how a library's catalog is indexed, keyword searches can identify topic words in a number of catalog record fields, including subject heading, title, author, publisher, and contents and notes fields. Keyword searches are most effective as a broad searching strategy, since they retrieve all of the records in which a researcher's topic words occur anywhere in the fields searched. Some library catalogs allow keyword phrase searching, which permits researchers to search for strings of keywords. If provided this option, researchers need to check which default operators, *and* or *or*, the catalog uses to connect strings of keywords. As described in chapter 1, the way a researcher executes a keyword search, as well as which fields are searchable in a catalog, affect the types of results retrieved. With these search parameters in mind, researchers can use keyword searches to refine their research topics by checking retrieved records for controlled subject headings that are relevant to their projects. When searching for secondary resources about an author of interest, researchers can conduct keyword searches for an author's name and an appropriate term such as *bibliography*, *biography*, *correspondence*, or *criticism*, as in *mcguckian and biography* or *mangen and criticism*.

Just as author and title searches scan a catalog's index of author and title fields in catalog records, subject searches scan the catalog's index of Library of Congress or other subject headings. In records in which an author's name appears as a subject heading, the heading often includes dates of birth and/or death, as well as a subject heading further describing what the work may be about: *McGuckian, Medbh, 1950—Criticism and interpretation*. A representative selection of Library of Congress subject headings for other subjects in Irish literature might include:

Irish poetry -- 20th century
English literature -- Irish authors
Literature and society -- Ireland -- History
Irish literature -- History and criticism -- Theory, etc.
Irish literature -- Middle Irish, 1100–1550 -- Translations into English
Yeats, W. B. (William Butler), 1865–1939 -- Correspondence
Theater -- Ireland

Along with author and title headings, subject headings have changed over time, as have the standards and rules that describe how to assign and use them in catalog records. In addition, cataloging practices vary from library to library, so it is not unusual, especially in the case of older authors and published works, to discover catalog records that do not have subject headings, or that feature very general subject headings such as "Irish literature," "Poets, Irish," or "Criticism" to describe items of considerably narrower focus. It is worth noting that assigned subject headings do not typically appear in records for creative works such as novels and short stories, although this practice has become more frequent in the last few years and continues to be a matter of debate among library professionals.

Becoming familiar with the format and typical elements of subject headings requires some practice, especially in light of changing cataloging standards for subject headings assignment. But when a researcher knows how to search for subject headings in a catalog, conducting refined searches becomes much simpler. Searching for a particular author as a subject, for example, is a useful strategy for identifying multiple subject headings about a writer. This strategy allows a researcher to see what kinds of resources a library owns about a particular author, as well as to discover principal areas of scholarly attention and research on an author's works. Figure 3.2 highlights multiple subject headings for Bernard Shaw and illustrates the volume of Shaw scholarship produced in different areas of interest.

Num	Mark	SUBJECTS (L.C.) (85-96 of 103)	Year	Entries 786 Found
85	☐	Shaw Bernard 1856 1950 Quotations		2
86	☐	Shaw Bernard 1856 1950 Relations With Women		2
87	☐	Shaw Bernard 1856 1950 Religion		7
88	☐	Shaw Bernard 1856 1950 Saint Joan		15
89	☐	Shaw Bernard 1856 1950 Saint Joan Bibliography	1930	1
90	☐	Shaw Bernard 1856 1950 Sources		2
91	☐	Shaw Bernard 1856 1950 St Joan	c1964	1
92	☐	Shaw Bernard 1856 1950 Stage History		15
93	☐	Shaw Bernard 1856 1950 Stage History 1950		2
94	☐	Shaw Bernard 1856 1950 Stage History China	c2002	1
95	☐	Shaw Bernard 1856 1950 Stories Plots Etc		3
96	☐	Shaw Bernard 1856 1950 Technique	c1991	1

Figure 3.2. Modified catalog display for Bernard Shaw as the Library of Congress subject heading. Source: Orbis Cascade Alliance, Summit union catalog.

UNION CATALOGS

Copac, at copac.ac.uk (accessed 31 March 2008).

Library of Congress and the National Union Catalog Subcommittee of the Resources Committee of the Resources and Technical Services Division, American Library Association. *National Union Catalog, Pre-1956 Imprints: A Cumulative Author List Representing Library of Congress Printed Cards and Titles Reported by Other American Libraries.* 754 vols. London: Mansell, 1968–1981.

WorldCat. Dublin, OH: OCLC. www.worldcat.org (accessed 31 March 2008).

At best, local library catalogs offer a view of the resources available on a research topic that are limited to the holdings cataloged for an individual OPAC. When researchers reach the limits of the local catalog, they can turn to union catalogs to find additional relevant resources and to identify where those resources can be found. Union catalogs make available the combined holdings of individual participating libraries in the form of a comprehensive print or electronic catalog. Union catalogs gather together the holdings of local academic and/or public libraries, state or regional consortiums, or national and international library partnerships and so provide researchers with a greater number of bibliographic records that can be viewed simultaneously in a printed volume or searched online in an electronic database. Large, well-known union catalogs, such as *Copac*, the *National Union Catalog* (*NUC*), and *WorldCat*, are particularly useful tools for identifying existing editions of authors' works and locating where to find them. Union catalog databases contain a vast number of records for holdings among multiple libraries, so the quality of cataloging exhibited in these resources varies.

Currently the largest union catalog available, ***WorldCat***, is an exhaustive, constantly updated database created and maintained by a major vendor of online library services and products, OCLC (Online Computer Library Center). Originally developed by OCLC as a collaborative resource to help library catalogers quickly create and maintain cataloging records that could be edited by member libraries and downloaded to local catalogs from a consistent, central source, *WorldCat* has evolved into an indispensable resource for scholars and researchers, as well as libraries. Available by subscription in most academic libraries, *WorldCat* presently makes available bibliographic information for almost 74,000,000 cataloged items held by over 41,000 member institutions the world over. The curious can even watch *WorldCat* "grow" in real time from OCLC's *WorldCat* website (http://www.oclc.org/worldcat), which links to screens that show when new records are added to the database (on an average of every ten seconds) as well as statistics about the database and its holdings, which currently exceed 1.1 billion. Despite these impressive numbers, *WorldCat* still only contains information that its participating members contribute to the database. It is important for researchers to remember, therefore, that *WorldCat* may not contain a given library's complete holdings.

In addition to its astonishing scope and size, *WorldCat*'s detailed searching options have become standard among countless other resources. Users can search by author, title, subject, series, keyword, ISSN, ISBN, publisher, publisher location, and material type, as well as narrower elements within these categories, such as phrases, notes, and genres. Researchers can further limit searches by date, language, holding institutions, and format. By default, *WorldCat* ranks search results in descending order according to the number of libraries that hold an item, though users can select different results ranking options such as by date and relevance. These options allow researchers to construct specific searches for resources relevant to very specific topics, as in a search for titles of literary periodicals published in Dublin during the first half of the twentieth century, for example.

As mentioned earlier, *WorldCat* was originally designed as a cataloging resource, and so performs author and subject searches most effectively when researchers identify and use authoritative headings. Fortunately, *WorldCat* features several "Find Related" options to facilitate the search for authoritative headings. Links to related subjects, authors, articles, journal articles, reference resources, and previous searches will retrieve sources that include the same author and title. Using *WorldCat*'s related searches feature is also a useful method for finding different editions and formats of an author's works, as well as secondary resources about the author. The following *WorldCat* record for a reprint edition of Nuala Ní Dhomhnaill's poetry collection, *The Astrakhan Cloak*, illustrates these options (figure 3.3).

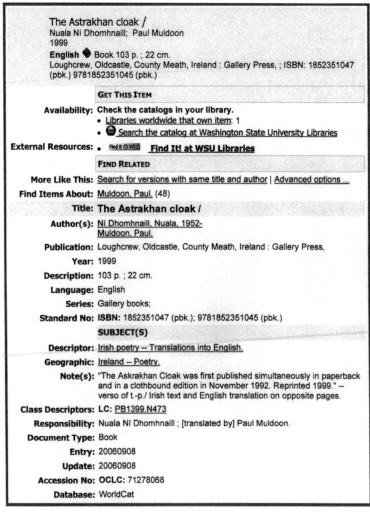

Figure 3.3. Modified *WorldCat* record for *The Astrakhan Cloak*. Source: *WorldCat*, via FirstSearch.

Each *WorldCat* record features a link to the number of libraries worldwide that have reported holdings for a given title. Yet, as described above, holdings reported to *WorldCat* do not necessarily correspond to a library's actual holdings. To verify whether a library holds a particular title in its collection, it is necessary to check the library's catalog directly, which itself contains only those titles and items that have been cataloged for inclusion in the online database. If the library does not hold the title sought, then researchers can use *WorldCat* to identify holding libraries and, if available, use *WorldCat*'s interlibrary loan request feature to borrow the title from an institution that owns the item.

Most of *WorldCat*'s records are also accessible to Web users through *WorldCat.org*, which is OCLC's online portal to *WorldCat* bibliographical record as well as some full-text and streaming digital content, including articles, maps, audio, and video. *WorldCat.org*'s potential as a bibliographic utility is remarkable. *WorldCat* is continuously updated, and scholars can conduct searches of tens of thousands of records, receive lists of locations of institutions that hold items of interest, avail themselves of the "Ask a Librarian" feature that connects searchers with local librarians for live assistance, and have the capability of reviewing or adding factual value to items described in records. Users may need to access this tool from an OCLC member library in order to view or download content or check out materials through *WorldCat.org*. *Google*, *Yahoo!Search*, *Windows Live Academic*, and other non-search engine sites devoted to bibliography and the book trades provide access to *WorldCat* records. When a Web user conducts a title search in, say, *Google* that matches a *WorldCat* title, the list of results retrieved by the search engine list will include a link to *WorldCat* data. Labeled "Find in a Library," the *WorldCat* link provides a brief bibliographic record and options to search holding libraries by postal code, state, province, or country. After conducting a geographic search for holding institutions, the user receives a list of local libraries that includes distance and contact information and, if available, links to online catalogs. Users can then check these catalogs to confirm if the local library of choice actually owns the sought item. Like the dedicated *WorldCat* database available in many libraries, participation in the *Open WorldCat* program is subscription-based, and only participating institutions have holdings displayed during Web searches. More information on OCLC's innovative *Open WorldCat* program is available on the Web. Recently, OCLC partnered with the Research Library Group (RLG) to integrate their respective online products and services, effectively eliminating overlap between holdings in the *RLG Union Catalog* and *WorldCat*. As a result, researchers can now access millions of holdings in multiple formats, including books, cartographic materials, electronic resources, sound recordings, music, serials, and photographs, previously not included in either database. Combined, *WorldCat* and the *RLG Union Catalog* serve as a powerful union catalog unmatched in the number of records available and the breadth and depth of items represented. And like *Copac*, *WorldCat* is now freely available to users via the World Wide Web.

Copac contains over thirty-one million records contributed by the twenty-seven member institutions of the Consortium of Research Libraries (CURL). Member institutions include significant research organizations and national libraries in Ireland and the United Kingdom such as the British Library, Cambridge University, the National Library of Scotland, the National Library of Wales, Oxford University, and the Trinity College Dublin Library, which will be discussed in the next section. As is the case with any union catalog, *Copac* only includes records that are available in its members' online catalogs. Researchers can review this information on individual library websites to gain a comprehensive understanding of each library's holdings. Most *Copac* records describe books, but periodicals and conference proceedings as well as nonprint items such as audio and visual recordings and electronic resources are also represented. Several contributors are august academic institutions with a few cataloged materials that date as far back as the twelfth century. Still, almost 40 percent of *Copac* records represent items published since the early 1980s.

Copac's default searching interface limits researchers to author/title or subject searches, options that search the entire catalog. From this interface, users can also select to narrow searches by material type to retrieve only periodicals or maps. Once a researcher selects the author search option, *Copac* provides additional fields useful for customizing searches, such as organization, title, publisher, ISBN/ISSN, publication date, language, and library. The subject search option allows scholars to limit by publication date, language, and library. Author searches only require first name initials as opposed to full or authoritative versions of authors' names to retrieve relevant results. Likewise, authoritative or controlled subject headings are not required to retrieve relevant results during a *Copac* subject search. Inputting the term *lady gregory* as a subject, for example, retrieves the same number of results as a subject search for *gregory lady*. Thus, while most of the controlled terms in *Copac* are Library of Congress subject headings, the catalog's indexing is flexible enough to accommodate searches for alternative subject headings.

Copac displays search results as a numbered list of brief citations with links in each line that allow users to tag (mark) or view "full record details" for each citation. Full record details include fields describing information found in most catalog records: publisher, physical description, standard number, notes, subject headings, added names, and, if available, links to holding libraries. Superscript asterisks by the names of holding institutions indicate that users can link to data in the holding library's catalog regarding the item's current location, classmark, and circulation status. The record in figure 3.4 illustrates differences between *Copac* and *WorldCat* records for the same item, such as the presentation of information (i.e., Muldoon is listed under "Other Names" rather than as an "Author"), slight variations in subject headings, different notes, and more detailed information regarding languages featured in the volume.

Copac offers several benefits to the researcher, namely, simple searching for unique resources at no cost. One drawback to using *Copac* is the availability of relevant items to distant users. Items located in *Copac* that cannot be found in *WorldCat* may be available to scholars through their local library's interlibrary loan service. Likewise, CURL and other scholarly research consortia sponsor digitization projects that may include versions of rare, relevant items sought by researchers. Reference librarians are an excellent resource to consult for more information regarding such projects and initiatives. Relevant items restricted for use and not available through interlibrary loan or as digital documents may be available in other ways. Researchers can directly contact holding libraries to discuss other options.

Main Author:	Ni Dhomhnaill, Nuala, 1952-
Title Details:	The Astrakhan cloak / Nuala Ni Dhomhnaill ; [translated by] Paul Muldoon
Series:	Gallery books
Publisher:	Loughcrew, Oldcastle, County Meath, Ireland : Gallery Press, 1992
Physical desc.:	103 p ; 22 cm
ISBN/ISSN:	1852351047 (pbk) 1852351055 (hbk)
Note:	Irish & English Irish text and English translation on opposite pages
Subject:	Irish poetry - 20th century - Translations into English Ireland - Poetry
Other Names:	Muldoon, Paul
Document Type:	Poetry
Language:	English Irish

For holdings information select a library from those below. Those marked with an asterisk give current availability. Held by: Aberdeen ; British Library ; Cambridge* ; Edinburgh* ; Glasgow* ; Liverpool* ; National Library of Scotland ; National Library of Wales ; Oxford* ; Sheffield* ; Southampton* ; Trinity College Dublin* ; UCL (University College London)* ; University of London - ULRLS*

Figure 3.4. Modified catalog record for *The Astrakhan Cloak*. Source: Copac.

Appropriate contacts are usually listed on library websites and online directories.

The previous discussion about online union catalogs may suggest that such comprehensive resources did not exist before the advent of Internet technology. The ***National Union Catalog, Pre-1956 Imprints*** (commonly referred to as the *NUC*), however, is a standard reference resource and extraordinary example of a print union catalog. The *NUC* is best suited for researching different editions of particular works published before the mid-1950s. The *NUC* consists of 754 volumes containing reproductions of library catalog cards representing over twelve million entries for items held at the Library of Congress and other libraries in the United States and Canada. Arranged alphabetically by author or editor name (personal or corporate), and then by title for items without names, the *NUC* does not lend itself to subject searches. In addition to these organizational limitations, the *NUC* also possesses a few features that researchers may find confusing. For example, the *NUC* consists of two separate alphabetical sequences. The first runs A to Z, from volumes 1 to 685. Volumes 686 to 754, on the other hand, list an additional alphabetical sequence of approximately 900,000 entries. Also, sections on major authors represented by several works are arranged by category rather than alphabetically by title. Finally, *NUC* cataloging quality varies from card to card and reflects the flexible and sometimes creative implementation of cataloging standards by libraries. As a result, variant descriptions of the same title appear in the *NUC* as separate editions, a fact that might confound the researcher seeking to trace distinct editions of a title. These irregularities and limitations aside, the *NUC* remains a valuable resource for scholars interested in locating items that may not be in a library's online catalog, as well as an indispensable supplement to online union catalogs that may not represent older, unique materials and editions potentially relevant to research projects.

NATIONAL LIBRARY CATALOGS

British Library Integrated Catalogue, at catalogue.bl.uk (accessed 31 March 2008).

Library of Congress Online Catalog, at catalog.loc.gov (accessed 31 March 2008).

National Library of Ireland Online Catalogues, at hip.nli.ie/ (accessed 31 March 2008).

Trinity College Library Online Catalogue, at www.tcd.ie/Library (accessed 31 March 2008).

Most national libraries are depository institutions, and as such, they receive a copy of each work published in the sponsoring country, including everything from titles published by commercial, academic, and specialized concerns to national government documents, as well as items from other countries. National library catalogs are exceptional research resources because of the breadth and depth of their holdings and for the range of services they provide, many at no cost to the user. In addition, national libraries often hold unique items produced by the institutions themselves, such as sound and video recordings of presentations, lectures, and readings that may be of particular interest to those studying modern literary authors, works, and topics.

The Library of Congress (LOC) maintains one of the largest library collections in the world, holding 130 million items in various formats, including print, audio and video recordings, photographs, cartographic materials, manuscripts, and electronic resources. The *Library of Congress Online Catalog* features standard interfaces for both basic and guided searching. The basic search interface allows users to search by title, author/creator, subject, keyword, command keyword (which provides for complex keyword searching with Boolean operators and index codes), LC call number, LCCN (Library of Congress Card Number)/ISBN/ISSN, series/uniform title, and author/creator sorted by title. During the course of a basic search, users have the option to limit title, keyword, command keyword, and standard number searches by date, language, material type, location within the Library of Congress, and place of publication. The guided search option allows users to set the search limits available in the basic search interface as well as to construct complex keyword searches of specific fields in a bibliographic record. A researcher, for example, could search for *heaney seamus* as a keyword in a personal name field and *tollund* as a keyword in a title field and further limit her results to items located in the LOC's Recorded Sound department to locate an audio recording of Seamus Heaney reading his poem "Tollund Man." While the Library of Congress maintains one of the world's largest library collections, it does not circulate many items to users not directly affiliated with the organization. Typically, other libraries fill user requests for items held by the LOC, unless it holds the only circulating copy of an item. The *LOC Online Catalog* is most useful to researchers as a resource to supplement *WorldCat* searches. For Irish literature scholars, the *LOC Online Catalog* is also useful for identifying relevant secondary material and unique or expanded subject headings for subsequent searches in local or union catalogs. And because the *LOC Online Catalog* is free to anyone with Internet access, it is a rich, high-quality research tool for identifying relevant resources for users who do not have access to subscription databases.

The British Library is the depository institution for the United Kingdom and as such holds a copy of each item published in the UK. It also serves as a depository for the Republic of Ireland, an arrangement outlined in Irish legislation that provides Trinity College Dublin Library with reciprocal depository rights to materials published in the United Kingdom. This arrangement contributes to the British Library's unparalleled status as an institution that maintains one of the largest and fastest-growing library collections in the world. Currently, the British Library holds more than one hundred and fifty million items, and adds three million items to its collections each year. In addition, the British Library maintains a Modern Irish Collection that includes major holdings in primary and secondary resources for the study of Irish history, literature, and language, as well as a significant collection of academic and literary periodicals relevant to Irish studies. The ***British Library Integrated Catalogue*** provides access to over twelve million items, including resources in the Modern Irish Collection, that were previously accessible in separate, subset sources, such as Reference and Document Supply catalogs, Serials and Periodicals, Newspapers, Cartographic, and Asia, Pacific, and Africa Collections. The default basic search interface allows users to search keywords or phrases in the author, title, publication year, publisher, subject headings (LC and others), ISBN/ISSN, and shelfmark fields. The advanced search interface is similar to that of *WorldCat*, and provides for searching across multiple fields as well as limiting searches by language, year, and format. The *British Library Integrated Catalogue* also features a "Catalogue Subset Search" interface that enables users to search one or more individual subset catalogs. The Newspapers collection is an exception to this feature, and must be searched separately, though newspaper holdings are searchable in the integrated catalog interface. Researchers who identify relevant items in the *British Library Integrated Catalogue* can often request copies for a fee. The library's "Information and Research Services" page outlines loan policies and procedures, as well as a range of document supply services and fees.

The Trinity College Library embodies several superlatives. Founded with the college in 1592, it is one of the oldest libraries in the West. It houses one of the most famous and recognizably "Irish" manuscripts in the world, the astonishingly beautiful *Book of Kells*. It is the largest library in Ireland and holds over four million volumes, with extensive holdings in Irish periodicals, manuscripts, maps, and music. As Ireland's counterpart to the British Library, Trinity College Library also serves as a primary national depository institution. The ***Trinity College Library Online Catalogue*** consists of four sections, Main Catalogue (From 1920), Periodicals, Early Printed Books (Before 1920), and Reserve Collection Indexes, that reflect the library's triple role as an academic library supporting rigorous college curricula, a research library that preserves and provides access to special and rare resources, and a depository library that provides information services to support national and civic interests. The catalog page notes that the Main Catalog and Early Printed Book sections provide access to items cataloged since 1968, and advises users who need resources cataloged outside this scheme to consult print catalogs maintained on campus. The default search interface is unique from others discussed in this chapter because it allows users to search alphabetically across several familiar search fields, such as title, author, and subject. Researchers can also select a keyword search option from the main catalog page that provides for searching by these fields as well as by series, publisher, ISBN/ISSN, and notes fields. Selecting the keyword search option also reveals additional search controls that allow users to conduct advanced keyword searches with Boolean operators, limit searches by date, language, and material type, and maintain a search history for the purpose of duplicating successful searches or to avoid repeating unsuccessful searches. Even though it provides access to the holdings of a national depository library, the *Trinity College Library Online Catalogue* differs widely from the LOC and British Library catalogs in terms of its reliance on the print catalogs maintained by the library. Also, the search interfaces, while unique, do not seem as flexible or intuitive as those provided by the other catalogs. Still, the *Trinity College Library Online Catalogue* remains a seminal resource for Irish literature scholarship, especially in respect to manuscript and primary sources.

Unlike the institutions described above, the National Library of Ireland is not a depository organization. However, it does serve Irish cultural as well as academic and research interests, and provides access to critical resources for the study of Irish literature that are not available in other institutions. In terms of numbers, it houses a relatively modest collection of just over a million printed books. Still, the National Library of Ireland is an institution rich in historical and cultural resources and maintains impressive Irish newspaper and periodical collections. The **National Library of Ireland Online Catalogues** are, as the name suggests, a group of catalogs organized according to format, with separate catalogs providing access to books and periodicals, photographs, prints and drawings, and manuscripts. The default search interface is identical among the separate catalogs, and presents scholars with an alphabetical index option similar to that of the *Trinity College Library Online Catalogue*. Likewise, researchers can select a more traditional keyword option from the default OPAC screen. In addition, users can browse each section of the *National Library of Ireland Catalogues* by familiar terms such as author, title, and subject, while individual sections offer specialized categories such as artist, series, publisher, and Irish publication date by year to facilitate narrower searching in specific formats. The *National Library of*

Ireland Catalogues page also provides links to newspaper, photograph, and manuscript databases that feature resources that may or may not be included in the main online catalog, as well as links to lists of new books published in Ireland over the course of the previous year. Like the *British Library Integrated Catalogue*, the *National Library of Ireland Catalogues* provide users with fee-based item reproduction services, all of which are described on the library's Services page.

CONCLUSION

The development of Internet access to online catalogs has facilitated unparalleled and unprecedented access to library holdings throughout the world. Online catalogs provide increased access to relevant resources by means of traditional author, title, and subject searches, as well as the capacity to search other bibliographical record fields by keyword. While most online catalogs do not contain a library's complete holdings, they do provide for more flexible and dynamic searching of items that have been cataloged for online formats. Online union catalogs further extend the parameters of identifying and locating relevant materials, while most national library catalogs provide free access to considerable collections. Researchers still have access to significant print resources like the *NUC* to identify and locate older materials that are not available in online catalogs. As scholarship in the field becomes more sophisticated and complex, Irish literature scholars can avail themselves of an impressive selection of tools to identify and locate sources and secondary material for the next era of Irish literature research.

Chapter Four

Print and Electronic Bibliographies, Indexes, and Annual Reviews

The word "bibliography," defined according to its etymological roots, can be literally translated as "book-writing." In one sense, the term refers to a notion of authorship connected to a specific medium. It also evokes the idea of writing about books, of books as a scholarly subject in their own right. This chapter covers bibliography in the latter sense, especially in respect to books and other reference materials that are themselves lists of or directories to primary and secondary resources relevant to the study of Irish literature. Such bibliographies are commonly available in print or electronic formats, as well as other media, but all provide basic bibliographic information organized around a theme or topic chosen by the bibliography's compiler(s). A bibliography's subject may be broad in scope (e.g., modern Anglo-Irish literature, Irish women literary writers) or focus on a comparatively narrow area of interest (e.g., medieval Celtic literature, travel writing). Bibliographers may emphasize either primary resources (e.g., correspondence, diaries, drafts, first editions, journals) or critical secondary materials (e.g., book reviews, dissertations, journals and journal articles, scholarly monographs), while still others cover both primary and secondary resources.

Bibliographies, though varied in scope and application, are essential scholarly resources. Bibliographies of significant scope may require several years to compile, and may ultimately serve as comprehensive records of existing primary resources produced during a certain period of time or in a particular area of scholarship. Bibliographies encompassing such a massive scope typically supply bibliographic descriptions of items as well as indicate where these items are located. *A Guide to Irish Fiction, 1650–1900* is one notable example of a comprehensive bibliography that attempts to list all fiction about Ireland and the Irish, whether published in or outside the country, over a span of years.

While most bibliographies represent significant scholarly achievement, many do not possess the breadth of coverage exhibited in the *A Guide to Irish Fiction*. Indeed, scholarly bibliographies are often selective in scope and compiled to help scholars identify works relevant to the study of a subject area or academic discipline. As suggested above, many focus on themes and topics or emphasize particular authors, genres, literary periods, national literatures, publishers, or a combination of these selection elements. To illustrate, the *Modern Language Association International Bibliography* (*MLAIB*) provides bibliographical information about all modern languages and literatures, while *Seamus Heaney: A Reference Guide* covers primary and secondary resources relevant to the study of a single author's life and work.

Annual reviews are serial bibliographies that provide overviews of secondary literature (e.g., anthologies, critical editions, criticism, reference works, reviews) published over the course of a year. Annual reviews are typically published either as monographic series or journal supplements. Both formats have advantages and drawbacks. Book-length annual reviews are compiled by experts and scholars who select and comment upon the most credible and significant resources relevant to a particular academic area or discipline published during the year. Yet, as a result of this rigorous selection and annotation process, these types of annual reviews may reflect a considerable time-lag between the publication dates of the bibliography and the items described within. Annual reviews published in journals, on the other hand, tend to convey more timely information about work produced during the previous year, but may lack the scholarly apparatuses available in book-length annual reviews.

In addition to bibliographies, this chapter also discusses indexes, resources that provide access to the contents of a single item or multiple publications by means of access points such as author, subject, and title. A few major research resources function as both bibliographies and indexes. The *MLAIB* and the *Annual Bibliography of English Language and Literature* (*ABELL*) both serve as bibliographies as well as indexes. Like bibliographies and annual reviews, these databases list citations to books, book chapters, dissertations, and journal articles published during the course of a year. They also permit access to these records by means of author/editor, title, and subject indexes based on assigned, controlled vocabularies.

Traditionally, short-title catalogs and other standard literary bibliographies were formidable print resources, often available only at larger research institutions and requiring special skills and knowledge to use. Increasingly, however, electronic and Web-based media have facilitated unprecedented access to these important resources. Online versions of *MLAIB* and *ABELL* are now available and scholars can retrieve the resources in them by means of the typically indexed access points of author, title, and subject, in addition to other fields which can be combined for advanced searches. To illustrate, researchers using the online version of the *MLAIB* can search for records by keyword, literary work, article title, publication date, journal name, full text, author, author as subject, literary theme, genre, publisher, and document type. They can further limit searches by publication type, most recent citation, and language. Some databases are available through multiple vendors and are thus cross-searchable. Cross-searchable online resources permit users to link to electronic full-text versions of works in one database from bibliographical citations in another, or to link to the user's local library catalog in order to locate a copy of a needed item. *ABELL* is a component of the *Literature Online* database package, which offers full-text access to English and American primary literary resources, as well as full-text access to research resources such as literary journals and reference works. When available, *ABELL* provides links from bibliographic entries to full-text sources maintained in other sections of *Literature Online*. Databases such as *JSTOR* and *Project MUSE* supplement these functions by linking to full-text versions of the source described by the record and indexed in the database.

As mentioned, compiling bibliographies for publication is time-intensive work and print annual reviews sometimes lag behind expected publication schedules. Yet another advantage of online bibliographies is the capability to update contents quickly. Bibliographies of secondary resources are well-served by regular updating, usually on a monthly basis, which reduces publication delays and provides access to recent criticism. In addition to making new scholarship available in more timely ways, online bibliographies allow scholars to identify earlier critical works with ease. Users of the print indexes of *MLAIB* and *ABELL* have to browse each individual year's index for relevant information. In contrast, the online version of *MLAIB* permits users to search its annual bibliographies from the 1920s to the present; access prior to 1926 is selective. Similarly, the online version of *ABELL* provides selective access to records for items published between 1892 and 1926 and cumulative access to bibliographic records from the late 1920s to the present. Scholars also benefit from the multiple access points available in the online versions of these standard works. Online bibliographies of primary resources and short-title catalogs continue to add relevant materials to the databases as previously unrecorded items are discovered, described, and cited.

Despite the benefits discussed above, online bibliographies possess a few shortcomings. Namely, access to most of these resources is available only to subscribing institutions and individuals. Fortunately, most university libraries subscribe to one or more full-text literature resources. In addition, other subscription-based general databases often available in many smaller academic libraries, such as EBSCO's *Academic Search Premier*, index selected literary criticism. Useful literary and specialized bibliographies also appear on the Web. Formerly available in print, the Celtic Studies Association of North America now publishes its cumulative bibliography on the Web. Updated on an ongoing basis, the *Celtic Studies of North America (CSANA) Online Bibliography* indexes scholarly books, periodicals, Festschriften, proceedings, and other publications relevant to the study of Irish and other Celtic literatures. Users can search the bibliography by keyword, author, title, and subject, and it even includes an index of controlled subject headings. The *CSANA Online Bibliography* is only one example of such a Web-based bibliographic tool. Chapter 10, "Web Resources," discusses in more detail this and other online bibliographies covering both primary and secondary resources.

The publication of various kinds of Irish literature bibliographies suggests the diverse nature of the field. It would be difficult to pinpoint the first major bibliography dedicated to Irish literature or a single, definitive resource on this promethean literary subject. Still, scholars can avail themselves of a wide range of resources for bibliographical information relevant to Irish literature research. Many journals devoted to Irish authors and literature, for example, publish annual bibliographies of and indexes to the previous year's contents. These annual bibliographies are excellent resources for identifying current research into specific topics and authors. Likewise, some national and university presses specializing in Irish literary resources publish catalogs and annual lists of relevant titles. On the other hand, many print bibliographies devoted to Irish literature or Anglo-Irish literature in general are also available. Though many of these general resources were published several years ago, they remain relevant due to their specialized focus and in-depth coverage of this subject.

Bibliographies' unique status as "writing about books" necessarily requires specialized knowledge and skills to use them effectively, whether researchers are using print or electronic versions of these resources. Though sometimes overlooked, a bibliography's front matter, introduction, or "About" links are essential reading; compilers typically outline a bibliography's parameters in these sections. In addition to learning about the scope of the resource from this material, scholars can determine its purpose and arrangement, learn why and how compilers selected the items included, discover what has been excluded and why, and determine if and how often the bibliography is updated. Compilers might also explain the elements cited for each bibliographic record (e.g., author, title, owning institution), offer suggestions for using the bibliography and indexes, and acknowledge inconsistencies or particularities, if known.

Though bibliographies can be arranged in a variety of ways, print bibliographies are commonly organized by subject. Bibliography compilers and readers may not necessarily agree on the subject of a cited work, however. In light of this prospect, scholars should consult indexes in addition to the subject categories to identify valuable resources that may be listed in unexpected places. Likewise, users of online bibliographies should become familiar with the controlled vocabularies particular to each database so that they can search with appropriate subject headings. Online bibliographies, like other electronic databases and catalogs, provide examples of successful search strategies on their help screens to facilitate effective use of these resources.

While it seems obvious, scholars benefit most when they choose bibliographies that best serve their research needs in a particular context. Researchers trying to identify first editions of well-known Irish literature authors writing after 1880, for example, can consult *A Bibliography of Modern Irish and Anglo-Irish Literature* for lists of works published by Yeats, Joyce, Shaw, and Beckett, among others. Scholars seeking an overview of criticism on the work of these writers, however, are better served by a resource like *Recent Research on Anglo-Irish Writers* (see chapter 2), which describes relevant secondary sources about these and other Irish authors. Bibliographies devoted to the work of a single author typically provide similar types of information regarding primary and secondary resources. Likewise, information about authors associated with particular genres may be available in genre-specific bibliographies. Short-title catalogs provide citations to primary sources published during the eighteenth and early nineteenth centuries, while the online versions of *ABELL* and *MLAIB* are useful tools for identifying criticism and other secondary resources published since the first half of the twentieth century. Researchers wishing to evaluate the most recent scholarship on a specific author or subject can consult annual publications such as the *Year's Work in English Studies* (*YWES*). In the end, it is helpful to remember that bibliography is a specialized, non-standardized field of scholarship. Each bibliography is unique and possesses its own strengths and weaknesses. Scholars who acquire a solid working knowledge of a variety of these specialized resources will be able to utilize them to their fullest potential. This chapter describes several general and Irish literature bibliographies with the aim of helping researchers determine which ones will be most useful for their projects.

GENERAL LITERATURE BIBLIOGRAPHIES

Annual Bibliography of English Language and Literature (*ABELL*). Leeds: Maney Publishing for the Modern Humanities Research Association, 1921–. www.chadwyck.com.

Bateson, F. W., ed. *Cambridge Bibliography of English Literature*. 4 vols. Cambridge: Cambridge University Press, 1940. Watson, George, ed. Supplement. 1957.

JSTOR: The Scholarly Journal Archive. New York: JSTOR, 1995–. www.jstor .org/. *Modern Language Association International Bibliography of Books and Articles on the Modern Languages and Literatures (MLAIB)*. New York: Modern Language Association of America, 1922–. Annual. Available online through various vendors. Check www.mla.org/bib_ electronic for a list of online vendors.

Project MUSE. Baltimore, MD: Johns Hopkins University, 1993–. muse.jhu.edu.

Shattock, Joanne, ed. *The Cambridge Bibliography of English Literature*. 3rd ed. Vol. 4: 1800–1900. New York: Cambridge University Press, 1999.

Watson, George, ed. *The New Cambridge Bibliography of English Literature*. 2nd ed. 5 vols. Cambridge: Cambridge University Press, 1971.

Year's Work in English Studies. Oxford: Published for the English Association by Oxford University Press, 1921–. Annual. www3.oup.co.uk/ywes.

The literature bibliographies discussed in this section are standard research tools well-known to most literature scholars. For literature students and scholars in the United States, the **Modern Language Association International Bibliography *(MLAIB)*** is the primary bibliographic source for literary studies. Originally published under the title *American Bibliography* from 1921 to 1955, this standard bibliographic resource was published annually in issues of the periodical *Publications of the Modern Language Association of America (PMLA)* until 1968. The bibliography's original title accurately emphasizes the early scope of this publication, which generally focused on scholarship produced in the United States. In 1956, the bibliography widened its selection criteria to include more international scholarship. Most academic libraries own multi-volume reprints or microfilmed reproductions of these older bibliographies. In 1969, the bibliography was published in four volumes, each organized according to specific subject areas: 1) General, English, American, Medieval and Neo-Latin, and Celtic literatures; 2) European, Asian, African, and Latin-American literatures; 3) linguistics; and 4) pedagogy in foreign languages, as compiled by the American Council on the Teaching of Foreign Languages (ACTFL). Each volume features its own table of contents and indexes arranged by author/editor/compiler. In 1981, a fifth volume covering folklore was added, and author and subject indexes for the entire bibliography were compiled and published in a separate volume.

The MLAIB currently cites articles, books, and dissertations concerned with literature, linguistics, modern languages, and folklore published during a review year. Still published in the five-volume format initiated in 1981, the bibliography features a slightly altered arrangement: 1) British and Irish, Commonwealth, English Caribbean, and American literatures; 2) European, Asian, African, and Latin American literatures; 3) linguistics; 4) general literature, humanities, teaching of literature, and rhetoric and composition; and 5) folklore. A comprehensive subject index covering the contents of all five volumes is published separately. Irish literature scholars consulting the current print bibliography will find relevant citations in the "Irish literature" section of Volume 1, though other volumes may also prove useful for interdisciplinary and comparative research projects, and for projects about authors connected in some way to Ireland. Citations are comprehensive and entries are chronologically arranged by period (starting with criticism of fifth-century Irish literature) and then alphabetically organized by general studies, genre (e.g., theater, biography, criticism, drama, fiction, novel, poetry, prose), and finally by literary author/subject/work. Each citation features subject descriptors summarizing an item's contents.

The Modern Language Association provides the standardized descriptors assigned to works included in the bibliography. These headings are unique to the *MLAIB* and do not correspond to Library of Congress subject headings or other controlled vocabularies. Indeed, MLA descriptors possess their own structure and syntax. Sample Irish literature descriptors include: "By women poets. Romantic period. Relationship to English-Irish relations"; and "Postmodernist novel. Treatment of Irish politics; cultural identity; relationship to postcolonialism." The subject index, on the other hand, shares features with other kinds of resources organized by subject and "provides access to names of persons, languages, groups, genres, stylistic and structural features, themes, sources, influences, processes, theories, and other related topics" (2005; xxiv). Headings relevant to Irish literature encompass a range of subjects, from the general ("Interview," "Short Story," "Irish Gaelic language literature," "Irish nationalism") to the specific ("Gothic conventions; relationship to ghost; Great Famine (Ireland)," "Treatment of education in Northern Ireland compared to Muldoon, Paul"). The subject index cross-references entries in all volumes, and provides "see also" references to narrower, preferred, and related subject terms. In addition, the subject index allows scholars to check topics and authors against the entries that appear in the classified sections pertinent to their research to identify relevant works that may be listed in other sections of the bibliography, which does not duplicate citations.

An online version of the *MLAIB* providing access to entries from the 1920s to the present is available from various vendors. In this chapter, descriptions of this resource and its features are based on the Thomson Gale's *InfoTrac* version. The "Advanced Search" screen is the default interface, which permits

users to select a variety of familiar and distinct access points, including: keyword; literary work; article title; publication date; journal name; article author; author as subject; subject; language; literary theme; genre; publisher;
document type; and ISBN/ISSN. In addition, researchers can limit searches to
refereed publications, citations to the most recent database update, and within
a specific date range. As these options suggest, the online version of the
MLAIB features refined and robust indexing that allows users the potential to
conduct and control detailed searches. Researchers can also select less-de-
tailed but familiar author, subject, or title search options. Help screens offer
detailed suggestions for conducting effective searches in each available option. Results display as brief citations listed in reverse chronological order according to publication date, while full records list general subject areas and
subject terms. Each entry in the database includes detailed subject areas such
as subject literature, period, primary subject author, genre, and subject terms
that describe the item's contents (see figure 4.1).

Compiled since 1921 under the auspices of the Modern Humanities Research Association, the ***Annual Bibliography of English Language and Literature*** (*ABELL*) is the British counterpart to the *MLAIB*. Worldwide in
scope, *ABELL* lists books, book reviews, collections of essays, critical editions of literary works, journal articles, and unpublished doctoral dissertations

Dotterer, Ronald L. "Flann O'Brien, James Joyce, and *The Dalkey Archive*." *New
Hibernia Review/Iris Éireannach Nua: A Quarterly Record of Irish Studies*, 8:2 (2004
Summer), pp. 54-63.
http://muse.jhu.edu/journals/new_hibernia_review/v008/8.2dotterer.html.

Subject Terms:	Irish literature; 1900-1999; O'Nolan, Brian (1911-1966): The Dalkey Archive (1964); novel; treatment of Joyce, James (1882-1941).
Language:	English
Document Type:	Journal article
ISSN:	1092-3977
Peer Reviewed:	Yes
MLA Update:	200401
MLA Sequence:	2004-1-8535
MLA Record Number:	2004872062
Source Database:	© *MLA International Bibliography*. New York: Modern Language Association of America, 1963- .
Gale Record Number:	N2811954911

Figure 4.1. Modified *MLAIB* record for "Flann O'Brien, James Joyce, and
The Dalkey Archive." Source: *MLAIB* via InfoTrac.

(for the period 1920–1999) published in any language. This resource covers all aspects and periods of English language and literature and represents British, American, and Commonwealth literatures. Print volumes are organized into several categories: bibliography; scholarly method; language, literature and the computer; newspapers and other periodicals; the English language; traditional culture, folklore, and folklife; and English literature. This last section is subdivided into general literary studies, old English, and Middle English and fifteenth century, and then by period up to the twenty-first century. Sections are subsequently arranged by genres (including children's literature, cinema, and broadcast media, where appropriate), related studies, literary theory, and authors. Entries are listed alphabetically by critic within each category. Some entries include cross-references or cite reviews. Unlike the *MLAIB*, *ABELL* does not organize national literatures into their own sections. Irish literature scholars, therefore, are obliged to consult the appropriate section for the period they study and review all the entries listed in a given category for relevant works. While *ABELL* does provide indexes organized by authors and film directors as well as by scholars, subject indexing was discontinued with the seventy-fifth volume of the bibliography (published in 2000).

Electronic versions of *ABELL*, published by Chadwyck-Healey, are available in online and CD-ROM formats. The online version provides coverage from 1920 the present, with selective coverage of retrospectively indexed items published between 1892 and 1919. While the print and CD-ROM version are published annually, new bibliographic records are loaded to the online version on a monthly basis. Depending on the subscribing library, *ABELL* online is available either as a stand-alone database or as a component of *Literature Online*, a resource that permits users to link from bibliographic records to electronic full-text versions of resources when available. The *ABELL* interface provides researchers with a selection of searchable access points: keyword(s); title keyword(s); subject; author/reviewer(s); publication details; journal; ISBN; ISSN; and publication year. Users can further limit their searches to return only citations to articles, books, reviews, or combinations of these publications. Main search fields include links to a browse feature that allows scholars to look for index terms to cut-and-paste into a search, as well as alphabetical lists of additional search terms from which to select more specific terms to further refine searches. Numerous headings relevant to the study of Irish literature appear in these lists. Subject headings in *ABELL* bibliographic records, on the other hand, are very general and arranged according to a hierarchical formula that subdivides literary or language headings by period and author: English Literature: Twentieth Century: Authors: (name of specific author). More detailed headings are further subdivided by genre and general or relational descriptions: English Literature: General Literary Studies: Related Studies; or English Language: Medium and Register: Stylistics of Literary Texts. Figure 4.2 shows examples of both standard and additional search terms in *ABELL*. Author subject headings are cross-referenced; when a researcher conducts a search for *o'nolan brian*, for example, he will retrieve every entry that includes the authoritative heading "English Literature: Twentieth Century: Authors: O'Nolan, Brian." In this example and the sample record below, the heading "English literature" refers to British as well as non-British literature (e.g., Irish, Scottish, American, etc.). Search results display in reverse chronological order, with the most recent publications appearing at the top of the list.

While some entries in *ABELL* overlap *MLAIB* citations, these bibliographies are very different from one another. Researchers utilizing both databases will conduct more comprehensive searches with results representing a variety of sources published in both North America and Britain. James Harner, discussed in chapter 2, underscores the geographic dimension to breadth of coverage by describing *ABELL*'s thorough indexing of British books and for providing access to articles published in small British periodicals. In addition, *ABELL* indexes book reviews and provides electronic access to scholarship published between 1920 and 1963. In the past, scholars (including Harner) have recognized the *MLAIB* as the stronger resource in respect to coverage of recent scholarship, especially research published since 1980. In addition, until recently, the *MLAIB*'s entries were updated more frequently and contained citations to scholarship published within the current year, while *ABELL*'s online coverage primarily corresponded to the contents of the most recent print edition. Now, however, both databases are updated on a regular basis, though a lag between citations from periodicals indexed by

ABELL
Author: Dotterer, Ronald L.
Title: Flann O'Brien, James Joyce, and *The Dalkey Archive*.
Publication Details: New Hibernia Review / Iris Éireannach Nua (8:2) 2004, 54-63.
Publication Year: 2004
Subject: English Literature: Twentieth Century: Authors: Joyce, James
English Literature: Twentieth Century: Authors: gCopaleen, Myles na (Flann O'Brien, Brian O'Nolan)
English Literature: Twentieth Century: Authors: O'Nolan, Brian (Flann O'Brien, Myles na gCopaleen)
English Literature: Twentieth Century: Authors: O'Brien, Flann (Myles na gCopaleen, Brian O'Nolan)
Reference Number: 2004:17580; 2004:18703
Additional Search Terms: Influence, The Dalkey Archive

Figure 4.2.   Modified *ABELL* record for "Flann O'Brien, James Joyce, and *The Dalkey Archive*." Source: *ABELL*, via Literature Online.

both bibliographies may reflect the geographic strengths of each (i.e., citations to articles published in British periodicals often appear in *ABELL* before they do in the *MLAIB* and vice versa).

Slight differences in indexing and subject access between the two databases, on the other hand, remain distinctive. In the *MLAIB* record for the journal article "Flann O'Brien, James Joyce, and *The Dalkey Archive*," for example, subject terms appear directly after the citation and are listed separately according to subject literature, period, primary subject author, primary work, genre, followed by distinctive subject terms that further describe the content of the article: "treatment of Joyce, James (1882–1941)." In contrast, the *ABELL* record describing the same article displays subject content as single headings structured according to the *ABELL* heading formula: "English Literature: Twentieth Century: Authors: Joyce, James," "English Literature: Twentieth Century: Authors: gCopaleen, Myles na (Flann O'Brien, Brian O'Nolan)." As in the *MLAIB* record, unique search terms supplement these formulaic headings. While both records indicate that Flann O'Brian is a pseudonym for Brian O'Nolan, only the *ABELL* record makes this relationship clear, in addition to providing yet another of O'Nolan's pen-names, the musical Myles na gCopaleen. In the *MLAIB*, a keyword search for *gcopaleen* retrieves seven hits, while a keyword search for *myles na gcopaleen* returns six results. A keyword search for *gcopaleen myles na* results in no hits. Conducting the same searches in *ABELL*, on the other hand, yields 199 and 192 entries, respectively. Even though subject indexing and access is comparable between these two bibliographies, these examples suggest significant differences that emphasize the utility of searching both for records unique to each database, as well as variant search results.

The *MLAIB*, *ABELL*, and other large online bibliographies are excellent resources for comprehensive research projects such as literature reviews and research prospectuses. These bibliographies, however, index a far greater number of resources than most university and research libraries own and getting access to many titles of interest can be a frustrating experience for the scholar. While both databases offer limited access to full-text versions of some sources, most *MLAIB* and *ABELL* users will find it necessary to supplement the full-text articles they find with interlibrary loan requests for remaining citations. Full-text databases, on the other hand, are an option for the researcher interested in "one-stop shopping" for recent criticism on particular topics, as well as electronic access to journal back issues that may not be available at one's local library. Like the *MLAIB* and *ABELL*, most full-text resources are subscription-based and so primarily available in university and research libraries. ***Project MUSE*** is a highly regarded online database that provides full-text access to more than three hundred scholarly humanities, arts, and social sciences titles. More than ninety literary journals are available, including relevant Irish literature titles such as *Éire-Ireland*, *Joyce Studies Annual*, *New Hibernia Review*, and *SHAW: The Annual Review of Shaw Studies*. Coverage for each title varies, though *Project MUSE* typically provides access to between one to five years for each unique title. Some titles, such as the *Joyce Studies Annual*, are available only as archived issues. The "Advanced Search" interface allows users to search by keyword over the entire *Project MUSE* database, a specific subject collection such as "Irish studies" or "Literature," or an individual journal. Researchers can also opt to search by all text, all fields except text, article text, article author, article title, Library of Congress subject heading, and journal title. Limiting options include document type (e.g., article, review, poetry, fiction, or drama), date, and journals by subscription, title, and subject. Search results display as lists of citations, many of which include subject headings. From this list, scholars can link to HTML and sometimes PDF versions of full-text articles, as well as browse an electronic document that shows all occurrences of search terms within a particular article's text. Providing more information than an abstract or summary, this feature is an especially useful tool for scholars who wish to scan an article's actual contents to get an idea of how their own search terms and ideas occur and are used in the context of a published scholarly work.

Additionally, *Project MUSE* users can reciprocally browse twenty-five selected titles also available in another subscription-based, full-text resource: **JSTOR: The Scholarly Journal Archive**. This feature allows researchers to peruse the contents of entire journal runs from a single interface, rather than searching multiple databases for the complete contents of individual serials, which are often available only in specific date ranges. Coverage of these and other titles available through *JSTOR* and *Project MUSE* varies between libraries, based on the subscriptions held by individual institutions.

As indicated by its title, *JSTOR* provides access to scholarly journal articles, but emphasizes coverage of significant academic titles older than most of those indexed in *Project MUSE*. In some instances, *JSTOR* offers digitized versions of serials that began publication in the nineteenth century, as well as cross-indexing and tracing for titles that have undergone changes in title, publisher, and publication frequency over several years. *JSTOR* was originally designed to serve as an online archive of digitized copies of entire journal runs for libraries and other information organizations seeking to supplement or complete their print journal holdings. One great advantage of such a resource is its capacity to show the complexities of how ideas are transmitted and shaped over time in the context of scholarly publishing, as well as to reveal the intricacies of academic literature in general and how these conventions change. Currently, twenty-five scholarly journals are cross-linked between *JSTOR* and *Project MUSE*. Cross-indexed titles in *JSTOR* make available previous years of publication and include several journals useful for Irish literary study such as *boundary 2* (1972–1999), *ELH* (1934–1994), *MLN* (1962–1994), *Modern Language Notes* (1886–1961), *New Literary History* (1969–1994), and *Studies in English Literature, 1500–1900* (1961–2002). Unlike *Project MUSE*, *JSTOR* does not include a separate Irish studies or Irish literature subject collection. Yet language and literature journals are richly represented in both of these databases, and scholars researching multidisciplinary and comparative topics can avail themselves of holdings in other subject collections, including art, economics, history, philosophy, religion, and women's studies.

The *Cambridge Bibliography of English Literature* (*CBEL*) selectively covers primary and secondary works by and about British literary authors. First published in 1940, the *CBEL* remains a standard print reference source and is relevant to Irish literature scholarship especially for citations to older criticism of Irish authors and literature. It also serves as an example of how Irish literary sources and scholarship were historically understood in the contexts of British literary scholarship and criticism. The *CBEL* has been published in its entirety in two complete editions, the second published as *The New Cambridge Bibliography of English Literature* (*NCBEL*). A third edition is currently under preparation. Each edition is organized chronologically by genre and author and covers all periods of English literature. Generally, the *CBEL* and *NCBEL* incorporate citations for many Irish authors, including Edgeworth, Moore, Wilde, Joyce, and Beckett, in the main text of the appropriate period volume. The third volumes of these first two editions, however, also include separate sections covering Anglo-Irish literature (as well as other "literatures of the dominions"); additional material on Anglo-Irish literature appears in the Supplement (Volume 5) to the first edition. These divisions organized around national literatures follow the chronological arrangement of the *CBEL* and *NCBEL*, and further subdivide citations by types of secondary sources (e.g., bibliographies, histories, biographies, etc.) and genre (e.g., Gaelic sources, poetry, and drama). In both editions, Irish literature coverage focuses on general philological, critical, and historical literary works, and authors considered by the editors to be specifically affiliated with Irish literary revival movements. Yeats and Synge have their own subdivision in the Anglo-Irish literature sections of both editions, while Joyce, O'Casey, and Beckett all receive their own unique, substantive sections in volume 4 of the second edition.

Though only volume 4, covering the nineteenth century, of the third edition of the *CBEL* has yet been published, it clearly marks a departure from the previous editions in terms of its selection criteria and organization. Basically, the most recent edition of the *CBEL* endeavors to be more inclusive than previous incarnations of the bibliography, and features more entries on women, minority, and other previously unrepresented authors, as well as citations to non-print and electronic resources. The first and second editions, for example, distinguished between major and minor authors, a practice that has been abandoned in the third edition. In addition, Irish, Scottish, and Welsh authors have been integrated into the bibliography's main divisions, and appear in the volumes representing the time period during which their significant literary output appeared rather than in the volumes corresponding to dates of birth. Thus, entries on Shaw, Synge, and Yeats are set to appear in volume 5. Despite these changes, the scope and purpose of the *CBEL* has been fairly consistent throughout all three editions. While primary resources receive chief emphasis, selected secondary and reference resources are also cited. Descriptions and arrangement of organizational categories vary between editions, yet all essentially cover the following topics where and when applicable: general works; book production and distribution; literary relations with the Continent; poetry; the novel (including children's books); drama; prose; history; political economy; philosophy and science; religion; English studies; travel; household books; sport; education; and newspapers and magazines. Poetry, drama, and non-fiction categories are further sub-arranged by early-, middle-, and late-century period divisions. As mentioned earlier in this chapter, authors appear alphabetically within the genre or subject division in which they published a majority of their work or with which they are most readily identified. Relevant secondary sections include cross-references to main entries. Though the third edition has dispensed with distinctions between major and minor authors, it is obvious in this most recent incarnation of the *CBEL* that some writers have received considerably more critical attention than others. As a result, author entries necessarily present a variety of primary and secondary sources for scholars to negotiate. Entries for widely published, studied, and collected writers, for example, may include references to and locations of manuscript collections, bibliographies and other author-specific reference works, collections and selections of an author's works, contemporary reviews, and translations into other languages. Typically, however, author entries are divided into published primary and secondary resources. Primary resources are listed chronologically by date of first publication, and may also list diaries, journals, notebooks, letters, periodical and collaborative contributions, prefaces or introductions, translations, and pseudonymous works, as well as misattributed and spurious works. Users of these resources might note that some full titles have been abbreviated and that periodical citations feature volume and year information but do not feature page numbers. Secondary resources may provide lists of influential criticism, textual and bibliographical criticism, and authoritative bibliographies. Major author entries may also cite obituaries, author-specific periodicals, and film, radio, and television adaptations.

Published annually since 1920, *Year's Work in English Studies* (*YWES*) is a highly regarded, selective guide to significant English-language and literatures scholarship. *YWES* is a hybrid publication, a serial bibliography that provides critically robust reviews of scholarly works (primarily books) published during the year. An online version of this title providing access to issues published since 1996 is available to subscribing institutions and individuals, while subscribers of the Oxford Journals Digital Archive have access to the entire run of this title. Users of the online bibliography also have short-term access to issues published before 1996 on a pay-per-article basis.

Both print and electronic versions of this title are organized into chronologically arranged subjects, from Old English to modern literature. Coverage of American literature is split between that written before and after 1900. While recent issues of *YWES* contain a separate chapter, "New Literatures," encompassing scholarship of the literatures of Africa, Australia and New Zealand, Canada, the Caribbean, the Indian subcontinent and Sri Lanka, topics and subjects relevant to Irish literature research are covered in the various English language, literature, and critical chapters: "English Language"; "Old English Literature"; "Middle English: Excluding Chaucer"; "Middle English: Chaucer"; "The Sixteenth Century: Excluding Drama after 1550"; "Shakespeare"; "Renaissance Drama: Excluding Shakespeare"; "The Earlier Seventeenth Century: General, Women's Writing"; "Milton and Poetry, 1603–1660"; "The Later Seventeenth Century"; "The Eighteenth Century"; "The Nineteenth Century: The Romantic Period"; "The Nineteenth Century: The Victorian Period"; "Modern Literature"; and "Bibliography and Textual Criticism." Both versions of *YWES* are indexed by "critic" and "authors and subjects treated," which facilitates quick searching for relevant citations. While most chapters are divided into sections based on genre, some issues include chapters with separate sections devoted to Irish subjects. Several scholars contribute descriptions of significant additions to the field published during the year to each chapter, and titles reviewed include books, critical editions, essays or book chapters, journal articles, and on occasion, reference books published in Britain, Canada, and the United States.

Despite the inevitable time lag between the publication of the scholarly works reviewed and *YWES* itself, this bibliography is an indispensable tool for assessing critical and scholarly trends in literary studies. Because of its selective nature, *YWES* is very useful as a preliminary or initial research resource. Scholars who begin the research process by searching *YWES* can expand the scope of their projects by consulting other bibliographical resources, such as *ABELL* and *MLAIB*, to identify other relevant works.

IRISH LITERATURE BIBLIOGRAPHIES

Eager, Alan R. *A Guide to Irish Bibliographical Material: A Bibliography of Irish Bibliographies and Sources of Information*. Westport, CT: Greenwood Press, 1980.

Harmon, Maurice. *Select Bibliography for the Study of Anglo-Irish Literature and Its Backgrounds: An Irish Studies Handbook*. Port Credit, Ontario: P. D. Meany, 1977.

IASIL (International Association for the Study of Irish Literatures). *Bibliography Bulletin*, published annually in *Irish University Review*. 1972–.

Kersnowski, F. L., et al. *Bibliography of Modern Irish and Anglo-Irish Literature*. San Antonio: Trinity University Press, 1976.

Loeber, Rolf, and Magda Loeber, with Anne Mullin Burnham. *A Guide to Irish Fiction, 1650–1900*. Portland, OR: Four Courts Press, 2006.

McKenna, Brian. *Irish Literature, 1800–1875: A Guide to Information Sources*. Detroit, MI: Gale, 1978.

Mikhail, E. H. *An Annotated Bibliography of Modern Anglo-Irish Drama*. Troy, NY: Whitston Publishing Co., 1981.

O'Malley, William T. *Anglo-Irish Literature: A Bibliography of Dissertations, 1873–1989*. New York: Greenwood Press, 1990.

The bibliographies described here represent a range of Irish literature bibliographies published in the late twentieth century, though several excellent Irish literature bibliographies pre-dating these titles have been published and remain relevant, especially as references to older primary and secondary sources. Each suggests various approaches to and conceptions of the discipline. Some bibliographies are comprehensive in scope, others selective, and many address materials relevant to a specific era, genre, place of publication, theme, or a combination of these and other organizing principles. Irish literature bibliographies are particularly compelling examples of scholarship because definitions of "Irish literature" vary between compilers. Titles treated in this section were selected to illustrate these notions as well as to highlight the strengths of various bibliography formats.

Eager's *A Guide to Irish Bibliographical Material: A Bibliography of Irish Bibliographies and Sources of Information*, originally published in 1964, remains a standard index listing bibliographies and reference works relevant to Irish studies in general. More than 9,500 numbered entries cite books, parts of books, journal articles, periodicals, and manuscripts. Contents are arranged into thirteen sections by subject: general works, philosophy, religion, sociology, philology, science, useful arts, fine arts, geography and travel, biography, and history. While the scope of this work is broad, Eager devotes a section exclusively to literature. A great starting point for research into secondary sources, this bibliography is also a convenient resource for exploring interdisciplinary topics and questions. Author and subject indexes facilitate quick and flexible navigation of the guide's contents. Most of the items listed are of Irish origin and may be difficult for scholars to locate at local libraries. Researchers are encouraged to work with interlibrary loan departments to verify what is available.

A Guide to Irish Bibliographical Material provides comprehensive coverage of a variety of primary and secondary sources. O'Malley's ***Anglo-Irish Literature: A Bibliography of Dissertations, 1873–1989***, on the other hand, is a unique resource focusing on a specific type of academic literature. Because theses and dissertations often document detailed evidence of research (e.g., literature reviews, defense of a critical argument, citations to works cited, bibliographies, and peer review), they are excellent scholarly resources. In addition to providing a convenient listing of resources produced at more than 350 universities in twenty-eight different countries, including Canada, Great Britain, Ireland, and the United States, O'Malley's book offers a fascinating overview of how the study of Irish literature has evolved over a one-hundred-year period, especially in respect to which authors and topics have been widely represented or neglected in secondary literature and criticism during specific eras. Citations to more than four thousand dissertations address Anglo-Irish literary topics and the lives and work of Irish authors primarily writing between 1600 and 1965 in a wide range of genres, including criticism, drama, fiction, history, journalism, poetry, and prose. Interestingly, many of the titles listed in this work are devoted to the work of individual authors. Most entries are arranged by author as subject, while general and topical studies are listed in a separate section. Entries cite dissertation authors, titles, institutions, and dates, but are not annotated. "See-also" references in citations direct readers to other relevant entries. Indexes to dissertation authors and subjects conclude the volume. *Anglo-Irish Literature: A Bibliography of Dissertations, 1873–1989* is a useful tool for scholars who wish to identify original areas of research, or for those who seek a survey of non-published research on well-documented Irish authors and Anglo-Irish literary topics.

Though Harmon's bibliography suggests a more personalized arrangement and tone than most bibliographies, scholars may still find his ***Select Bibliography for the Study of Anglo-Irish Literature and its Backgrounds: An Irish Studies Handbook*** useful for its breadth of coverage as well as its several citations to parts of books and generous sampling of early twentieth-century resources. As its subtitle suggests, this book offers slightly more information than lists of entries or citations to primary or secondary sources, though these represent a majority of the contents. In addition, Harmon includes literary maps and a brief, selective chronology comparing the publication of significant literary works in Ireland with similar literary events in other Western countries occurring between 1765 and 1976. Dividing the contents into general reference works, background materials, and literature sections, Harmon lists entries in broad categories. The literature section groups entries under general studies, poetry, fiction, drama, individual author bibliographies, and literary periodicals. While entries follow academic citation conventions (author, title, publication information, and date), the annotations sometimes exhibit an editorial flavor revealing Harmon's particular preferences and proclivities. The lack of an index further underscores the general scope and personal character of this resource.

Narrower and more scholarly in scope than *Modern Irish Literature, 1800–1967*, McKenna's ***Irish Literature, 1800–1875: A Guide to Information Sources*** approaches its subject from two angles. Part one, "Background and research," groups entries according to types of literature: anthologies; periodicals; bibliography, biography, and criticism; and supplementary subjects ("Current awareness and research," "Irish literature and Irish antiquities," "Irish history," and "Songs and folklore"). Part two, "Individual authors," is a selective, alphabetical list of more than one hundred nineteenth-century Irish authors. Author entries conform to a common format that arranges citations according to secondary works (bibliography, biography, and criticism) followed by citations to primary sources, which are in turn grouped by genre according to the literary form most identified with a particular author. Citations to secondary works are annotated throughout, while primary sources are sporadically described. Author, title, and subject indexes direct researchers to contents. McKenna's work is most notable, perhaps, for his attempt to record consistent bibliographical information for each author listed. His annotations, in particular, suggest considerable familiarity and knowledge of the secondary literature regarding the authors included.[1]

Published as the first volume of a projected two-volume bibliography covering Irish literature through 1950, McKenna's *Irish Literature, 1800–1875* remains a useful reference for scholars researching nineteen-century Irish literature. Though *Irish Literature, 1876–1950* was never published, Kersnowski's ***Bibliography of Modern Irish and Anglo-Irish Literature*** serves as a viable surrogate. Addressing Irish writers published between 1880 and the mid-1970s, authors identified with or influenced by the Irish Literary Renaissance receive primary attention. Contents are organized alphabetically by author. Entries list general bibliographies, bibliographies of secondary criticism, collected works, individual works arranged by genre, and biography and criticism. Many of the writers included were widely published in anthologies and may not be represented by individual publications.

Annotated bibliographies can yield relevant and sometimes invaluable information concerning the contents of a cited work. Of course, as mentioned in regard to Harmon, bibliography compilers hold differing opinions regarding how much objectivity or detail an annotation requires. Mikhail has compiled several bibliographies dedicated to Irish literature and authors, and has developed a distinctive though brief annotation style. His *An Annotated Bibliography of Modern Anglo-Irish Drama* significantly expands an earlier work published by the University of Washington Press in 1972, *A Bibliography of Modern Irish Drama 1899–1970*, with the addition of annotations and an updated index. Organized into six sections—bibliographies, reference works, books (including parts of books and chapters), periodical articles, dissertations, and library collections—this work covers criticism and secondary sources published between 1899 and 1977. Citations to selected later publications also appear. Arranged alphabetically by authors, 1,775 entries consist of citations followed by annotations. Scholars perusing this resource will discover, however, that Mikhail's annotations are not evaluative and may consist of a single word (e.g., "survey," "recollections") or short, sometimes cryptic phrases ("reflections on the Irish drama," "during shooting an Irish film") or significant quotes ("'The drama of low life is only now being written. Previously it was sentimentalised'") that must be understood in reference to the title of the work cited. Titles deemed sufficiently self-explanatory do not have annotations. Separate name (of both authors and subjects) and subject indexes permit researchers to navigate the book's contents.

Despite its comparative brevity, *An Annotated Bibliography of Modern Anglo-Irish Drama* does provide credible scholarly information as well as apparatuses (arranged contents, indexes) that ably assist researchers who wish to utilize its contents. Loeber and Loeber's *A Guide to Irish Fiction, 1650–1900* is a rich bibliographic resource that presents a stark contrast to the other bibliographies previously described. A deeply learned work, this book is an "annotated bibliography of all known books of fiction by Irish authors and foreign authors writing about Ireland and the Irish" (lxviii). This vast standard for selection corresponds to the compilers' interest in the historical, as opposed to the literary, dimensions of Irish literature. It also considerably widens the scope of Irish literary studies to include works possibly excluded from literary study, such as propaganda and popular and didactic works. In this sense, *A Guide to Irish Fiction, 1650–1900* possesses a cultural significance that transcends the scholarly parameters of many literary bibliographies. The *Guide* is organized into four sections: "Anonymous Authors of Only One Work"; "Anonymous Authors of More Than One Work of Fiction"; "Authored Works"; and "Addenda." Sections arrange entries alphabetically by title or author. Entries consist of standard information such as citations, location and source information, and detailed commentary. Where appropriate,

entries include biographical sketches of authors, sources for biographical
sketches, book identification numbers, a note indicating whether or not the
compilers have seen the book, publication details, sources of publication details, and sources for commentary information. This elaborate methodology
emphasizes the comprehensive nature of this singular work. It also provides
a documentary foundation for other scholars who may wish to locate both primary and secondary sources cited in the *Guide*, as well as to expand on its
contents. Over one hundred pages of introductory material describe this project in detail and provide other valuable information such as figures and tables
illustrating, for instance, "Nationality of foreign authors writing about Ireland
and the Irish" (Figure 3, lxxxiv) and "Examples of earliest known works of
fiction with Irish content," which lists when the first treatments of "Irish
dandies and women seducers in London" and "Horror fiction featuring vam-
pires," among other themes, were published (Table 4, c). A glossary and indexes of persons, book titles, historic periods, themes, and settings, publishers, and places relating to authors supplement this bibliography. It is possible
that *A Guide to Irish Fiction, 1650–1900* will be a standard bibliography for
generations of researchers. In this respect, it is a unique, discrete publication
representing years of rigorous scholarly work upon which future bibliographers can build.

The *Irish University Review* (described in chapter 5) publishes the annual bibliography of the International Association for the Study of Irish
Literature (IASIL). International in scope, this resource features contributions submitted by scholars of Irish literature from all over the world. Originally published in this journal as the International Association for the
Study of Anglo-Irish Literature's ***Bibliography Bulletin***, this annual publication has streamlined its format over the years and now organizes entries
alphabetically by author according to the categories "General Studies" and
"Individual Authors." The former includes citations to journal articles,
books, and selections from monographs covering topics potentially relevant to Irish literary study, such as film, folklore, and language. Criticism
of English authors with Irish connections (e.g., Spenser, Thackeray, and
Trollope) is also cited here. The latter section specifically covers criticism
about Irish authors. From the beginning of its publication, this bibliography has cultivated an international scope and is particularly strong in entries citing translations of Irish authors and works into languages other
than English, as well as criticism appearing in foreign-language periodicals. Submission standards are very specific and emphasize literary and
cultural significance and scholarly documentation.

IRISH LITERATURE AUTHOR BIBLIOGRAPHIES

Laurence, Dan H. *Bernard Shaw: A Bibliography*. SoHo Bibliographies. New York: Oxford University Press, 1983.
———. "A Supplement to Bernard Shaw: A Bibliography." *SHAW: The Annual of Bernard Shaw Studies* 20 (2000): 1–124.
———. "Selective Index to 'A Supplement to Bernard Shaw: A Bibliography.'" *SHAW: The Annual of Bernard Shaw Studies* 20 (2000): 124–128.
Mikhail, E. H. *Lady Gregory: An Annotated Bibliography of Criticism*. Troy, NY: Whitston Pub. Co., 1982.
Durkan, Michael J., and Rand Brandes. *Seamus Heaney: A Reference Guide*. New York: G. K. Hall, 1996.
Wearing, J. P., Elsie Bonita Adams, and Donald C. Haberman. *G. B. Shaw: An Annotated Bibliography of Writings about Him. An Annotated Secondary Bibliography Series on English Literature in Transition, 1880–1920*. DeKalb, IL: Northern Illinois University Press, 1986.

Irish literature scholars working on individual authors have access to a number of bibliographies specifically devoted to the work and criticism of their subject, especially if researching widely read, canonical Irish writers, Yeats, Joyce, and Beckett among them. Consulting general resources such as the *Cambridge Bibliography of English Literature* and Finneran's *Anglo-Irish Literature: A Review of Research* (described in chapter 2) can help researchers identify useful bibliographies as well as describe the scope of a potential source. In addition, searchers can browse any of the bibliographies discussed in this chapter or a union catalog such as *WorldCat* to locate other relevant resources (chapter 3 outlines strategies for finding author bibliographies in library catalogs). Author bibliographies seldom follow a standard format. Some focus on an author's primary works; others list citations to secondary resources. Still others cover both primary and secondary resources, or focus on a particular aspect of an author's life and work, such as theme, location, or a significant character. Bibliographies are published in a variety of formats and media and frequently appear as books, journal publications, and websites. The works discussed in this section are selected examples of bibliographies published as monographs (though Web-based bibliographies relevant to Irish literature appear in chapter 10, "Web Resources"). While this chapter primarily examines comparatively recent resources, older bibliographies often remain relevant for their coverage of earlier and contemporary sources relevant to the study of a particular author's life and work. In addition, *MLAIB*, *ABELL*, and *YWES* permit users to identify more recent criticism to supplement the citations available in older resources.

Laurence's ***Bernard Shaw: A Bibliography*** is the standard resource for primary sources from the pen of this prolific author. Published as a title in the esteemed *Soho Bibliographies* series from Oxford University Press, Laurence's study is an exhaustive listing of everything Shaw wrote, may have written, or was attributed to have written. Organized into thirteen sections over two volumes, *Bernard Shaw: A Bibliography* includes approximately eight thousand entries for books and ephemeral publications, rough proofs/ rehearsal copies, contributions to books, works edited by Shaw, contributions to periodicals and newspapers, postcards, blurbs, broadcasts, recordings, wraiths and strays (potential leads to unaccounted-for Shaw writings), manuscripts, works on Shaw, and misattributed works (a single item) published between 1875 and 1983. Descriptions of books and ephemeral publications receive the most pages, including citations to all known editions and translations of each of Shaw's works. In addition to listing Shaw's works and their various editions and translations, the chapters devoted to books, ephemera, and rough proofs/rehearsal copies present citations according to descriptive bibliographic conventions intended to represent an item's physical attributes, including descriptions of its physical dimensions, binding and cover material, typeface, and paper. Laurence organizes most sections chronologically by year and further arranges descriptions of multiple editions and translations of individual works to appear next to each other in succeeding order of publication. Citations to secondary sources consist of a chronological checklist of "published books and pamphlets, in all languages, concerned with the life, work, and philosophy of Shaw" published between 1905 and 1983, excluding dissertations (899). Serials dedicated to Shaw studies and study guides on individual plays are also listed, while scholarly articles published in academic periodicals or as book chapters are not included. In 2000, Laurence's "A Supplement to Bernard Shaw: A Bibliography" (including a selective index) to *Bernard Shaw: A Bibliography* appeared in volume twenty of *SHAW: The Annual of Bernard Shaw Studies*. The supplement follows the format of the original bibliography, and new entries are cross-referenced with those previously published under separate cover.

Bernard Shaw: A Bibliography represents an extraordinary scholarly achievement, especially in terms of the astonishing volume and variety of primary resources described. However, scholars seeking Shaw criticism and other secondary sources must turn to other bibliographies for such information. ***G. B. Shaw: An Annotated Bibliography of Writings about Him***, published around the same time as *Bernard Shaw: A Bibliography*, is a worthy counterpart to Laurence's standard work. Arranged chronologically over three volumes, this work covers the years 1871–1980 and consists of more than eight thousand annotated entries to Shaw criticism published in all languages in various formats, including books, parts of books, journal and newspaper articles, and dissertations. In contrast to Laurence's descriptive entries, the citations in this book adhere to scholarly citation formats and are followed by detailed, critical descriptions of each entry. Each volume features thorough indexes referencing authors, titles of secondary and primary works, periodicals and newspapers, and foreign languages. While other Shaw bibliographies have subsequently appeared to supplement works discussed here, these earlier titles remain seminal scholarly research resources.

The Shaw bibliographies described above are comprehensive in scope and exemplify works that mark the culmination of years of scholarly study, research, and preparation. Other author bibliographies, however, may be more modest in scale and purposefully compiled to exclude works documented in previously published resources. Mikhail's *Lady Gregory: An Annotated Bibliography of Criticism*, for example, gathers a highly selective listing of secondary and critical sources pertinent to the study of this influential but traditionally neglected literary figure and her work. Historically, Lady Gregory has received much scholarly attention in Yeats criticism, but comparatively little devoted exclusively to her own life and work. Mikhail's bibliography results from an interest to address burgeoning critical interest in Lady Gregory in the early 1980s, and so dispenses with references to secondary literature devoted to Yeatsian topics in order to focus on Lady Gregory criticism ("Preface"). To achieve this end, he cites sources sometimes excluded from author bibliographies such as book reviews of both primary and secondary works as well as other bibliographies. Coverage in this volume encompasses more than two thousand entries spanning criticism published in the late-nineteenth century through 1979. Broadly organized into three sections ("Bibliographies," "Published Books by Lady Gregory and Their Reviews," and "Criticism on Lady Gregory"), citations are sub-arranged by types of publication: reviews of first editions; reviews of volumes of the (definitive) *Coole Edition of Lady Gregory's Works*; books; periodicals; dissertations; manuscripts; and reviews of produced plays. Sections are structured alphabetically by author, while reviews of dramatic productions are listed alphabetically by play title, followed by relevant reviews for each play. Annotations are brief and usually consist of a single line or phrase describing an entry's main topic or a work under discussion (e.g., "Interview with Lady Gregory during the Abbey Theatre's first American tour," "Hugh Lane's Life"). A general index permits scholars to browse contents by authors, titles, and subjects addressed.

While Lady Gregory's scholarly fortunes have surely increased in the twenty-five or so years since Mikhail's bibliography was published, Seamus Heaney has enjoyed a high-profile among critics, both casual and formal, throughout his celebrated career. In many ways, Durkan and Brandes' *Seamus Heaney: A Reference Guide*, chronicles how swiftly and expansively Heaney's critical esteem has grown since he began to publish in the mid-1960s. Though Heaney criticism has exploded since this book appeared in 1996, it remains a relevant resource essential to the study of this famous poet as well as an example of a selective bibliography compiled specifically to identify scholarly and academic resources to the exclusion of "trivial, unscholarly items" (xii). Despite such criteria, this bibliography includes citations to a wide range of publications: books; doctoral dissertations; essays in books; journal articles and reviews; newspaper articles, stories, and reviews; and interviews. Contents are arranged chronologically and cover Heaney criticism published between 1965 and 1993. Entry descriptions exhibit considerable knowledge of primary and secondary literature and, when appropriate, identify reprints and the contents of collections. *Seamus Heaney: A Reference Guide* also features a brief biographical chronology and a chronological list of Heaney's major works, and a general index provides names of authors, titles, and subjects.

CONCLUSION

While significant Irish literature bibliography has historically been included in English literature resources, scholars increasingly have access to sources specifically devoted to Irish authors, works, and literary history. Indeed, as the works described in this chapter suggest, bibliographies and indexes relevant to Irish literary studies have become increasingly sophisticated and specialized as the field evolves. In addition, online bibliographies permit more effective searching of both standard and new electronic and print resources, as well as greater access to both primary and secondary resources relevant to the study of authors and works representing a spectrum of critical attention.

NOTE

1. Harner suggests using McKenna to begin research on minor Irish writers. See James Harner, *Literary Research Guide: An Annotated Listing of Reference Sources in English Literary Studies* (New York: MLA, 2002), 342.

Chapter Five

Scholarly Journals

Academic journals are basic venues for the publication and transmission of literary research. Scholars use journals to keep abreast of recent trends and developments in the field and in areas of special interest both through articles and reviews of newly published books, to identify resources relevant to their own research projects, and to select appropriate forums for the transmission of their own work to other scholars. In respect to Irish literary research, relevant scholarly journals include periodicals devoted to Irish Studies in general, titles covering other disciplines such as history and politics, and resources devoted to specific time periods or literary eras. This chapter details major journals covering Irish literary authors, works, and topics. In addition, this chapter describes scholarly periodicals of more general scope relevant to the study of Irish literature and other journals that regularly address Irish literary authors, works, subjects, and issues. Grouped into three broad categories, the journals summarized here include titles devoted to Irish literature, Irish authors, and general literature journals that cover multiple literary traditions and periods (e.g., British literature, the Romantic era). Each description follows a format that outlines a journal's scope, indicates types of pieces published in each issue (e.g., articles, review essays, notes, book reviews), and provides examples of article topics, typically gathered from the journal's most recent issues. In addition, journals featuring Web-accessible content such as tables of contents and article abstracts are noted as such in their descriptions, and Web addresses are listed in the citations that precede each section.

Generally, articles are the most commonly published type of scholarly journal contributions. They are usually substantive examples of scholarly work based on research and close reading of primary and secondary texts relevant to the study of authors, works, literary movements, and events. While scholarly articles vary in length, those published in the titles presented here frequently run from ten to forty pages. Review essays may be no less scholarly or lengthy than articles, but focus specifically on analyzing scholarly texts often connected by common themes or topics. Notes tend to be much shorter in length, from a few paragraphs to several pages, and typically address narrow areas of scholarly interest, such as an author's use of a specific term in her work, or an illuminating biographical or textual detail that reveals new insights into the study of a writer or work. Book reviews are brief, descriptive commentaries about recently published titles of scholarly interest that fall within a journal's scope.

Most of the journals discussed here are indexed in the *MLA International Bibliography* and *ABELL: Annual Bibliography of English Language and Literature*. *MLAIB* title abbreviations and former titles appear in citations, when applicable. Scholars can verify if a title is included in *ABELL* or *MLAIB* and if so, what years of coverage are available by conducting a journal search in either database. In *MLAIB*, users select "journal name" from one of the drop-down menus on the "Advanced Search" screen and conduct a search for the journal of interest. The database returns a list of citations from the journal searched, which displays in chronological order beginning with the most recently indexed volume. Correspondingly, citations from the oldest indexed volume appear at the end of the list. By consulting the first and last citations in a list of results, users can generally verify the extent of a journal's coverage in *MLAIB*, since coverage between beginning and end dates can be sporadic. A "journal name" search for *Journal of Irish Literature*, for example, returns a list of 156 citations. The first citation in the list is for an article by José Lanters about the novels of Olivia Robertson, published in September 1993. The last citation is for a piece by Robert Hogan about Paul Vincent Carroll, published in 1972. *MLAIB* coverage of the *Journal of Irish Literature*, then, extends from 1972 to 1993. Though Hogan's article is the final citation listed, scholars will note that the page numbers suggest that it is not the first to appear in the issue, and so may not be chronologically accurate or consistent with later citations in the list. This discrepancy illustrates differences between indexing practices; older citations are chronologically listed by volume, and then alphabetically sub-arranged by title. That "An Interview with Juanita Casey" (alphabetized articles is another throw-back) is the first citation listed for the first volume of the *Journal of Irish Literature* underscores this idea. *ABELL* permits scholars to conduct similar "Journal Name" searches. The criticism search screen includes a "journal" search option as well as a drop-down list of journal titles. Lists of citations are chronologically sorted latest volume to earliest, and sub-arranged alphabetically by author. As with lists of citations in *MLAIB*, users can surmise the extent of journal coverage from the dates provided in the earliest and most recent citations. *ABELL* also covers the *Journal of Irish Literature*, from 1973–1974, 1988–1989, and 1991–1993. Users only discover these gaps in coverage, however, upon review of the *ABELL*'s results list, which numbers only forty-one citations from the *Journal of Irish Literature*.

Neither *ABELL* nor *MLAIB* provide summaries that outline journal imprints, dates of coverage, or submission guidelines. Depending on a library's *MLAIB* subscription, users may also conduct searches for journal citations providing such data in a companion resource, the *MLA Directory of Periodicals*, while working in an open *MLAIB* session. The print version of the *Directory* ceased in 1999, and is now available as a component of the online *MLAIB*. If available, researchers can link to the default *Directory* search from *MLAIB* search screens. The *Directory* presents detailed outlines of the journals indexed in *MLAIB*. These citations communicate crucial information about scholarly journals, such as MLA title abbreviations, contact data, editorial details (e.g., editor(s), first publication date, ISSN(s), scope, frequency, status), electronic availability (whether full text or tables of content and abstracts only), subscription details, and submission guidelines (e.g., maximum word count, time between acceptance and publication). Though former titles and closing dates for inactive titles do not appear in these citations, they remain useful documents for scholars navigating the *MLAIB*. Full-text electronic versions of many titles indexed in both *MLAIB* and *ABELL* are available in other resources such as *Project Muse*, *Academic Search Premier*, *JSTOR*, and *Ingenta*. Depending on library subscriptions, users can typically link directly to electronic full-text articles from *MLAIB* and *ABELL* databases. In addition, electronic journal and database publishers are more frequently providing RSS feeds, summaries delivered to Internet browsers and RSS readers, to notify subscribing users of content and performance updates.

Scholarly journals dedicated to Irish literature began to appear in the latter half of the mid-twentieth century. Notable titles appearing at this time include the *Irish University Review* (1970) and the *Journal of Irish Literature* (1972). Many Irish literature journals publish both primary and secondary materials, and several titles currently focus on scholarly research and criticism, such as the *Irish University Review*, which initially published imaginative content, such as original poetry and creative prose. Articles concerning widely read Irish writers, both those writing as British subjects (e.g., Swift, Goldsmith, Edgeworth) and those who rose to prominence as writers representing a distinctly Irish literature (e.g., Yeats, Joyce, O'Faolain), have appeared in standard literary and philological journals since the early twentieth century, several of which continue to be valuable resources for Irish literary scholarship.

While the following section outlines several journals nominally devoted to Irish Studies, all of these publications contain a significant body of Irish literary research. After all, Irish literature is a cornerstone of Irish Studies, and a great deal of evidence supporting previous and current perceptions of the Irish cultural record arise from Irish literary history and biography. While most of the journals outlined here treat all literary periods, modern Irish literature, particularly authors writing and literature produced and published during the nineteenth and twentieth centuries, receives the most critical attention in their pages.

IRISH LITERATURE JOURNALS

ABEI Journal: The Brazilian Journal of Irish Studies (ABEIJ). Brazilian Association of Irish Studies (ABEI), 1999–. Annual. ISSN: 1518-0581.

An Sionnach: A Journal of Literature, Culture, and the Arts (AnSionnach). Creighton University Press, 2005–. 2/yr. ISSN: 1554-8953. www.an-sionnach .com/index.html.

Australian Journal of Irish Studies. Centre for Irish Studies at Murdoch University, Perth, Australia, 2001–. Annual. ISSN: 1444-5409. www.soc .murdoch.edu.au/cfis/ajis.html (Not in *MLAIB*).

Canadian Journal of Irish Studies/Revue Canadienne d'Études Irlandaises (CJIS). University of Alberta, 1975–. 2/yr. ISSN: 0703-1459. www.irish studies.ca/CJIS.html.

Celtica (Celtica). Dublin Institute for Advanced Studies, 1946–. Irregular. ISSN: 0069-1399. www.celt.dias.ie/publications/celtica/.

Dublin Review. Dublin, Ireland, 2000–. Quarterly. ISSN: 1393-998X. www.thedublinreview.com/index.html (Not in *MLAIB*).

Éigse: A Journal of Irish Studies (Éigse). National University of Ireland, 1939–. Annual. ISSN: 0013-2608. www.nui.ie/eigse/.

Éire-Ireland: A Journal of Irish Studies (Éire). Irish American Cultural Institute, 1966–. Quarterly. ISSN: 0013-2683.

Estudios Irlandeses (EstudiosI). The Spanish Association for Irish Studies/Asociación Española de Estudios Irlandeses (AEDEI), 2005–. Annual. ISSN: 1699-311X. www.estudiosirlandeses.org/indexnavy.htm.

Études Irlandaises (EI). Les Presses Universitaires du Septentrion, 1972–. 2/yr. ISSN: 0183-973X. etudes-irlandaises.septentrion.com/.

Field Day Review. Field Day Publications, in association with the Keough-Naughton Institute for Irish Studies of Notre Dame, 2005–. Annual. ISSN: 1649-6507. marketplace.nd.edu/fielddaybooks/Field_Day_Review_C1 .cfm (Not in *MLAIB*).

Irish Journal of Gothic and Horror Studies. School of English, Trinity College Dublin, 2006–. 2/yr. irishgothichorrorjournal.homestead.com/index .html (Not in *MLAIB*).

Irish Review. Cork University Press, University College, Cork, 1986–. 2/yr. ISSN: 0790-7850. www.corkuniversitypress.com/ (Not in *MLAIB*).

Irish Studies Review (ISRev.). British Association for Irish Studies, 1992–. Quarterly. ISSN: 0967-0882. EISSN: 1469-9303. Former title: Irish Studies in Britain (N.d.–1989). www.tandf.co.uk/journals/titles/09670882.asp.

Irish University Review. "A Journal of Irish Studies" (IUR). Irish University Press, 1970–. 2/yr. ISSN: 0021-1427. Former title: *University Review* (1954–1968).

Journal of Irish Literature (JIL). Proscenium Press, 1972–1993. ISSN: 0047-2514.

New Hibernia Review/Iris Éireannach Nua: A Quarterly Record of Irish Studies (NHRev). University of St. Thomas, 1997–. Quarterly. ISSN: 1092-3977. www.stthomas.edu/irishstudies/nhr.htm.

Nordic Irish Studies (NIS). Centre of Irish Studies Aarhus (CISA), 2002–. Annual. ISSN: 1602-124X. www.hum.au.dk/engelsk/cisa/en/publications .html and users.du.se/~ehm/DUCIS/Nordic%20Irish%20Studies.htm.

As previously mentioned, many of the journals encompass a broad scope and include essays on several aspects of Irish culture, the arts, drama, history, literature, and social sciences among them. Most exhibit a standard scholarly publication format (i.e., contents are attributed and documented) and typically include several lengthy essays, book reviews, and other critical pieces such as review essays and notes. Falling within this category is ***Éire-Ireland: A Journal of Irish Studies***, which many scholars consider the premier journal of Irish Studies. Published by the Irish American Cultural Institute since 1966, issues of *Éire-Ireland* feature a wide range of scholarly articles from all areas of the arts, humanities, and social sciences relating to Ireland and Irish America. Creative submissions also appear. Though described as a quarterly, individual numbers are published together, twice a year; issues 1 and 2 are published in the Spring/Summer, while issues 3 and 4 appear in the Fall/Winter. Each number presents ten to twelve articles. Submissions exemplifying interdisciplinary approaches to historical and cultural matters relevant to Irish Studies are favored over narrower analyses or interpretations of literary authors, figures, and works. Robust academic considerations of Irish colonization, post-colonialism, nationalism, immigration, and identity provide strong critical and theoretical foundations for many contributions, especially in issues published during the last five years. Recent article titles include: "Ghosting the Llangollen Ladies: Female Intimacies, Ascendancy Exiles, and the Anglo-Irish Novel," "James Farrell's *Studs Lonigan Trilogy* and the Anxieties of Race," and "Women Writers and the Death of Rural Ireland: Realism and Nostalgia in the 1940s." Scholars studying the historical and cultural forces that have shaped Irish literature and authors are well-served by the consistently high-quality, interdisciplinary material available in *Éire-Ireland: A Journal of Irish Studies*.

Though also subtitled "Journal of Irish Studies," *Irish University Review* primarily covers modern Irish literature; articles display a variety of critical approaches and interdisciplinary contexts. Two numbers appear each year, the Spring–Summer issue devoted to a specific author or theme while the Fall–Winter publication is general in scope. John Banville, Lady Gregory, and the Irish Literary Revival, for example, have been subjects of Spring–Summer numbers, while "Nation and Gender in Jennifer Johnston: A Kristevan Reading," "Race, Cosmopolitanism, and Modernity: Irish Writing and Culture in the Late Nineteen Fifties," and "'Slightly out of Synch': Joycean Strategies in Ciaran Carson's *The Twelfth of Never*" are titles of essays that have appeared in Fall–Winter issues. Fall–Winter publications also include the annual bibliography compiled by the International Association for the Study of Irish Literatures (formerly known as the International Association for the Study of Anglo-Irish Literature, or IASAIL). In addition, this title is a recommended resource for descriptive Irish author bibliographies and checklists. Published in its current incarnation since 1970, the *Irish University Review* grew out of another publication simply titled *University Review* which was published by the Graduates Association of the National University of Ireland between 1953 and 1968. The current title has become a leading scholarly journal of Irish literary studies and is one of the most widely held academic periodicals available to scholars.

The *Field Day Review* is another premier Irish Studies publication. Co-edited by the influential Irish author and critic Seamus Deane and the esteemed Irish historian Breandán Mac Suibhne, this journal annually publishes academic articles and review essays on Irish literary and political culture. Regular contributors include well-known and highly regarded artists, critics, and scholars such as Ciaran Carson, Terry Eagleton, Maud Ellman, and Stephen Rea. Each issue contains approximately ten articles and ten to twelve review essays. Articles consist of interdisciplinary explorations of Irish cultural matters, interviews, reminiscences, and commentary. Review essays treat various items of Irish interest, such as considerations of ideology, interpretive readings of literary works, and analyses of historical events. Researchers can peruse tables of contents on the journal's website.

New Hibernia Review/Iris Éireannach Nua: A Quarterly Record of Irish Studies, published under the auspices of the Center for Irish Studies at the University of St. Thomas (Minneapolis), is a multidisciplinary journal featuring Irish literary and historical scholarship, book reviews, some creative work, and occasionally, interviews and personal essays. A relatively new title among scholarly journals devoted to Irish Studies, *New Hibernia Review* has been in publication since 1997. The contents of each issue vary, though submissions emphasize nineteenth- and twentieth-century topics and subjects and literary scholarship is well-represented in every volume. Imaginative contributions typically consist of new poetry from recognizable writers such as Eavan Boland, John Montague, and Michael Longley, or translations from the Irish. Critical essays on Irish music frequently appear in the pages of this journal, as well as interpretive articles on contemporary Irish cinema. Irish visual arts are promoted in the very design of each individual number, the covers of which feature color reproductions of Irish art accompanied by brief descriptive essays. In general, *New Hibernia Review* is an ideal resource for scholars seeking a general cross-section of Irish Studies research.

Originally titled *Irish Studies in Britain*, which ceased publication in 1989, **Irish Studies Review** is a scholarly quarterly published by the British Irish Studies Association since 1992. This title's publication frequency has varied over the years. Between 1992 and approximately 1998, only two issues appeared each year, with three numbers a year published between 1998 and 2004. Since 2005, four numbers have been issued yearly. Interdisciplinary in scope, *Irish Studies Review* aims to be "an indispensable resource for all those engaged in Irish Studies and related disciplines." Articles address a wide range of disciplines, including literary, cultural, gender, and media studies, archaeology, history, economics, politics, music, and the arts. Individual issues consist of refereed articles, book reviews, and topical debates and interviews. Contributions exemplify traditional disciplinary scholarship and are rigorously researched and documented, and many focus on Anglo-Irish contexts and events. Essays recently published in *Irish Studies Review* have been "Ireland and the Geopolitics of Anglo-Irish Relations," "The Victorian Fathers of the Irish Literary Revival," and "Digging for Darwin: Bitter Wisdom in *The Picture of Dorian Gray* and 'The Critic as Artist.'" Books selected for review often possess a historical or political theme.

Several unique periodicals have shared the title **Dublin Review**. One version published during the nineteenth century will be described in greater depth in chapter 6, "Contemporary Reviews." The title under discussion here has been in circulation since 2001 and is not necessarily a scholarly journal in the traditional, peer-reviewed sense of the term, though it does publish high-quality, scholarly content. Published four times a year, issues feature both creative and critical content usually divided between approximately ten submissions. Similar in scope to literary publications such as *The Paris Review* and *Granta*, critical essays explore topics relevant to contemporary Irish life and letters. *The Dublin Review* is an excellent resource for primary contributions from significant living Irish writers such as Heaney, Muldoon, and Tóibín, as well as new authors. In addition, rare or previously unpublished texts, correspondence, and reminiscences by widely studied authors such as Beckett, Joyce, and O'Connor appear in some numbers. This title is a particularly rich resource of critical and investigative commentary by notable Irish literary writers; to date, issues have included submissions from John Banville on the controversial French novelist Michel Houellebecq, Colm Tóibín on John Butler Yeats, and Edna Longley on scholarship of the Irish Literary Revival. Critical and creative works by influential scholars and critics such as Terry Eagleton and Roy Foster also appear on a regular basis. Since the *Dublin Review* is not indexed in the *MLA International Bibliography*, interested Irish literary researchers can browse this journal's website for lists of the complete contents for each issue, as well as links to selected contributions.

Like the *Dublin Review*, Cork University's **Irish Review** shares its title with previous publications and is not indexed in the *MLAIB*. Begun in 1986, the *Irish Review* was published twice a year through 2003. It appears from information posted on the Cork University Press website, however, that single issues of this journal have been published each year since 2004. Original critical and imaginative content are regularly featured in its pages, and articles often address contemporary cultural concerns. Contributions represent a broad spectrum of writers, from well-known and highly regarded authors such as Roy Foster, Seamus Deane, and Edna Longley to work from up-and-coming thinkers and artists. Older issues present a balanced selection of scholarly articles, creative works, and book reviews. More recent issues exhibit a loose, thematic organization that emphasizes critical commentary and review of significant themes (e.g., Scottish literature, Sean O'Faolain, globalization, Irish post-nationalism) with an emphasis on topics relevant to Cork and environs. Similar in scope to the *Dublin Review*, the *Irish Review* complements other titles such as *Éire-Ireland* that publish interdisciplinary explorations of traditional and popular culture. Titles of recent articles include: "Boyz to Menz (own): Irish Boy Bands and the Alternative Nation," "Exclusion and Inclusion in Swift's *Gulliver's Travels*," and "Edward Said and the Cultural Intellectual at Century's End."

An Sionnach: A Journal of Literature, Culture, and the Arts is yet another interdisciplinary journal emphasizing contemporary Irish literature and culture, published by Creighton University Press since 2005. Issues tend to emphasize a unifying theme or subject and present both critical and creative works. Number (3.1), for example, is devoted to the life and work of contemporary Irish poet Gerald Dawe and features appreciations and criticism of his work, as well as an interview with the author. Other issues have focused on the life and work of Irish-American poet James Liddy and connections between Irish and South Asian art and culture. Though Irish authors and works (e.g., Beckett, Kavanagh, Mahon, Banville's *The Sea*) frequently treated in criticism are addressed in its contents, *An Sionnach* is a particularly useful resource for information on living Irish authors and interdisciplinary research into non-traditional, non-literary subjects potentially relevant to Irish literary scholarship. Recent articles have explored music-making in Alan Parker's film *The Commitments* (based on Roddy Doyle's novel of the same title), Buddhist themes in the poetry of Paula Meehan, and the role Irish guitar-god Rory Gallagher played in introducing blues to his native shores.

Interdisciplinary in scope with a focus on work featuring a "Canadian dimension," the **Canadian Journal of Irish Studies/Revue Canadienne d'Études Irlandaises** has a complex publishing history. Founded in 1975, this official journal of the Canadian Association of Irish Studies has been edited at the University of British Columbia, the University of Saskatchewan, Memorial University, and Concordia University. Its current home is the University of Alberta. Each issue contains approximately a dozen articles covering all aspects of Irish life, though contributions addressing Irish literature, especially twentieth-century works and authors, generally outnumber research in other disciplines. Some creative work, poetry in particular, graces the pages of particular issues. Volumes of *CJIS* also feature a robust selection of multiple book reviews. Since 2000, editors of *CJIS* have sought to expand the journal's scope to include a more varied selection of scholarship, and actively solicit research, in English, French, and Irish, on a broad range of subjects relevant to Irish Studies, anthropology, economics, folklore, material culture, music, and women's studies among them. Currently, issues of *CJIS* are published as guest-edited special issues organized around a unifying theme such as Irish cinema, the nineteenth century, and Irish-Canadian literature.

The only publication discussed here devoted to a specific genre, the **Irish Journal of Gothic and Horror Studies** is a free, interdisciplinary electronic journal that appears twice each year. As its title makes plain, it is devoted to gothic and horror literature, film, television, and new media, and inclusively treats everything from literary and genre theory to comic books and B-movies. Though only two issues have been published at the time of writing, each presents five articles and several reviews of books, film, television, and multi-media relevant to the journal's scope. The current issue also includes a "Lost Souls" section, which profiles "neglected & underrated personages of Horror, from the 19th Century Gothic novelist Francis Lathom to the 1950s Scream Queen Susan Cabot [*sic*]." This journal's electronic format is ideally suited to the presentation of value-adding elements such as color illustrations, portraits, and facsimiles that accompany the scholarly content. Though the reviews address a wide range of relevant gothic and horror materials, Irish subjects so far have been well-represented in the articles, recent titles of which include: "Irish Gothic: A Theoretical Introduction," "Vamping the Woman: Menstrual Pathologies in Bram Stoker's *Dracula*," "Rebel Yells: Genre Hybridity and Irishness in Garth Ennis and Steve Dillon's *Preacher*," and "Irish Gothic: A Rhetorical Hermeneutics Approach." The *Irish Journal of Gothic and Horror Studies* website is easy to navigate and provides full-text, printable access to all of its contents.

Among the scholarly journals described in this chapter, the **Journal of Irish Literature** is the only title no longer in circulation. Published three times a year between 1972 and 1993, the back issues of this journal remain an excellent source of Irish literary scholarship, especially in respect to comparative readings of Irish authors and works. Early numbers feature creative as well as critical content, while later numbers include more critical and theoretical contributions. Over its twenty-year publication history, the *Journal of Irish Literature* also published a number of interviews with Irish authors and other literary figures as well as rare correspondence and reminiscences. In addition, like the *Irish University Review*, useful bibliographies and checklists frequently appear in its pages. Curiously, the 1992 IASAIL annual bibliography, which typically appears in the Fall–Winter number of the *Irish University Review*, was published in the *Journal of Irish Literature*. Especially strong in coverage of nineteenth-century authors such as Le Fanu and Mangan, this journal also promotes scholarship of the Irish Literary Revival and eighteenth-century literature, literary production, and literacy.

The scholarly journals described above are published in Great Britain, Ireland, and North America. But the allure of Irish literary scholarship transcends the bounds of these traditional centers of study. Several scholarly publications devoted to matters Irish, some of them innovative in presentation and distribution, have recently emerged from other parts of the world where Irish influences are often overlooked or ignored. Of these journals, *Études Irlandaises* is perhaps the most traditional in scope and presentation. A peer-reviewed journal publishing articles in English and French, its contributions explore all aspects of Irish literature, history, and culture from ancient times to the present. Essays frequently address a wide range of interdisciplinary subjects such as drama, film, music, politics, economics, and social studies. Published in the spring and fall, volumes consist of two issues, one general in content and the other a special issue organized around a particular theme. Topics of recent special issues include: "The Peace Process" (1999); "The Irish Language" (2001); "Early Medieval Ireland" (2002); "Ireland and the United States" (2003); "Irish Space(s), Zones and Margins" (2004); "Ireland

and Europe" (2005); and "Irish English: Varieties and Variations" (2006). Each number features a section devoted to comprehensive reviews of recently published material on Ireland. Similar in scope and format to *Études Irlandaises*, **Nordic Irish Studies** represents a collaborative publication effort by the Centre for Irish Studies in Aarhus (CISA), Aarhus University, Denmark; Dalarna University Centre for Irish Studies (DUCIS), Dalarna University College, Sweden; and the Nordic Irish Studies Network (NISN). Published annually, issues consist of approximately ten articles divided between contributions devoted to literary research and political scholarship. Book reviews conclude each number. Essays on literature tend to emphasize theoretical readings of modern Irish texts and authors. Critical readings of contemporary Irish poets and their work, in particular, receive many pages in this journal. Scholars of Boland, Carson, Durcan, Heaney, McGuckian, Muldoon, and Ní Dhomhnaill, in particular, will discover a wealth of insightful commentary on these significant writers and their poetry.

In circulation since 1999, **ABEI Journal: The Brazilian Journal of Irish Studies** (*ABEIJ*) is a comparatively recent Irish Studies publication exhibiting a broad topical and critical scope. Issues typically include between ten and fifteen scholarly articles examining Irish art, criticism, biography, dance, drama, fiction, poetry, music, and travel literature, as well as book reviews and news and announcements concerning the Brazilian Association of Irish Studies. *ABEIJ* emphasizes connections between Irish and South American, especially Brazilian, history and culture. Articles appear in English and, less frequently, Portuguese and Spanish. Some issues include creative work from contemporary Irish authors and Portuguese translations of English-language Irish poems and prose. In addition to its unique focus on Irish-South American topics, *ABEIJ* publishes articles dealing with Irish literature and authors of all literary periods that represent a wide spectrum of critical viewpoints. Contemporary authors especially, both those widely read and those less well-known, receive rigorous critical attention in the pages of *ABEIJ*, as suggested by the following titles from recent issues: "Demystifying Irish History in Roddy Doyle's *A Star Called Henry*," "The 'Tinker' Figure in the Children's Fiction of Patricia Lynch," and "The Hindu Celticism of James Cousins (1873–1956)."

Estudios Irlandeses is a comparatively new addition to the list of scholarly Irish Studies periodicals. Published once a year in March under the auspices of the Spanish Association for Irish Studies since 2005, this journal is a peer-reviewed, open access electronic publication. As such, it is a high-quality, free academic journal independently edited and published by experts in the field and not distributed by a for-profit publisher. Articles appear in English or Spanish, though abstracts are printed in both languages. *Estudios Irlandeses* seeks to cultivate an international scope both in respect to its content and its readership. Issues typically include twelve to fifteen essays addressing all aspects of Irish literature, history, arts, and the media. Numbers also feature sections dedicated to Irish book, cinema, and television reviews, as well as lists of books relevant to Irish Studies published in Spain during the previous year. Interviews and conference and publication announcements appear in some issues. The editors encourage submissions that explore connections between Irish and Spanish culture. Contributions are eclectic and innovative, and address a wide range of topics, including interpretations of Irish popular culture, especially music and film. The 2007 issue of *Estudios Irlandeses*, for example, presents essays that compare Joyce's views on Irish nationalism with Elvis Costello's response to Thatcherism on his classic 1986 album *King of America*, examine the Irish voting record at the UN General Assembly, and explore the portrayal of Irish emigration in John Ford's 1952 film *The Quiet Man* and the big-screen adaptation of Frank McCourt's *Angela's Ashes*.

Also published annually, the **Australian Journal of Irish Studies** presents a diverse selection of essays "embracing research on the Irish in Australia and New Zealand as well as Irish Studies in the more traditional sense of Irish history, language, literature and other cultural forms." Issues also feature book reviews and announcements of theses and dissertations on relevant Irish Studies research produced at Australian and New Zealand universities. Diverse in scope, this journal emphasizes contemporary affairs and developments, particularly the Northern Ireland peace process, the Irish economy, and Ireland's new and emerging roles in the European Union and the international community. Recent contributions treat contemporary Irish writing, painting, and film, as well as explore substantial social changes that have transformed Ireland over the last two decades, especially the status of women. Tables of contents and subscription information are available on the journal's website.

In contrast to the other scholarly journals discussed here, **Celtica** primarily addresses topics relevant to the study of philology, including Irish, Welsh, Scottish, Gaulish, and other Celtic languages. Irregularly published since 1946 by the Dublin Institute for Advanced Studies, volumes typically feature twelve to fifteen essays examining the history of Celtic languages in their spoken, written, and literary forms. Scholars researching influences on modern and contemporary Irish authors and texts may find of particular interest the frequent contributions on Irish folklore and mythology, as well as imagery and symbolism in Irish language. Some issues are honorary or memorial volumes dedicated to influential Celtic language scholars, while others include review essays and book reviews of recent scholarship. Again, researchers are advised to observe that issues of *Celtica* are often published several years apart, and so are best utilized as sources for background information rather than as a resource for recent developments in the field.

Though subtitled "A Journal of Irish Studies," the annual *Éigse* is similar in scope to *Celtica* and primarily covers Irish literature and language. In print since 1939, this journal often makes available previously unpublished Old Irish and modern-language texts in prose and verse, including items transcribed from oral narration. In addition, *Éigse* regularly prints scholarly articles on grammar, lexicography, paleography, metrics, and the history of the Irish language, as well as contributions on a wide variety of Irish literary topics. Studies of all aspects of the study of the language and literature of Modern Irish, especially, are emphasized, and each volume features scholarly reviews of books and other major publications in the field of Irish Language and Literature Studies. Due to the highly specialized and scholarly nature of *Éigse's* contents, this title is recommended to Irish literary scholars as a superior source for research on the use of Irish language in contemporary works.

AUTHOR-SPECIFIC JOURNALS

Hypermedia Joyce Studies: An Electronic Journal of James Joyce Scholarship (HJS). Prague James Joyce Centre, 1995–. 2/yr. ISSN: 1324-0625. hjs.ff.cuni.cz/main/hjs.php?page=index_page.

James Joyce Quarterly (JJQ). University of Tulsa, 1963–. Quarterly. ISSN: 0021-4183. EISSN: 1938-6036. www.utulsa.edu/jjq/.

Journal of Beckett Studies (JBeckS). Patrick Cole Books, 1976–1989; Department of English, Florida State University, 1992–. 2/yr. ISSN: 0309-5207. www.english.fsu.edu/jobs/default.htm.

Yeats Eliot Review: A Journal of Criticism and Scholarship (YER). Murphy Newsletter Service, 1978–. Varies. ISSN: 0704-5700.

Shaw: The Annual of Bernard Shaw Studies (ShawR). Pennsylvania State University Press, 1951–. Annual. ISSN: 0037-3354.

Yeats Annual (YeA). Palgrave Macmillan, 1982–. Annual. ISSN: 0278-7687.

Yeats: An Annual of Critical and Textual Studies (Yeats). University of Michigan Press, 1983–. Annual. ISSN: 0742-6224.

The journals summarized here are devoted to specific Irish authors. Influential literary authors often receive a great deal of critical and casual attention, and Beckett, Joyce, Shaw, and Yeats have been popular subjects of study for decades. Given his enduring status as a literary visionary and pioneer of postmodernism and textual innovation, it is fitting that ***Hypermedia Joyce Studies: An Electronic Journal of James Joyce Scholarship*** should emerge from burgeoning critical interest in Joycean considerations of hypertextuality.

According to the preamble of *Hypermedia Joyce Studies* volume 2, number 1 (Summer 1999), this journal:

> publishes all its articles electronically on the World Wide Web and its form of publication makes it different from and a complement to other outlets for Joyce scholarship. HJS takes advantage of the unique opportunities the Web offers for hypertext writing (non-linear writing in which screens of text are connected by links, often with several links leading in different directions from a single screen) and for articles that incorporate multimedia elements (illustrations, video, sound). (http://hjs.ff.cuni.cz/archives/v2/about.html)

As this statement indicates, electronic delivery of scholarly contents allows for dynamic linking of references as well as to resources in a variety of media formats. While issue design varies, contents typically consist of at least five articles covering all aspects of Joyce's life and art. The journal's homepage features links to an archive providing full access to all back issues, to bibliographies of hypermedia, video, and audio resources and products relevant to Joyce Studies, to other James Joyce websites (including links to other print and electronic publications dedicated to Joyce scholarship, most of which are defunct), and an author index.

Currently published in a traditional print format, the **James Joyce Quarterly** publishes "a wide array of critical and theoretical work focusing on the life, writing, and reception of James Joyce." Each issue of this journal provides a selection of peer-reviewed essays, as well as notes, reviews, letters, a comprehensive checklist of recent Joyce-related publications, and editor's comments. Plans are in the works to supplement the print journal with a variety of electronic scholarly resources, including an archive of past issues, a calendar of Joyce events, and an on-line checklist. Currently, scholars who visit the *James Joyce Quarterly* website can browse the contents of recent issues, and can access the complete text of the most current James Joyce checklist, which lists citations to primary, secondary, and multimedia resources relevant to the study of this influential Irish writer. Since 1963, this publication has been the premier scholarly resource for James Joyce scholars, students, and enthusiasts.

Issued in the spring and autumn of each year, the current incarnation of the **Journal of Beckett Studies** has been in print since 1992 and is sponsored by the Florida State University English Department. Between 1976 and 1989, a version of this journal was published as a joint venture between Cole Books in the United States and the Beckett Archive at the University of Reading in the United Kingdom. Contents have remained consistent between both old and new series, and articles contributed by international Beckett scholars represent a wide array of critical viewpoints and approaches to Beckett's life and

work, including reviews of and commentary on play performance and production. Some numbers are guest edited or thematically organized and may
feature notes, book reviews, interviews, and reminiscences. The most recent
issue appeared in 2005 and combines the summer and autumn numbers.

Most of the scholarly journals discussed in this chapter are affiliated with
academic institutions, organizations, or associations. The *Yeats Eliot Review:
A Journal of Criticism and Scholarship*, however, is unique among the other
titles featured here because it is currently an independently owned and published enterprise. Historically, the *Yeats Eliot Review* has always been a modest publication. Founded by modern literature scholar Professor Shyamal
Bagchee of the University of Alberta, this journal was originally devoted exclusively to Eliot research, first as the *T. S. Eliot Newsletter* (1974) and then
as the *T. S. Eliot Review* (1975–76). While this review has retained its current
title and scope since 1978, it has undergone several other changes. Namely,
frequency has varied over the years and the imprint has migrated from Professor Bagchee's office in Edmonton to the Milestone Press based in Little
Rock, Arkansas, a private publishing concern owned and operated by *YER's*
current editor and publisher, Russell Elliott Murphy. Contributions per issue
may feature a single essay or several articles, and usually consist of critical
readings of works, including lesser-known pieces, from these two influential
Modernists that assume a scholarly knowledge of their lives and texts.

Similar in scope and tone to the *Yeats Eliot Review*, the *Yeats Annual*
(YeA) and *Yeats: An Annual of Critical and Textual Studies* (Yeats) both
publish scholarly articles on the life and work of this seminal Irish literary
figure. Edited by the notable Yeats editor Richard J. Finneran, *Yeats: An Annual of Critical and Textual Studies* has been published since 1983 and presents articles, notes, reviews, and an annual bibliography of criticism relevant
to Yeats scholarship. Finneran also edited the first two volumes of the *Yeats
Annual*, a publication begun in 1982, each issue of which features articles,
notes, forums on thematic topics, reviews, and a section on bibliographical
and research materials. Though described as annuals, both publications
demonstrate irregularities in frequency. Given the nearly identical dates for
these titles, scholars may find searching their respective contents confusing.
For example, both journals are indexed in *MLAIB* and conducting a search for
the journal name "yeats annual" retrieves citations from both publications.
Irish literary researchers interested in browsing the contents of either title
might consider conducting *MLAIB* searches under ISSN number.

Mentioned in chapter 4, "Print and Electronic Bibliographies, Indexes, and
Annual Reviews," *Shaw: The Annual of Bernard Shaw Studies* publishes
general articles, reviews, notes, and the "Continuing Checklist of Shaviana,"
an authoritative list of publications, products, and productions relevant to the

study of Bernard Shaw and his milieu. In addition, previously unpublished or rare primary works by Shaw occasionally appear in its pages. The editors organized some volumes around a theme, of which "Shaw and Science Fiction," "Shaw and History," and "Dionysian Shaw" are only a few examples. Published by the Pennsylvania State University Press, this title has enjoyed a continuous run since 1981. While the journal is primarily devoted to Shaw studies, literary scholars researching Victorian literature, drama, and politics may find that the thematic volumes contain content relevant to their studies.

GENERAL LITERATURE JOURNALS

boundary 2: An International Journal of Literature and Culture (BoundaryII). Duke University Press, 1972–. 3/yr. ISSN: 0190-3659. E-ISSN: 1527-2141. Former title: boundary 2: A Journal of Postmodern Literature and Culture (1972–1990). boundary2.dukejournals.org/ and muse.jhu.edu/journals/boundary/.

Comparative Literature Studies (CLS). Pennsylvania State University Press, 1963–. Quarterly. ISSN: 0010-4132. E-ISSN: 1528-4212. www.cl-studies .org/ and muse.jhu.edu/journals/comparative_literature_studies/.

Costerus (New Series). "Essays in English and American Language and Literature." (Costerus) Rodopi, 1974–. ISSN: 0165-9618. Former title: Costerus (1972–1973). www.rodopi.nl/senj.asp?SerieId=COS.

ELH (ELH). Johns Hopkins University Press, 1934–. Quarterly. ISSN: 0013-8304. Former title: ELH: A Journal of English Literary History (1934–1955). muse.jhu.edu/journals/elh.

Essays in Criticism: A Quarterly Journal of Literary Criticism (EIC). Oxford University Press, 1951–. Quarterly. ISSN: 0014-0856. www3.oup.co .uk/escrit.

MLQ: Modern Language Quarterly: A Journal of Literary History (MLQ). University of Washington, 1940–. Quarterly. ISSN: 0026-7929. Former title: *Modern Language Quarterly* (1940–1992). depts.washington.edu/mlq.

Modern Language Review (MLR). Modern Humanities Research Association, 1905–. Quarterly. ISSN: 0026-7937. Former titles: Modern Language Quarterly (1900–1904); Modern Quarterly of Language and Literature (1898–1899); Modern Language Quarterly (1897). www.mhra.org.uk/Publications/Journals/mlr.html.

New Literary History (NLH). Johns Hopkins University Press, 1969–. Quarterly. ISSN: 0028-6087; E-ISSN: 1080-661X. muse.jhu.edu/journals/nlh.

Philological Quarterly (PQ). University of Iowa, 1922–. Quarterly. ISSN: 0031-7977.

PMLA: Publications of the Modern Language Association of America (PMLA). Modern Language Association of America, 1888–. 6/yr. ISSN: 0030-8129. Former titles: Transactions of the Modern Language Association of America (1885/1885); Transactions and Proceedings of the Modern Language Association of America (1886–1887). www.mla.org.

Review of English Studies: A Quarterly Journal of English Literature and the English Language (RES). Oxford University Press, 1925–. Quarterly; 5/yr. in 2003. ISSN: 0034-6551. www3.oup.co.uk/revesj.

SEL: Studies in English Literature, 1500–1900 (SEL). Rice University, 1961–. Quarterly. ISSN: 0039-3657. www.sel.rice.edu/ and muse.jhu.edu/journals/studies_in_english_literature.

Women's Writing (WoWr). Triangle Journals Ltd., 1994–. 3/yr. ISSN: 0969-9082. www.triangle.co.uk/wow.

This section highlights journals that cover multiple literary periods and areas of research, including British, European, and American literature. In addition, the titles examined here are typically interdisciplinary or multidisciplinary in scope, and frequently address Irish literary figures and topics. They are also resources highly regarded by scholars, and considered standard journals in the field. Still, this list of sources is intended to be representative rather than complete or definitive, and serves only as a starting point for further research. In the course of searching *MLAIB* or *ABELL*, scholars will surely discover that many other journals occasionally publish compelling, high-quality articles relevant to Irish literary studies.

Originally devoted to postmodern literature and theory, **boundary 2** has evolved into a scholarly and political forum dedicated to the identification and analysis of "tyrannies of thought and action spreading around the world." Though still subtitled "an international journal of literature and culture," *boundary 2* currently covers the study of national and international culture and politics through literature and social sciences from various historical, political, and theoretical perspectives. As suggested by the deliberate tone of this journal's mission and scope, it presents rigorously researched and documented explorations of complex, multidisciplinary topics. Contributions from international scholars often cover matters relevant to Irish literary studies, as revealed in a sampling of titles of recent and archived submissions: "The Poetry of Origins and the Origins of Poetry: Norman O. Brown's Giambattista Vico and James Joyce," "The Production of Cultural Space in Irish Writing," and "The Irony of Tradition and W. B. Yeats's Autobiography: An Essay in Dialectical Hermeneutics." Some numbers are published as special issues, such as the "Contemporary Irish Culture and Politics" issue (31:1, Spring 2004) co-edited by noted Irish literature scholar and author Seamus Deane and Irish historian Kevin Whelan.

As its title indicates, ***Comparative Literature Studies*** features comparative articles on literature and culture, critical theory, and the cultural and literary connections between African, Asian, European, and American traditions, and coverage spans from ancient to modern literature. A number devoted to East-West literary and cultural relations is published every two years. Each issue includes between four and nine essays and reviews of significant books, though notes are not accepted. Articles comparing modern Irish literary figures and topics with authors and works from other traditions frequently appear, as suggested by titles such as "The Poetics of Recontextualization: Intertextuality in a Chinese Adaptive Translation of *The Picture of Dorian Gray*" and "Refining the Artist into Existence: Pygmalion's Statue, Stephen's Villanelle, and the Venus of Praxiteles."

Costerus is a monographic series published between three and five times a year. Each volume bears a unique title, addresses a particular theme, and is either authored or edited by individual scholars or co-contributors. Several numbers consist of literature conference proceedings. In general, this title features essays on all periods and genres of English and American literature. Because issues are structured around themes, many submissions are solicited or commissioned. Unlike most of the other journals outlined here, *Costerus* emphasizes heavily researched, fully documented articles on authors' lives, writings, and professional careers over critical or interpretive essays. Original source materials, including manuscripts and correspondence, often appear, as well as contributions focusing on textual, bibliographical, and canonical scholarship. Over the years, several volumes in this series have been devoted to Irish literature. Titles of edited volumes gathering a selection of articles include: *Back to the Present: Forward to the Past: Irish Writing and History since 1798* (162, 2 vols.); *Ireland in Writing: Interviews with Writers and Academics* (115); *Politics and the Rhetoric of Poetry: Perspectives on Modern Anglo-Irish Poetry* (102); *Troubled Histories, Troubled Fictions : Twentieth-Century Anglo-Irish Prose* (101); *Tumult of Images: Essays on W. B. Yeats and Politics* (100); *Ritual Remembering: History, Myth and Politics in Anglo-Irish Drama* (99); *Forging in the Smithy: National Identity and Representation in Anglo-Irish Literary History* (98); *The Crows Behind the Plough: History and Violence in Anglo-Irish Poetry and Drama* (79). *Costerus* has also published individually authored volumes relevant to Irish literary study, many of which represent expanded doctoral dissertations. They have been omitted in this chapter to emphasize material that more closely corresponds to conventions of scholarly journal publication.

Primarily publishing critical essays on major figures of the British literary tradition from Chaucer to contemporary authors, the highly respected journal ***ELH*** also features research on Irish and American literatures. Each issue typically contains nine to eleven lengthy articles. Shorter critical pieces, such as notes and book reviews, are not included. Essays exploring the lives and work of Burke, Edgeworth, Joyce, Stoker, Swift, Wilde, and Yeats have appeared in the latest issues. Interdisciplinary studies on the notion of birthplace, ghost stories, allegory in modern poetry, and gothic genealogy that heavily utilize Irish authors and works have also been published in recent numbers.

Founded in 1951 by the eminent literary scholar F. W. Bateson, *Essays in Criticism: A Quarterly Journal of Literary Criticism* covers English literature from the time of Chaucer to the present day. In addition to one to three articles, each issue offers comprehensive book reviews and a "Critical Opinion" section featuring topical debate and commentary on a wide range of literary issues. The April issue includes the text of the annual F. W. Bateson Memorial Lecture. While submissions treating Irish literature and authors appear only once a year, on average, essays are thoughtful and judiciously researched and documented. Recent contributions with an Irish literary focus have addressed Heaney's use of pastoral, Shakespearean comedy in Joyce's *Ulysses*, and Swift's critique of slavery in "A Modest Proposal." Other essays touch on matters and themes possibly relevant to critical discussions of Irish literary study, such as the British canon and critical implications of captivity narratives in eighteenth-century literature.

According the brief publication history posted on its website, *Modern Language Quarterly* is "dedicated to scholarship that illuminates texts of the recent and the distant past. It is devoted to those texts as the representations, agents, and vehicles of change." Three to six articles treating British, American, and European literatures, from the middle ages to the current era, appear in each issue. Annually, one number of this journal is designated a special issue addressing a theme. Recent special issues include: "Globalism on the Move" (2007), "Genre and History" (2006), "Postcolonialism and the Past" (2005), and "Feminism in Time" (2004). The *Modern Language Quarterly* website provides links to tables of contents for volumes from 1990 to the present, as well as access to abstracts for articles published since 2000. While articles on Irish authors and works are infrequent, this journal remains a valuable resource for scholars seeking interdisciplinary research into the historical forces (people, events, documents, etc.) that continue to shape perceptions and understandings of national literatures, literary identity, and ways in which literature and culture intersect and interact.

Modern Language Review, the flagship journal of the Modern Humanities Research Association, possesses a wide scope. Articles published in its pages predominantly cover medieval and modern English, French, Germanic, Hispanic, Italian, and Slavonic literatures, as well as linguistics, comparative literature, and critical theory. Each issue includes nine to thirteen essays of varying length and over one hundred book reviews. Though expansive in content, articles treating Irish authors and texts often appear in this title. As is the case with other general scholarly journals, contributions devoted to Beckett, Joyce, Swift, and Yeats outnumber those covering other Irish subjects, though Le Fanu, Maturin, and Stoker have also received some critical attention, as have Irish folklore, hagiography, and mythology. Issues of *Modern Language Review* conclude with article abstracts, and the MHRA website provides access to a sample article and to the current issue's table of contents.

Emphasizing literary theory and interpretation, **New Literary History** publishes articles that explore the "reasons for literary change, the definitions of periods, and the evolution of styles, conventions, and genres." Towards fulfilling this end, some issues examine a theme or question such as reading and healing, literature and technology, or human science and science fiction. Articles comparing Irish literary topics to other national literary figures and works are frequently published, as are theoretical considerations of the social, cultural, and philosophical contexts of Irish literature. Recent titles covering Irish literature include "Decadence from Belfast to Byzantium," "A Study of the Imagination in Samuel Beckett's *Watt*," and "The Way of the Chameleon in Iser, Beckett, and Yeats: Figuring Death and the Imaginary in *The Fictive and the Imaginary*."

Founded in 1921, **Philological Quarterly** is a standard source for scholarly articles on classical and modern languages and literatures, with an emphasis on research that explores textual analysis, contexts for the contents of literary texts, and studies of language and rhetoric employed by literary authors in their published and private works. Submissions tend to emphasize canonical, pre-twentieth-century English literary figures and works. Each issue publishes five or six articles and a list of books received. Essays on Irish authors and works regularly appear, with critical attention primarily focused on widely read figures such as Beckett, Burke, Joyce, Swift, Yeats, and Wilde. In addition, this journal is a superb resource for bibliographical scholarship.

PMLA, the primary scholarly publication of the Modern Language Association of America, presents a broad range of essays by MLA members treating language and literature from "all scholarly methods and theoretical perspectives." Issues contain between three and eight articles, MLA announcements and news, and shorter pieces that address various scholarly areas, such as "the changing profession," "little-known documents," "theories and methodologies," and transcripts of the Nobel Prize in Literature lectures. This journal's wide scope assures that articles concerning Irish literature appear on occasion. Recently published titles include "Wilde and Wilder," "Clearing the Stage: Gender, Class, and the Freedom of the Scenes in Eighteenth-Century Dublin," "The Changing Profession: Lessons in Blindness from Samuel Beckett," "Burke, Boredom, and the Theater of Counterrevolution," and "'Abroad and at Home': Sexual Ambiguity, Miscegenation, and Colonial Boundaries in Edgeworth's *Belinda*." *PMLA* is a reliable resource, in particular, for scholars interested in interdisciplinary and historical considerations of Irish literary topics.

Covering English literature and language, including American and postcolonial literatures in English, from the earliest period to the present, *Review of English Studies* emphasizes "historical scholarship rather than interpretative criticism, though fresh readings of authors and texts are also offered in light of newly discovered sources or new interpretation of known material." Most articles focus on canonical authors and works from the English literary canon, though Irish literary figures and texts also receive critical attention. Titles of recent contributions relevant to Irish literary scholarship suggest a growing interest in authors and works outside the modern Irish canon: "Maturin, Archibald Constable, and the Publication of *Melmoth the Wanderer*," "The Meaning of the 'Sublime and Beautiful': Shaftesburian Contexts and Rhetorical Issues in Edmund Burke's *Philosophical Enquiry*," and "Mantles, Quirks, and Irish Bulls: Ironic Guise and Colonial Subjectivity in Maria Edgeworth's *Castle Rackrent*." Each issue typically presents four to six articles and twenty to twenty-five reviews, as well as an occasional review essay.

SEL: Studies in English Literature follows a unique publication format. Each quarterly issue is devoted to a literary period: the winter issue covers the English Renaissance, spring treats Tudor and Stuart drama, summer focuses on the Restoration and the eighteenth century, and autumn addresses the nineteenth century. Each issue contains eight to ten articles, a critical evaluation of recent studies in the relevant literary period, and a list of books received. Essays relevant to Irish literature appear in all four numbers. For example, the 2006 eighteenth century issue features a study of Burke's correspondence with Richard Shackleton, while the 2002 English Renaissance issue includes an essay titled "Spanish Lessons: Spenser and the Irish Moriscos." The *SEL* website provides access to tables of contents (1961–present), while users can access the first page of all articles published through 2000 via *JSTOR* links.

Women's Writing focuses primarily on British women's writing up to the end of the nineteenth century and features essays presenting "theoretical and historical perspectives, and contributions that are concerned with gender, culture, race and class." Each issue contains seven to nine articles and several book reviews. Some numbers are devoted to special topics, usually a concept or theme such as "Still Kissing the Rod?" (concerning the future of the study of early modern women's writing) or an individual literary figure such as novelist Marie Corelli. Studies of general subjects pertaining to Irish literature, such as Romantic poetry and fiction, as well as critical articles on Irish women writers including Anna Jameson, Charlotte Riddell, and Mary Davys, are frequently published. The journal's website features a comprehensive list of all articles and forthcoming material.

CONCLUSION

Hopefully, this overview of scholarly journals pertinent to the study of Irish literature will assist scholars to become familiar with the principal journals in the field and obtain a sense of each journal's theoretical stance and scope. Though more and more journals have websites listing tables of contents and abstracts, searching *MLAIB* and *ABELL* allows researchers to identify a wider range of articles relevant to a literary topic or figure of interest. Again, journals are often the first forum presenting new scholarship. As such, they serve a vital function in most literary research by establishing a record of the current trends, authors, and theoretical approaches receiving critical and scholarly attention in Irish literary studies at any given time. Along similar lines, journals are a crucial component to understanding how Irish literary scholarship emerged from the study of English literature, as well as how it has changed and developed over time. Finally, journals serve as forums to which emerging as well as experienced scholars can contribute and possibly expand the intellectual life of the discipline.

Chapter Six

Periodicals, Newspapers, and Reviews

The previous chapter considered scholarly journals as a chief source of information for literary research. Yet other kinds of periodicals, such as magazines and newspapers, are also credible resources. While academic journals are often valued due to following specific standards and conventions, periodicals not necessarily published for scholarly purposes can serve as viable research materials as well.

Typically published for quick consumption by general audiences, periodicals do not fulfill the particular research and editorial standards of scholarly journals, which require time, attribution and citation, and peer-review for publication. Yet, magazines, newspapers, and other types of periodicals cover a wide variety of information that appeals to diverse readerships. These materials may offer researchers information providing documentary evidence, as well as texture, nuance, depth, and unique critical angles that may not be available in other publications. They are also potentially rich sources of primary materials by contemporary authors, many of whom regularly review and write for various serials. The Booker Prize-winning Irish novelist John Banville, for example, frequently contributes to the *London Review of Books* as well as to the *New York Review of Books*. Despite their potential utility, magazines and newspapers do not replace scholarly publications. They can, however, enhance and supplement information gathered from other sources.

Standards for publishing magazines and newspapers vary in regard to frequency, scope, audience, and complexity. Serials, both popular and scholarly, are a notoriously volatile type of publication because they can begin, cease, change title and frequency, and merge with or split from other titles for administrative or practical reasons. In addition, electronic and Internet media offer alternatives to traditional publishing platforms. Serials publishers may now offer titles in multiple formats, cease print versions of their titles to publish exclusively online, and/or supplement print content with expanded, companion, or exclusive online features.

Publication frequency marks a significant distinction between scholarly journals and other kinds of serials. Most of the journals described in chapter 5, for example, are published one to four times a year. In contrast, periodicals and newspapers often appear daily, weekly, or monthly, and publishers can update electronic serials even more frequently if necessary, as well as automatically notify readers of new material by means of email notices and RSS feeds. Frequency also influences content. While writers may conduct research for newspaper and magazine articles that are, in turn, submitted for editorial review before publication, these items mainly report background, events, and statements of topical relevance, or investigate an ongoing issue, rather than defend a thesis, document historical evidence, or synthesize scholarly conclusions and trends. In addition, distinctions between serials formats are often unclear. For example, the distinguished London weekly, *The Economist*, markets itself as a "newspaper," though its international scope and analytical content exceed the quotidian matters usually treated in most community-based weeklies and dailies. Yet, newspapers are valuable historical resources for this very reason; they offer researchers a record of day-to-day realities that can inform a critical reading of a literary work, contextualize entries in an author's diary, or contain the raw material from which a writer may have crafted a plot or character.

Periodicals manifest the times in which they are published. Therefore, understanding the cultural, political, social, and economic aspects of the climate in which a magazine or newspaper exists, as well as their targeted and rival audiences, sheds light upon the contents of particular publications and publishing trends. These issues also impact the strategies scholars use for researching these types of materials. For example, no single, comprehensive directory listing the titles of all serial publications exists. Rather, multiple reference works attempt to address specific aspects of serials publishing, such as audience, format (e.g., newspapers, magazines), geographic area, and time period. Researchers will find that indexes and finding aids to periodical contents are limited and typically provide access to articles primarily published in the most well-known monthly and quarterly periodicals. Articles in dailies and weeklies, on the other hand, may be harder to find due to the massive challenge of attempting to index materials published so frequently. While more and more titles, both current and archived, appear online, scholars still require a combination of print, electronic, and Web-based resources to identify and access serials, especially those researching pre-twentieth-century topics.

Other chapters in this book describe and discuss several standard and specialized databases and print references designed specifically for scholarly research in serials and periodicals. Some of these resources, notably *MLAIB* and *ABELL*, cover academic sources almost exclusively. In many ways, the task of identifying scholarly serials published according to scholarly standards is simpler than categorizing other periodicals because definitions of magazines, newspapers, and reviews have changed and continue to change over time. Reference tools devoted to describing periodicals tend to reflect these ambiguities in scope and coverage. To fully utilize the vast body of periodical literature available, researchers must rely on multiple resources delivered in different formats such as traditional print references, electronic subscriptions, and Web-based sources to identify and access these materials.

This chapter presents Irish literature scholars with a selection of print and electronic resources covering and providing access to periodicals and newspapers. As is the case with many of the reference sources covered in this volume, several of the titles mentioned here refer to British literature as a term inclusive of Irish literary work. Resources treating historical publications as well as contemporary sources are also discussed in order to accommodate research in various time periods, and standard reference works such as *Poole's Index to Periodical Literature* receive particular attention. In addition, some of the sources covered focus on Irish themes and topics, while others exhibit a wider scope. Sources addressed in other chapters, especially those featured in chapters 7 and 8, "Microform and Digital Collections" and "Manuscripts and Archives," respectively, may also prove useful to the researcher seeking historical periodicals and newspapers. This chapter begins with an overview of strategies for locating relevant serial publications and summarizes a selection of reference sources, then goes on to describe resources useful for identifying a broad range of periodicals. The chapter closes with a brief discussion about strategies for finding and resources covering contemporary and current reviews.

IDENTIFYING PERIODICALS AND NEWSPAPERS

Balay, Robert. *Early Periodical Indexes: Bibliographies and Indexes of Literature Published in Periodicals before 1900*. Lanham, MD: Scarecrow Press, 2000.

Center for Research Libraries (U.S.), Kristine Smets, and Adriana Pilecky-Dekajlo. *Foreign Newspapers*. Chicago: Center for Research Libraries, 1998. www.crl.edu/content.asp?l1=5&l2=23&l3=44&l4=27.

Copac Academic and National Library Catalogue. www. copac.ac.uk.

English Short Title Catalogue (ESTC). London: British Library. estc.bl.uk.

Hayes, Richard J. *Sources for the History of Irish Civilisation: Articles in Irish Periodicals*. 9 vols. Boston: G. K. Hall, 1970.

Irish Newspaper Archives. [Ireland]: Irish Newspaper Archives, Ltd, 2006. irishnewspaperarchives.com/.

North, John S., ed. *The Waterloo Directory of English Newspapers and Periodicals, 1800–1900*. 10 vols. Waterloo, Ont.: North Waterloo Academic Press, 1997.

——. *The Waterloo Directory of Irish Newspapers and Periodicals, 1800–1900*. Waterloo, Ont.: North Waterloo Academic Press, 1986.

——. *The Waterloo Directory of Scottish Newspapers and Periodicals, 1800–1900*. 2 vols. Waterloo, Ont.: North Waterloo Academic Press, 1989.

O'Toole, James, and Sara Smyth. *Newsplan Report of the Newsplan Project in Ireland*. London: British Library, 1998. Available online as the *NEWSPLAN Database*. www.nli.ie/en/catalogues-and-databases-printed-newspapers.aspx.

Stewart, James D., Muriel E. Hammond, and Erwin Saenger. *British Union Catalogue of Periodicals*. 4 vols. Hamden, CT: Archon Books, 1968.

Titus, Edna Brown, ed. *Union List of Serials in Libraries of the United States and Canada*. 3rd ed. 5 vols. New York: H. W. Wilson, 1965.

WorldCat. Dublin, OH: OCLC. www.worldcat.org/.

Identifying relevant periodicals and newspapers for literary research can seem like an overwhelming task due to the volume and variety of sources available. The reference literature devoted to organizing and providing access to these materials is as substantial and diverse. Scholars of Irish literature setting out to locate and identify these kinds of resources with a specific idea of what they seek will more successfully navigate these complex resources. For example, a researcher wanting to learn more about local coverage of the beginnings of Seamus Heaney's writing career while a student at Queen's University, Belfast, may decide from the outset to locate only Irish newspapers and university periodicals published in Northern Ireland between 1957 and 1961. Identifying a few definite details as access points, such as a personal name, location, types of publication, and a span of years, frees the scholar to search for resources relevant to the topic. In this instance, catalogs, directories, and indexes of twentieth-century Irish periodicals and newspapers are all viable sources. Northern Ireland is part of the United Kingdom, so locating resources devoted to twentieth-century British publications may also be useful. Finally, browsing biographical references related to Heaney, including bibliographies, checklists, and guides, may yield yet more citations to pertinent periodicals and newspapers.

A familiar and reliable place to begin identifying available periodical and newspaper titles is a library homepage. Many library websites feature clearly marked links to lists of newspapers as well as search screens that permit users to browse online article indexes, citation databases, and electronic journals. Researchers favoring a more direct approach and in search of relevant newspapers held at their local libraries can conduct title searches for publications of interest in the library catalogs. Alternatively, they can conduct subject searches by means of standardized subject headings. "Irish newspapers" and "Irish periodicals" are frequently used Library of Congress subject headings, and searches for either return records describing bibliographies, directories, histories, indexes, union lists, and other scholarly works devoted to Irish publications, most of which contain valuable information about publication time spans, title changes, and coverage. Conducting a subject search for a particular geographic location, such as "Belfast (Northern Ireland)," followed by the heading "newspapers" or "periodicals," is another strategy that allows researchers to browse publications produced in or relevant to a specific region in Ireland.

In addition to local library catalogs, online union catalogs such OCLC's *WorldCat* and *Copac*, and union lists of serials in print, such as the *Union List of Serials* and *British Union Catalogue of Periodicals*, are secondary reference sources useful for verifying titles, dates, and possible locations of materials. *WorldCat* offers researchers search limits ideally suited to identifying periodicals, including place of publication, range of dates, and type of publication (serial). Searches in this resource will retrieve records for print and microform materials. The *English Short Title Catalogue*, freely available via the British Library website, is a standard reference bibliography of titles published between 1473 and 1800, including thousands of newspapers and serials, many of which were published in Ireland or relevant in some way to Irish history, literature, and politics. A sophisticated searching interface enables scholars to conduct basic or advanced searches over multiple indexes, and to limit results by language, date, range of years, format, and country. In addition, records retrieved list publication locations and specify whether microform titles are part of a larger collection. Chapter 8 addresses locating microform collections in more detail.

Several online resources are available for researchers attempting to survey a range of potentially useful periodicals. The Center for Research Libraries' *Foreign Newspapers* database is a searchable list of advertisers, bulletins, journals, newspapers, and other periodicals published outside of the United States. Coverage of periodicals published in Ireland and Northern Ireland extends from the seventeenth century to the mid-1980s. The search interface is straightforward and permits users to conduct combined searches for publication title, city, county, region, language, years, and frequency. This database is particularly valuable for tracing publication dates and title changes, as well as identifying materials published in specific locations. Retrieved records include information regarding place, publisher, frequency, language of publication, and OCLC record numbers when available, which permits researchers to search *WorldCat* to verify which libraries hold desired titles. CRL no longer updates *Foreign Newspapers* as a separate resource, but scholars seeking information on foreign periodicals published since the mid-1980s can limit searches to newspapers in the *CRL Catalog*.

Though not originally intended to serve as a bibliographic resource, the National Library of Ireland's *Newsplan Database* is the searchable online version of the **Newsplan Report of the Newsplan Project in Ireland**. The Newsplan Project is an ongoing, co-operative newspaper preservation project between the United Kingdom and Ireland begun in the mid-1980s for the purpose of microfilming newspapers held by national libraries, public libraries, academic libraries, private libraries, and newspapers in both countries. The project is organized into ten geographic regions and titles are microfilmed according to priorities set within each region. In this resource, Ireland and Northern Ireland comprise one region, and the print report of the project in Ireland lists all extant files of Irish newspapers held in the National Library of Ireland, the British Library, public libraries, universities, archives, and newspaper offices. While much of the title coverage in the online tool overlaps with that of the *Foreign Newspapers* database, the *Newsplan Database* includes unique functions and information, such as a feature that allows users to search by the locations of original files from which reproductions have been made, as well as notes regarding the quality of originals and detailed descriptions of title changes and variations.

Though more limited in coverage than either of the two resources discussed above, the **Irish Newspaper Archives** currently supplies digitized images of twenty-five contemporary Irish newspapers, *The Irish Independent*, *The Freeman's Journal*, and the *Irish Farmer's Journal* among them. Access to this resource is fee-based, though interested researchers can register for free and receive complimentary, limited access to files of their choice. Digital reproductions are of high quality and represented by 1.5 million pages of content covering Irish news from the eighteenth century to the present day. Each page image has been scanned, and contents have been indexed and are searchable. Plans are in the works to add additional significant national, regional, and out-of-print titles on an ongoing basis. While a few of the titles available from this resource maintain websites where readers can access current content for free, the *Irish Newspaper Archives* provides digital reproductions of significantly older issues that may otherwise be available only at libraries and archives, or in microform.

The Waterloo Directory of English Newspapers and Periodicals, 1800–1900**, **The Waterloo Directory of Irish Newspapers and Periodicals, 1800–1900**, and **The Waterloo Directory of Scottish Newspapers and Periodicals, 1800–1900 represent an ongoing work-in-progress ultimately intended to comprise a fifty-volume directory of nineteenth-century newspapers and periodicals covering all subjects to be released in five series. The first series, published in print as a ten-volume set and online as a subscription-based database, lists over twenty-seven thousand entries. The second series, available in print as a twenty-volume set and online by subscription, effectively doubles the contents of the inaugural series and includes revised and expanded entries from that resource, as well as twenty-five thousand additional entries. Significantly, *The Waterloo Directory* contains detailed entries for all nineteenth-century titles featured in the *NEWSPLAN Project* described above. The editors project that the fifth series will list over 125,000 nineteenth-century serial titles and supersede all previous editions.

Entries in this directory adhere to a format that organizes data into several categories. These fields have expanded with each subsequent series and now include: title; alternate titles; title changes; volumes; dates; place of publication; editor; proprietor; publisher; printer; contributors; names; size; price; circulation; frequency; illustration; issuing body; indexing; departments (e.g., sections, columns); orientation (e.g., political or religious perspective); description and comments; merges; sources; histories; and selected locations for holdings. While print versions of both the English and Scottish directories include selections of title page facsimiles, the Irish directory does not. In general, the Web-based version of the English directory accommodates flexible searching and permits users to compile lists of titles arranged by date and location. This capability is particularly valuable for scholars researching serials published in a particular location over a specific range of years. So a researcher interested in surveying contemporary opinions about Irish immigration to Liverpool during the 1840s, for example, can assemble a list of serial publications produced in that city between 1840 and 1850. Though the title of the *The Waterloo Directory* specifies 1800 and 1900 as the beginning and ending dates of coverage, titles ceasing or beginning (or both) in the nineteenth century are included. Consequently, influential eighteenth-century literary titles such as *The Monthly Review* (1749–1844) and Smollett's *Critical Review* (1756–1817) are also listed.

At present, *The Waterloo Directory* is the most comprehensive and thorough reference covering nineteenth-century periodicals. No equivalent resource currently exists for pre-nineteenth-century publications, though other sources, such as Balay's ***Early Periodical Indexes: Bibliographies and Indexes of Literature Published in Periodicals before 1900***, provide selected coverage of these eras. This work is an annotated bibliography of bibliographies and indexes of periodical literature published prior to 1900. Balay categorizes and annotates a broad spectrum of standard and obscure resources providing varying levels of access to periodical articles from around the world. Historically, the indexing of periodical articles exhibits significant inconsistencies and gaps, so *Early Periodical Indexes* also addresses several bibliographies covering books and other publications in addition to articles. Balay has organized the volume into six categories: General; Humanities; History and Area Studies; Social and Behavioral Sciences; Science and Technology; and Library and Information Science. Each category is subdivided by country, and subject divisions feature separate sections arranged according to discipline (Literature under Humanities, for example), specialization within the discipline (e.g., Comedy, Rhetoric, Science Fiction), or geographic location (Europe to Britain). In addition to literature, the compiled reference sources cover research in many fields of study, including art, biology, chemistry, education, history, languages, law, medicine, music, philosophy, religion, sociology, as well as many others. Still, *Early Periodical Indexes* contains multiple references to relevant sources and concludes with a valuable "Dates of Coverage" section that arranges most of the cited bibliographies and indexes in a broad chronological order according to the periodicals indexed. While most of these sources date from the Victorian era and later, this volume also uncovers some hard-to-find, alternative resources. Balay's annotations are intelligent and informative, and address a work's content, analyze its strengths and weaknesses, and offer suggestions for effectively using difficult and arcane reference materials. Though broad in scope, this work cites only one resource directly related to Irish studies, Hayes' massive *Sources for the History of Irish Civilization: Articles in Irish Periodicals* in nine volumes.

Richard J. Hayes served as the Director of the National Library of Ireland from 1940 until the late 1960s. He is also one of the most significant Irish bibliographers of the twentieth century. His **Sources for the History of Irish Civilisation: Articles in Irish Periodicals** is a multi-volume index to approximately 120 English-language historical, literary, and scientific periodical articles published in Ireland between 1800 and 1969, including the transactions and proceedings of learned societies. An impressively thorough and comprehensive resource, Hayes' wide-ranging work organizes entries into three sections: persons, subjects, and places. The first volume lists titles indexed. Entries under any one heading are arranged in chronological order, earliest date of publication to most recent. Though not a widely held resource, scholars who have access to this index should be aware that it exhibits some inconsistencies. For example, appropriate entries are cross-referenced. Yet, some entries requiring cross-referencing only appear in one section. Therefore, researchers may have to check under more than one entry point to verify citations of interest. *Sources for the History of Irish Civilisation* is an excellent source for book reviews.

FINDING ARTICLES AND REVIEWS

Critical Heritage Series. London: Routledge, 1967–.

Gale Research Company, and Gale Group. *Book Review Index.* Detroit: Gale Research Co., 1965–. gale.com/BRIOnline/.

Houghton, Walter E., ed. *The Wellesley Index to Victorian Periodicals, 1824–1900.* Toronto: University of Toronto Press, 1966–1989.

H. W. Wilson Company. *Book Review Digest.* Bronx, N.Y.: H. W. Wilson, 1906–.

———. *Book Review Digest Retrospective.* Bronx: H. W. Wilson, 2000–.

———. *Book Review Digest Plus.* Bronx: H. W. Wilson, 2002–.

Library Association. *British Humanities Index.* Bethesda, MD: Cambridge Scientific Abstracts, 1962.

Poole, William Frederick. *Poole's Index to Periodical Literature.* 6 vols. 1802–1906. Boston: Houghton, 1888–1908. Rev. ed. Boston: Houghton, 1891. Reprint, New York: Peter Smith, 1938. www.paratext.com/ and www.proquest.com/.

ProQuest Information and Learning Company, Chadwyck-Healey, Inc, and Bell & Howell Information and Learning. *Periodicals Archive Online.* Ann Arbor, MI: ProQuest Information and Learning Company, 2001. pao .chadwyck.com.

ProQuest Information and Learning Company, and Chadwyck-Healey, Inc. *Periodicals Index Online* [Cambridge, UK]: Chadwyck-Healey, 1990s. pio.chadwyck.com.

Ward, William S., comp. *Literary Reviews in British Periodicals, 1789–1797: A Bibliography with a Supplementary List of General (Non-Review) Articles on Literary Subjects.* New York: Garland, 1979.

———. *Literary Reviews in British Periodicals, 1798–1820: A Bibliography with a Supplementary List of General (Non-Review) Articles on Literary Subjects.* 2 vols. New York: Garland, 1972.

———. *Literary Reviews in British Periodicals, 1821–1826: A Bibliography with a Supplementary List of General (Non-Review) Articles on Literary Subjects.* New York: Garland, 1977.

In addition to helping researchers identify relevant periodicals and newspapers, some of the resources addressed in the previous section, such as the *NEWSPLAN Project* and the *Irish Newspaper Archives*, also serve as sources of articles and reviews. This portion of the present chapter further expands the list of resources scholars can utilize to access articles and reviews published in serials. Significantly, some of the standard print reference resources described here, including *Poole's Index to Periodical Literature*, have been digitized and are available from multiple vendors. Because several of these titles are widely held in print in academic and research institutions, the following summaries generally focus on the scope and contents of these resources and do not examine the specific features and functions of their online versions. Still, readers are encouraged to explore which versions of these titles are owned by their local libraries and to consult with reference librarians or subject specialists regarding the most effective ways to use them successfully.

Poole's Index to Periodical Literature and *The Wellesley Index to Victorian Periodicals, 1824–1900* are currently the core nineteenth-century magazine article indexes. Both offer limited, but invaluable, access to the contents of major nineteenth-century journals. Scholars consulting either of these research tools, both in print and subscription-based electronic versions, will be well-served if they allow themselves time, perhaps in consultation with a reference librarian, to learn how to use them. Both exhibit unique peculiarities posing challenges to researchers.

For example, while **Poole's Index to Periodical Literature** provides subject access to 479 nineteenth-century periodicals published between 1802 and 1906, its index possesses idiosyncrasies that make it difficult to use at times. Problems in the index include: non-standardized subject headings, which potentially require users to search under multiple terms; entries do not record full article titles, but rather abbreviated or reassigned title words intended to convey the contents of the article cited; author indexing is inconsistent, at best, and names are often unverified or irregularly spelled; references cite only the first page of an article, and do not indicate article length; Poole indexed stories, poems, and plays by title, reviews of fictional works by authors, and reviews of non-fiction work by subject, irregularities that have largely been corrected in the electronic version of this work; and finally, in an attempt to regularize the inconsistent journal numbering and title changes, Poole assigned his own unique numbering scheme for periodical volumes and employed only the most well-known journal titles. As a result, scholars must verify volume and title information in order to locate desired articles. Fortunately, two reference works, *Poole's Index Date and Volume Key* and the *Transfer Vectors for Poole's Index to Periodical Literature*, demystify Poole's unique systems by listing the actual publication titles, volumes, and years. As suggested above, researchers who have access to the online version of *Poole's Index* can avail themselves of integrated author and subject indexing, citations containing dates, and corrected inaccuracies.

The Wellesley Index to Victorian Periodicals, 1824–1900 lists the tables of contents of forty-three significant British and Irish monthlies and quarterlies, including *The Dublin Review* and *The Dublin University Magazine*. Entries for journals are prefaced by introductory essays describing each title's history, editorial practices, and political biases. Information about authors is particularly valuable in this work because compilers studied publisher records, archives, and other resources to identify the most accurate information possible based on contemporary resources. Titles that reveal little about an article's contents are accompanied by subjects in brackets. Additional notes that provide evidence to support authorship follow authors' names. As a result, author indexing and access to article titles via tables of contents are the stand-out features of this resource. As in the case of *Poole's Index*, various shortcomings of this resource have been redressed in subsequent print volumes as well as a CD-ROM and online versions. Specifically, the electronic incarnations of *Wellesley* have incorporated the corrections published in subsequent volumes of the five-volume print edition, facilitated and improved author indexing and keyword searching of tables of contents, and seamlessly linked periodical contents and contributor information.

Periodicals Index Online (*PIO*) and *Periodicals Archive Online* (*PAO*) are companion resources that originally appeared as the online databases *Periodicals Contents Index* and *PCI Full Text*, respectively. Access is by subscription only. Unprecedented in scope and coverage, *PIO* indexes over fifteen million articles published between 1665 and 1995 in over 4,600 arts, humanities, and social sciences periodicals from around the world. Some of the subjects covered include archaeology, fine arts, economics, folklore, geography, history, humanities, linguistics/philology, literature, music, performing arts, philosophy, political science, religion/theology, social sciences, and women's studies. In addition, journals in languages other than English—German, Italian, French, and Spanish to name a few—are represented. While *PIO* emphasizes twentieth-century periodicals, those that extend back to the seventeenth, eighteenth, and nineteenth centuries are indexed from their earliest volumes. *PAO* allows users to link to full text articles retrieved from a *PIO* search. Though its backfile of several hundred periodicals continues to grow, *PAO* currently provides access to over 1 million articles. In general, this coverage presently extends back to nineteenth-century titles. Together, these online tools are an excellent source for book reviews published in journals over the last two centuries, and the *PIO* interface allows researchers to limit searches to these types of documents.

Book reviews represent a distinct kind of literary criticism because they appear around the time review books are published. For this reason, they are valuable resources for literary research, especially for scholars interested in assessing the contemporary critical reception of authors and works, or tracing the evolution over time of popular and cultural tastes for certain kinds of writers and literary forms and practices. Book reviews are also comparatively ubiquitous and appear in a wide variety of academic, popular, and specialized journals, magazines, and newspapers, and book reviews frequently provide content for televised, broadcast, and Internet programming. Given their high profile, publications and reference tools devoted to publishing and accessing book reviews, especially those appearing in print, are widely available. Of course, enterprising researchers will consult several different resources (e.g., bibliographies and indexes devoted to specific authors and subjects, online periodical and newspaper databases, secondary sources, indexes to scholarly journals) to locate such publications. However, the resources discussed below serve as useful starting points for scholars seeking to survey book review documentation. As with many reference works relevant to the Irish literary study, these sources do not typically address Irish literature directly.

Book Review Index (*BRI*) is a standard reference tool held in many libraries. In print since 1965, *BRI* currently contains more than five million citations to book reviews published in thousands of titles, including refereed journals, general interest publications, and newspapers. Each annual volume includes citations to reviews published the year before. Since 2001, this resource has been available in an online version, *BRI Online*, that includes the entire backfile of the print edition and is searchable by author of book reviewed, title of book reviewed, publication date, reviewer, title of review, review length, journal, refereed publications, and reading level. In general, *BRI* indexes reviews of general fiction and non-fiction, the humanities, and the social sciences published in contemporary scholarly and popular North American English-language journals, though a few well-known international titles also appear. Indexed titles of potential interest to researchers of Irish literature include *Choice*, the *Irish Literary Supplement*, *Library Journal*, the *Times Literary Supplement* (*TLS*), *Women's Review of Books*, and *World Literature Today*. For book reviews published before 1965, researchers can consult ***Book Review Digest*** (*BRD*), which has cited and selectively excerpted reviews of books published or distributed in Canada or the United States since 1906. This resource covers periodicals published in Canada, Great Britain, and the United States, and focuses on current English-language fiction and non-fiction books, including children's books. The requisites for inclusion in *BRD* are specific. For example, non-fiction books must be reviewed in at least two of the titles covered and fictional works must be reviewed in at least three of the periodicals indexed to receive mention. In addition, reviews must have appeared within eighteen months after a title's publication, and at least one review must be from a periodical published in Canada or the United States. While there is no limit to the number of review citations, excerpts are typically restricted to three for fiction and four for non-fiction. Books deemed to be of extraordinary significance or controversial are an exception to this rule, and additional excerpts reflecting multiple points of view on these works are included. *BRD* is also available online by subscription as ***Book Review Digest Plus***, which provides selected full-text access to book reviews published since 1983, and ***Book Review Digest Retrospective***, which covers reviews published between 1905 and 1982.

Both *Books Review Index* and *Book Review Digest* offer scholars a wide selection of book reviews primarily published in North America during the twentieth century. However, for a more complete picture of English-language book reviews useful to Irish literary study, researchers might also consult British resources covering Irish authors, works, and subjects. Appearing annually in print since 1962 and available as a CD-ROM product since 2003, the ***British Humanities Index*** (*BHI*) is a standard source for articles and reviews published in major British newspapers, magazines, and scholarly journals, including the *Economist*, the *Guardian*, the *Independent*, the *Times* (London), *New Statesman*, and *TLS*. A list of abstracted journals prefaces each print volume. Organized alphabetically by subject, contents consist of numbered entries featuring citations and brief article abstracts. In general, titles with rigorous publication frequencies, such as daily newspapers and monthly magazines, receive selective abstracting. So book reviews, interviews, and author profiles appearing in these kinds of serials may not be summarized in the *BHI*. Still, this resource is invaluable for identifying and locating articles and reviews composed, and interviews conducted by, contemporary literary figures. Subject, author, and source indexes conclude each volume of the *BHI*, and facilitate the swift discovery of such items. Scholars seeking citations to and abstracts of articles published in significant British periodicals before 1962 will need to consult the *Subject Index to Periodicals*, the original publication from which the *BHI* split. Though published annually between 1919 and 1961 (with some irregularities), the *Subject Index to Periodicals* actually begins its coverage with citations to articles published in 1915.

While it indexes almost a century of periodical publishing, the *BHI* focuses primarily on titles produced in Great Britain. As a result, reviews and articles on topics pertinent to Irish literary research appearing in periodicals published elsewhere are not represented. Given the dizzying numbers of periodicals appearing the world over, especially in respect to daily and monthly serials, this fact seems reasonable if not inevitable. Another potential limitation for scholars is the time span covered.

Ward's *Literary Reviews in British Periodicals, 1789–1797: A Bibliography*, *Literary Reviews in British Periodicals, 1798–1820: A Bibliography*, and *Literary Reviews in British Periodicals, 1821–1826: A Bibliography*, for example, focus on topics relevant to late eighteenth- and early nineteenth-century literary study. Specifically, these three volumes index contemporary reviews of literary works and critical essays addressing authors and genres. Coverage is exclusive to British (including Irish) fiction, poetry, drama, and non-fiction prose published between 1789 and 1826. Literary reviews published in over ninety periodicals and in the *Champion* and the *Examiner* newspapers are indexed. Though Ward does not list the periodicals indexed, a detail that complicates the task of verifying periodical titles, this omission does not compromise either the breadth of journal coverage or the value of having access to a wide variety of contemporary responses to authors writing and works published during the first two decades of the nineteenth century.

The works described above represent only a modest sample of the resources researchers can use to find articles and reviews. Many others exist, however, and scholars of Irish literature have several choices, available both in print and electronically, at their disposal to supplement their work with other resources. Antonia Forster's *Index to Book Reviews in England, 1749–1774* and *Index to Book Reviews in England, 1775–1800*, for example, list citations to reviews of works by Irish authors who published in seminal British journals such as *The British Magazine*, *The Critical Review*, and *The Town and Country Magazine* during the latter half of the eighteenth century. Forster's works are particularly useful for identifying multiple reviews on literary works. In addition, several digital collections offer users at subscribing institutions direct access to primary materials. The *Seventeenth and Eighteenth Century Burney Collection Newspapers* from Gale is a collection of over one thousand newspapers, pamphlets, and proclamations gathered by Reverend Charles Burney and now housed at the British Library. Most of the materials in this collection were published in London, though it also includes examples of English provincial, Irish, Scottish, and a few American colonial papers. Adam Matthew Publishers' *Eighteenth Century Journals* is a worthy complement to the Burney collection. Currently consisting of two parts, content and coverage continue to expand and plans are in the works to add periodicals and newspapers from Scotland, Ireland, India, Canada, and the West Indies held by diverse libraries. The first iteration of *Eighteenth Century Journals* presents rare journals, both major and minor titles, published between 1714 and 1799, which are part of the Hope Collection housed at Oxford's Bodleian Library. This collection covers a wide range of topics and exhibits particular strength in writings on the British colonies and eighteenth-century drama. The second part features works from the Harry Ransom Humanities Research Center, University of Texas at Austin, which includes a wide variety of rare newspapers and periodicals, many of which exist only in short runs and are not available anywhere else. Libraries may subscribe to either version of *Eighteenth Century Journals* or a portal providing access to both parts. Consequently, researchers may have to verify with librarians to which portions of these collections they have access. *British Periodicals* from ProQuest/Chadwyck-Healey is also available in two separate parts or as a package and "offers facsimile page images and searchable full text for nearly 500 British periodicals published from the 17th through the early 20th centuries." Collection I covers literature, philosophy, history, science, the fine arts, and the social sciences and consists of more than 160 journals drawn from the *Early British Periodicals* microfilm set. Collection II presents writings devoted to literature, music, art, drama, archaeology, and architecture originally published in more than 300 journals reproduced in the *English Literary Periodicals*, *British Periodicals in the Creative Arts*, and additional microfilm collections.

Finally, volumes in the **Critical Heritage Series** from the British publisher Routledge are valuable resources for finding critical overviews of individual authors over time. Each title in the series is thoroughly documented and points readers to a range of primary and secondary sources. Currently, scholars of Irish literature can avail themselves of individual volumes devoted to major writers such as Beckett, Goldsmith, Joyce, Shaw, Sterne, Swift, Wilde, and Yeats.

CONCLUSION

Periodicals and newspapers are viable sources for book reviews and offer researchers information that may contextualize literary authors, works, and subjects. Still, a lack of standard indexes to this literature creates challenges for scholars, and those seeking sources for research in Irish literature must utilize many resources that do not directly focus on this area. This chapter addresses strategies for identifying and locating periodical and newspaper articles and reviews, both contemporary and historical. It also discusses selected print and online reference tools that provide access to citations, and in some instances full text, to these materials. In many ways, the sheer diversity of print and electronic periodical indexes corresponds to the multitude of periodical and newspaper titles published over time. Some of these resources possess unique organizational or editorial features that may at first seem arcane and prohibitive to effective research. In addition, researchers must often consult multiple reference tools to discover as many relevant resources as possible. Fortunately, librarians can assist scholars attempting to negotiate these resources, as well as recommend a combination of Web-based and traditional print indexes, bibliographies, online catalogs, and other sources for the purposes of identifying and locating pertinent articles and reviews.

Chapter Seven

Microform and Digital Collections

Scholars working with historical sources relevant to Irish literary study or researching the work of lesser-known authors and literary figures may require access to rare or unique primary resource materials typically available only in archives and special collections. Fortunately, such books, journals, newspapers, and documents are often available in microform and digital collections. As pointed out in the Introduction, Irish literature is an evolving area of study, and many resources devoted to English literature and criticism, especially older resources, do not distinguish between these disciplines and Irish literature sources and scholarship. So many microform and digital collections devoted to the study of English or British literature may include items useful in Irish literature scholarship.

During the twentieth century, microforms fulfilled a dual purpose: they preserved rare and fragile materials from damage incurred through excessive use while providing wider access to them. Over the last few years, the development of digital collections has challenged the primacy of microform as a preservation and access format. Digital collections fulfill the same crucial purposes of preserving and providing access to rare and unique sources as microforms, with the additional advantages of full-text accessibility and searching from Internet platforms. The advent of ready access to personal computing, hypertext formatting, and electronic delivery has presented researchers with alternatives to using microform readers, which typically require special training to use and are expensive to repair or replace. Additionally, preserving microforms themselves also poses problems, since they are sometimes subject to the same misuse and damage that often destroys the print resources preserved and distributed on them. In this respect, it makes sense that commercial vendors of digital collections first selected major microform collections as viable resources to convert to electronic formats. Colleges and universities, libraries, archives, and museums began to scan and make available high-value and at-risk works from their collections. In addition, individual scholars and other experts identified unconverted microform collections and used digital technology to capture images of these resources.

At present, the Irish literature scholar must work in a transitional information environment in which she will utilize a range of skills to access both microform and digitized resources in her search for relevant information. The migration from microform to digital collections is not complete, and questions persist regarding whether or not this scenario is even desirable. Making microform collections available in digital formats is time-consuming and expensive, and vendors still produce microforms because they remain a format easier to create, manage, and sell than digital resources.

First produced in the nineteenth century, microforms are currently available in a number of formats, film, fiche, micro-opaque, and ultra-microfiche among them. Of these formats, microfilm and microfiche are more widely used than micro-opaque and ultra-microfiche. Indeed, the latter two formats are no longer utilized for new microform projects, though researchers may still have access to micro-opaque and ultra-microfiche collections in some institutions. Reproducing materials in micro-opaque format required a highly specialized method of printing images on opaque white cards that could be reflected onto a screen. Also, the equally specialized technology required to access micro-opaque cards is no longer available, making nearly impossible the task of maintaining or replacing machines still in use. Likewise, ultra-microfiche could store more images than microfiche, but they were too small to view without powerful lenses that could adequately magnify the images to a usable standard. Despite these limitations, researchers can consult with their local libraries to verify if alternative viewing technologies, such as microfilm scanners, are available and can be used with data preserved in micro-opaque formats. Information organizations continue to invest in microfilm and microfiche, on the other hand, because these formats have proven easier to use and maintain than other microforms, and they consistently provide higher image quality than that available from other formats. In addition, the technology required to access microfilm and microfiche resources is readily available, requiring only an illuminating source (a light), a lens, and a screen upon which to project a relatively high-quality image of the information reproduced on the microform.

Over the last few years, the technology used to digitize microforms on an organizational level has also become available to individuals, a development which has ironically occasioned a recurrence of low-quality micro-image reproduction. Digitizing microform readers allow users to scan and save images of microform resources in several image file formats, including GIF, JPEG,

PDF, and TIF. With optical character recognition (OCR) software, users can convert these images into ASCII characters that can then be imported as searchable documents into word processing programs. OCR file conversion poses few problems in respect to images of recent or contemporary documents produced during the era of mechanized printing. The quality of images of older printed resources, on the other hand, especially those published during the eighteenth and nineteenth centuries, tends to diminish during the OCR conversion process on account of the unique, sometimes ornate appearance of hand-produced type. Still, digitization provides for more flexible management of microform resources, as well as more dynamic methods for storing, scanning, and searching within these materials.

Microform and digital collections are complex resources that often consist of multiple parts organized under a distinctive title, as in the case of *GRAIL: The Galway Resource for Anglo-Irish Literature*, a collection of more than five hundred individual titles reproduced on almost one thousand microfiche containing several hundred primary resources relevant to the study of Anglo-Irish literature. Cataloging each part included in such collections requires a lot of time and experienced personnel, both of which are usually dedicated to other cataloging priorities. To work around these common restrictions, libraries often choose to catalog an entire microform or digital collection on a single bibliographic record. While this "collection-level record" approach to cataloging provides general subject-level access and classification to microform and digital resources, it does not facilitate online searching of the individual titles or parts contained in a collection. Scholars who wish to search the contents of collections cataloged in this way must turn to print or electronic finding aids. Alternatively, libraries sometimes purchase and load into their catalogs records prepared by an outside vendor that describe the individual parts of a collection. These "title-level" records contain searchable access points such as author, title, publication information, and subject headings that describe individual works included in a collection. Multiple documents can be reproduced on a single microform, so these records also include the numbers of the microforms that contain titles of interest. Because specialized technology is required to access microforms, libraries typically designate a specific physical location for their storage and use. A few libraries assign call numbers to microform collections, though most arrange them by access numbers, which correspond to the order in which a library acquires a microform set. Records for digitized resources, on the other hand, usually feature a link to the collection.

Libraries sometimes purchase parts of microfilm sets rather than entire collections. Libraries can also purchase individual newspapers and periodicals in microform. Catalog records for parts of microform sets can be confusing because they often contain the titles of complete microform collections, even though the library does not own the set in its entirety. Scholars who wish to use a whole microform collection but are unsure if the library owns the set can consult with a reference librarian to verify what is available. Likewise, researchers can consult microform collection finding aids to access the articles available in microform reproductions of newspapers and periodicals. Not all finding aids are created equal, however, and when finding aids do not provide article-level access to newspapers and periodicals on microfilm, researchers can search for articles in indexes and bibliographies. In comparison, digitization projects usually allow scholars to conduct keyword searches for article titles, and some feature full-text searching capabilities. Despite these improved functions, researchers may still need to use core indexes to supplement their article searches. Chapter 6 discuss techniques for conducting successful article-level searches of serials, regardless of format.

Finally, scholars may request microforms through interlibrary loan if their library does not own a needed collection. A researcher may want to make an interlibrary loan request for the finding aid before borrowing the microfilm since libraries that do not own specific microform sets seldom own the finding aids required to determine which microform reels or fiche contain the needed part or title.

FINDING MICROFORM AND DIGITIZED COLLECTIONS

"Bibliographies and Guides." *Library of Congress Microform Reading Room* at www.loc.gov/rr/microform/bibguide.html (accessed 31 March 2008).

CELT: Corpus of Electronic Texts, at www.ucc.ie/celt/index.html (accessed 31 March 2008).

Dodson, Suzanne Cates, ed. *Microform Research Collections: A Guide*. 2nd ed. Westport, CT: Meckler Pub., 1984.

Frazier, Patrick, ed. *A Guide to the Microform Collections in the Humanities and Social Sciences Division of the Library of Congress*. Washington, DC: Library of Congress Humanities and Social Sciences Division, 1996. Online at www.loc.gov/rr/microform/guide/intro.html (accessed 31 March 2008).

Guide to Microforms in Print, updated annually. Munich: Saur, 1978–.

WorldCat. Dublin, OH: OCLC. www.worldcat.org/.

Almost any publication that exists in print can be digitized or reproduced as a microform. To survey the diversity of materials available in these collections, researchers can browse the websites of microform and digital publishers such as Adam Matthews, ProQuest (which now owns standard microform publishers Chadwyck-Healey and UMI), and Gale to discover which collections are available. Rare items and documents produced for relatively quick consumption by readers have been especially well-served by these technologies. As a result, many collections consist of early and rare books, newspapers, pamphlets, correspondence, and other unique kinds of literature. Further emphasizing the singular nature of many of these collections is the lack of a standard method of organizing them. Microform and digitized collections, like research bibliographies and other significant reference resources in print, embody the research practices and bibliographical values of those who create them, principles that are often expressed in a collection's scope, which may differ widely from other collections organized around similar materials or themes. Because of their unique contents and the specialized methods required to store and access microform collections, consulting a reference librarian is a recommended user strategy when embarking on a project that requires microforms. A reference librarian can describe the microform collections owned by a library and demonstrate how to use them. Scholars can also meet with librarians who specialize in specific subject areas to learn about a library's microform holdings in particular disciplines such as literature, history, and politics. Some libraries maintain a professional staff in microform areas to assist patrons with informational and use issues. Alternatively, researchers can browse a library's website to check for links to lists of microform or digitized collections.

Chapter 3 pointed out that not all items in a library's collection are necessarily represented in its catalog. Still, if a researcher knows the title of a microfilm or digitized collection, she could conduct a title search in her library's catalog to verify if it is held. Some library catalogs allow users to limit searches by format, though this method is most useful to gain a general overview of a library's microform holdings, most of which consist of periodicals and newspapers. Because microform and digitized collections are usually cataloged at the collection level, it is difficult and sometimes inefficient to identify specific titles or items in a collection through the catalog. To get the most out of a library's microform collections, researchers should plan to work closely with reference librarians and consult several reference resources, both in print and online, to discover what is available in collections of interest.

Reference librarians knowledgeable about microform collections can discuss projects with library users to identify relevant microform resources. In addition, they can suggest standard microform reference books that can assist the researcher in his quest to find microform collections that fit his research needs, as well as verify the scope of potentially useful collections. ***Microform***

Research Collections: A Guide has been a standard microforms reference work for more than twenty years and it is still relevant. Likewise, the annually updated *Guide to Microforms in Print* is a thorough and rigorously cross-indexed standard reference for microforms research. Online finding aids and guides to special collections are also excellent microform reference resources. Large research institutions that maintain manuscripts, archives, and special collections units typically make these resources available on webpages devoted to these unique collections. The *Bibliographies and Guides* webpage maintained by the Library of Congress Microform Reading Room, for example, features links to finding aids and summaries describing the library's microform collections. One such finding aid, *A Guide to the Microform Collections in the Humanities and Social Sciences Division of the Library of Congress*, is a standard reference work first published in print in 1996 and now available as a continually updated resource on the Library of Congress website. Broad in scope, this finding aid is a useful tool for identifying potentially relevant Irish literature resources, especially literary periodicals, biographical resources, and government documents. Scholars can consult this finding aid's subject index to locate headings such as "Ireland—Biography," "Ireland—Genealogy," "Ireland—Politics and Government," and "Northern Ireland—Politics and Government." (On the webpage, the subject index is split between two searchable links, *Index A–J* and *Index K–Z*.) Titles of relevant collections are listed under these headings.[1] To view summaries of these collections' scope and contents, researchers simply click on the first letter of the title of the collection in the alphabetical series of links at the top of the page. Descriptions are typically brief but thorough. The collection *British and Irish Biographies, 1840–1940*, for example, "Consists of two sections: the first is an index, on 93 microfiche, listing over 180,000 persons, including both prominent and non-prominent persons. The second consists of copies of the full sources, providing biographical entries for the names indexed." In addition, users are encouraged to check spelling variants to account for irregularities in the indexing for this title.[2] Access points that identify the name of the selector of the content (David Lewis Jones), the publisher and date of the collection (Chadwick-Healey, 1984–), the total number of microfiche comprising this collection (4397), the accession number of the guide corresponding to this collection (135), and subject headings ("England—Biography" and "Ireland—Biography") supplement this descriptive information. With this data, scholars can search their library catalogs to verify the availability of a collection. If local libraries do not own a needed collection, researchers can search union catalogs (e.g., *WorldCat*) to locate libraries from which parts of microform collections can be requested through interlibrary loan.

Directories and catalogs of digitized collections are not as readily available as those devoted to microform resources. Again, consulting with reference librarians and searching union catalogs are reliable methods of locating digitized resources. Browsing Irish literary websites with a scholarly focus is another viable way to discover relevant digitized resources. **CELT: *Corpus of Electronic Texts***, maintained by the University College Cork History Department, is a notable online resource of digitized texts. Currently, this project contains over 920 documents of historical, literary, and political interest representing works produced from the thirteenth century to the present. Resources are available in several languages, including English, French, Irish, and Latin, as well as translations from these languages into English. *CELT* features both scanned texts, such as Kuno Meyer's *A Primer of Irish Metrics* (London, 1909), as well as transcriptions of texts that can be viewed as HTML, SGML, or text files. Transcribed texts are rigorously documented and paginated to enable contextual searching, the creation of concordances, and other kinds of bibliographical and textual analyses. *CELT*'s "Frequently Asked Questions" section (linked from the main webpage) provides detailed information about digitization methodology, standards, and preferred viewing and functionality preferences to optimize the usability of this remarkable resource. Scholars of Irish literature will find an astonishing variety of primary resources, including electronic editions of canonical and lesser-known eighteenth-, nineteenth-, and twentieth-century Irish literary texts in English by widely studied authors such as Jonathan Swift, Sheridan Le Fanu, and Bram Stoker. Plans to add works by Laurence Sterne, Lady Gregory, and Emily Lawless, among others, are pending. Vast in scope, *CELT: Corpus of Electronic Texts* is an exceptional reference resource for digitized collections and texts relevant to Irish literary study, as well as a rich repository of documentation about the evolving discipline of digitization.

For many literary research projects, an entire microform or digital collection may not be as appropriate a resource as a microfilmed or digitized book or serial. In such instances, scholars can search for the relevant title in a library or union catalog to locate what is available either locally or through interlibrary loan. As mentioned previously, however, many libraries catalog microform and digitized collections at the collection level, which complicates the task of locating individual titles. Fortunately, finding aids listing the contents of collections are sometimes available. The widely consulted microfilm collection *English Literary Periodicals*, for example, includes a printed guide, *Accessing English Literary Periodicals*, that lists the titles in the collection. In addition, an accompanying CD-ROM provides access to article titles. Because cataloging policies and practices vary between libraries, scholars can search for individual parts of collections in union catalogs such as **WorldCat**.

Accordingly, knowing how to search for and interpret records for parts of microform and digitized collections are useful skills for the would-be user of microforms and digitized resources. Figure 7.1 is a *WorldCat* record for *The Irish Quarterly Review* (1851–1860), a literary periodical available on microfilm.

In this example, the bold, italicized text in the series note indicates that *The Irish Quarterly Review* is part of the *English Literary Periodicals* microform collection. The occurrence of both the periodical and collection titles in this record simplifies the task of finding it in the catalog. A researcher can first search her local library catalog for the periodical title and then for the collection title, depending on the success of her initial search. If the local catalog does not yield results for either the periodical or the collection title, a researcher can duplicate her periodical title search in a union catalog to identify pertinent interlibrary loan information. As shown in the example record for *The Irish Quarterly Review*, again in bold italics, the appropriate record will include the numbers of the reels needed to fill the request: 135–139.

A reference librarian can assist users to determine whether finding aids are available for titles that are parts of collections but have not been cataloged. *The Irish Quarterly Review* is part of the *English Literary Periodicals* collection. Yet, the collection-level record for *English Literary Periodicals* does not indicate this fact, as illustrated in figure 7.2.

Here, the title, description, and notes of the microform collection are highlighted in bold. While the record specifies that this collection consists of 969 microfilm reels, it does not mention the individual titles reproduced on these reels. If a scholar searches for but does not find an individual title, he can re-

---

The Irish quarterly review
1851-1860
English Serial Publication : Periodical : Quarterly (every 3 months) : Microform   36 v.
Dublin : W.B. Kelly
      Title: The Irish quarterly review
  Publication: Dublin : W.B. Kelly,
      Year: 1851-1860
  Frequency: Quarterly
  Description: No. 1 (Mar. 1851)-no. 36 (Jan. 1860) = v. 1-9.; 36 v.
    Language: English
      Series: Variation: ***English literary periodicals ;; 135-139***.
    Descriptor: Irish literature--Periodicals.
  Geographic: Ireland—Politics and government—19th century—Periodicals.
     Note(s): Reproduction: Microfilm./ Ann Arbor, Mich. :/ University Microfilms
              International,/ 1954./ 5 microfilm reels. 35 mm./ (English literary
              periodicals ; reels 135-139
  Accession No: OCLC: 7183371

Figure 7.1.   Modified *WorldCat* record for *The Irish Quarterly Review*. Source: *WorldCat*, via *FirstSearch*.

English literary periodicals
University Microfilms International.
1951-1977
English Book : Microform **969 microfilm reels** ; 35 mm.
Ann Arbor, Mich. : University Microfilms,
  Availability: Check the catalogs in your library.
       Libraries worldwide that own item: 58
      Title: English literary periodicals
Corp Author(s): University Microfilms International. ; Accessing English literary
      periodicals.
  Publication: Ann Arbor, Mich. : University Microfilms,
     Year: 1951-1977
  Description: 969 microfilm reels ; 35 mm.
   Language: English
     SUBJECT(S)
  Descriptor: English literature—Periodicals.
      English periodicals.
      Periodicals on microfilm.
    Note(s): Accompanied by printed guide with title: Accessing English
      literary periodicals.
Material Type: Microfilm (mfl)
Accession No: OCLC: 22860959

Figure 7.2. Modified *WorldCat* record for *English Literary Periodicals*.
Source: *WorldCat*, via *FirstSearch*.

quest through interlibrary loan the printed guide, *Accessing English Literary Periodicals* that contains information about the titles in the collection.

MICROFORM AND DIGITIZED COLLECTIONS

Act of Union Virtual Library: A Digital Resource for the Act of Union of 1800. Belfast, Northern Ireland: Queen's University at Belfast, 2002–, at www .actofunion.ac.uk/ (accessed 20 March 2007).

Early British Periodicals. 902 microfilm reels. Ann Arbor, MI: University Microfilms International, 1983. Available online via www.proquest.com.

Eighteenth Century Collections Online. Farmington Hills, MI: Gale Group, 2003. www.galegroup.com/EighteenthCentury/email/ecco.htm.

Elizabethan Ireland and the Settlement of Ulster: The Carew Papers from Lambeth Palace Library. 15 microfilm reels. London: World Microfilms Publications, 1978.

Elizabethan Ireland and the Settlement of Ulster: The Carew Papers from Lambeth Palace Library: List of Contents and Index to Reels. London: World Microfilms Publications, 1978, at www.crl.edu/ReferenceFolders/ ElizabethanIreland.pdf (accessed 31 March 2008).

English Literary Periodicals. 969 microfilm reels. Ann Arbor, MI: University Microfilms, 1951–1977. Available online via www.proquest.com.

GRAIL: The Galway Resource for Anglo-Irish Literature. 977 microfiches. Dublin, Ireland: European Micropublishing Services, 1988.

Hayes, Richard J. *Irish Newspapers Prior to 1750 in Dublin Libraries*. Ann Arbor, MI: University Microfilms, 1950.

Hoornstra, Jean, and Grace Puravs, eds. *A Guide to the Early British Periodicals Collection on Microfilm with Title, Subject, Editor, and Reel Number Indexes*. Ann Arbor, MI: University Microfilms International, 1981.

Irish Newspapers in Dublin Libraries, 1685–1754. 24 microfilm reels. Ann Arbor, MI: University Microfilms, 1950–1953.

Irish Script on Screen. Dublin, Ireland: School of Celtic Studies, Dublin Institute for Advanced Studies, 2000–, at www.isos.dias.ie/english/index .html (accessed 31 March 2008).

Mercier, Jacqueline. *GRAIL: The Galway Resource for Anglo-Irish Literature: Index to the Microfiche Set*. Chestnut Hill, MA: Boston College Libraries, 1997.

Northern Ireland Political Literature. 3179 microfiches. Belfast, Northern Ireland: Linen Hall, with European Micropublishing Services, 1989–.

Northern Ireland Political Literature on Microfiche. Catalog and Indexes. Phase 1, Periodicals, 1966–1989. Belfast, Northern Ireland: Linen Hall Library, with European Micropublishing Services, 1993.

Pollard, Alfred W., and Donald Goddard Wing. *Early English Books Online*. Ann Arbor, MI: ProQuest, 1999. eebo.chadwyck.com/home.

Project Gutenberg, at www.gutenberg.org (accessed 31 March 2008).

Puravs, Grace, Kathy L. Kavanagh, and Vicki Smith, eds. *Accessing English Literary Periodicals: A Guide to the Microfilm Collection with Title, Subject, Editor, and Reel Number Indexes*. Ann Arbor, MI: University Microfilms International, 1981.

This chapter opened with a reminder that, in the past, scholars and publishers often failed to distinguish Irish literature from British and English literary traditions. The scope and organization of some microform and digitized collections illustrates this idea. The previous section underscores this point by discussing several reference resources that are relevant to the study of Irish literature though ostensibly devoted to English literary works and resources. To provide a contrast to these past editing and publishing practices, this section focuses on describing a selection of microform and digitized collections almost exclusively organized around topics and themes relevant to Irish literature scholarship. Two exceptions to this scheme are the *Early British Periodicals* and *English Literary Periodicals* microfilm collections, both of which are standard resources for periodical literature published in England, Scotland, and Ireland between the seventeenth and twentieth centuries.

Sponsored by the School of Celtic Studies at the Dublin Institute for Advanced Studies, *Irish Script on Screen (ISOS)* is a digitization project that makes available images of Irish manuscripts held by several institutions, including the National Library of Ireland, the Royal Irish Academy, and Trinity College Dublin. Even though the materials selected for this collection are highly specialized and of potentially narrow scholarly interest, it is a fascinating resource to browse for information about the tremendous efforts that contribute to the creation of a high-quality digitization project. The critical apparatuses and commentary accompanying each part of the collection are excellent examples of robust archival and bibliographical scholarship and provide helpful data for navigating these materials. While general browsers have access to images of manuscripts reproduced on the *ISOS* website, users who seek greater access to these resources for scholarly purposes must register with the sponsoring institution for access to high-resolution images of the collection. Contents encompass an astonishing variety of works, including Irish grammars, religious rules, historical and mythical cycles, and poetic address. Researchers interested in book history topics such as bindings, endpapers, palimpsests, and scripts will discover in *ISOS* a treasure trove of primary evidence for their studies.

Elizabethan Ireland and the Settlement of Ulster: The Carew Papers from Lambeth Palace Library is a small but fascinating microfilm collection. Consisting of papers and documents either authored or preserved by Sir George Carew, an official representing the English crown in Ireland in various capacities between 1574 and 1603, this collection provides a unique record of early documentation concerning the "Irish question." Contents include examples of anti-Irish propaganda, personal and official correspondence and papers, genealogies, and historical works. Official documents regarding England's Ireland policies from the reigns of monarchs beginning with Henry VII to Elizabeth I may be of particular interest to researchers seeking to explore colonial and post-colonial matters in English and Irish literature of this and subsequent periods. A brief finding aid for this collection, *Elizabethan Ireland and the Settlement of Ulster: The Carew Papers from Lambeth Palace Library: List of Contents and Index to Reels*, is available in print and online.

The *Galway Resource for Anglo-Irish Literature (GRAIL)* is a significant microfiche collection that reproduces approximately 545 Anglo-Irish primary resources, including works of fiction, non-fiction, poetry, and drama. The result of collaborative efforts between University College, Galway, and the National Library of Ireland (Dublin), *GRAIL*'s holdings of nineteenth-century literary works are especially strong and feature popular authors of the era, many of whom were women. Selina Bunbury, Maria Edgeworth, Regina Maria Roche, and Mary Tighe, for example, are widely represented in this collection. *GRAIL* is particularly easy to use because all of the works in the collection have been cataloged at the title-level. The cataloging between records is remarkably consistent, especially in regard to reproduction notes pointing users to specific parts of the collection. A print finding aid for this collection, ***GRAIL: The Galway Resource for Anglo-Irish Literature: Index to the Microfiche Set***, is available. Users can also conduct a title search for "*GRAIL: The Galway Resource for Anglo-Irish Literature*" in *WorldCat* to browse individual titles in this collection. Other valuable sources of Irish documents are ProQuest's ***Early English Books Online*** (*EEBO*) and Gale's ***Eighteenth Century Collections Online*** (*ECCO*). *EEBO* contains over 1,200 records describing items published in Ireland between 1475 and 1700, sixteen of which represent Irish Gaelic language items. *EECO*, on the other hand, presents more than eleven thousand records for titles published in Dublin alone during this pivotal period in literary history, including seven Irish language items.

Michael Hart started ***Project Gutenberg*** in 1971 with the intention of providing free access to e-books: electronic versions of printed texts. Today, *Project Gutenberg* makes available well over twenty thousand electronic versions of literary texts. Unlike the manuscripts digitized for the *ISOS* project, described above, *Project Gutenberg* e-books are electronically reproduced text versions of printed works available in the public domain. Because this project emphasizes providing wide access to electronic texts, users who seek scholarly editions of literary works might be better served by other resources. Many of the copyright-free works digitized for *Project Gutenberg* do not necessarily represent the best editions of works available in other formats. This site utilizes simple text-based platforms to facilitate the submission of texts by volunteer contributors to the project as well as to make resources available to a large number of users. Scholars of Irish literature have access to many Irish authors, especially major figures like Joyce and Yeats, through *Project Gutenberg*. However, these texts may not be authoritative or academically credible. The site's general disclaimer offers users the best practical suggestion: "Use at your own risk!"

As previously indicated, the ***English Literary Periodicals*** (*ELP*) microfilm collection is a standard and substantial resource in literary scholarship. Based on a bibliography co-compiled by Katherine Kirtley Weed, a librarian, and Richmond Bond, a professor at the University of North Carolina, this collection is the result of a project Bond coordinated in the late 1940s. Bond approached various scholars and UMI to identify a broad yet extensive selection of periodicals for inclusion in this set. This decidedly open-ended charge accounts for the generally broad scope of the collection, which consists of 341 serial titles published from 1681 to 1914. In addition to the broad geographic coverage of this set, subjects are varied and feature drama, economics, history, literature, politics, and social sciences. Periodical runs range from titles that span a few issues to others spanning several decades. Dailies, annuals, and irregularly published periodicals represent only a few of the various publication frequencies present here. Titles in this collection comprise widely read publications, such as *Critical Review* and *London Magazine*, as well as humbler titles that circulated for only a few issues. The *ELP* consists of several titles potentially relevant to the study of Irish literature: *Irish Quarterly Review*, *Literary Journal*, and the *Dublin and London Magazine*. ***Accessing English Literary Periodicals: A Guide to the Microfilm Collection with Title, Subject, Editor, and Reel Number Indexes***, by Puravs, Kavanagh, and Smith, is the print finding aid to this collection. ELP is also available online from ProQuest's *British Periodicals* database, which partly consists of titles drawn from *English Literary Periodicals* microfilm collection.

Selected by Dr. Daniel Fader, a University of Michigan Professor of English Literature, ***Early British Periodicals (EBP)*** is a microfilm collection that supplements the *ELP*. It consists of 168 titles published between 1681 and 1921. The *EBP* represents an even wider scope of periodicals than the *ELP*. Subjects include art and esthetics, emancipation, history, literature, philosophy, and politics. In general, the titles in this collection offer broader social perspectives on issues than those explored in some of the titles contained in the *ELP*. Scholars interested in researching social attitudes towards women during Maria Edgeworth's lifetime, for example, could use articles available from titles in the *EBP* to supplement reviews and critical essays contained in periodicals available in *English Literary Periodicals*. Titles in this collection potentially relevant for Irish literature scholars are the *Dublin Saturday Magazine*, *Duffy's Hibernian Magazine*, and the *Irish Magazine, and Monthly Asylum for Neglected Biography*. Edited by Hoornstra and Puravs, ***A Guide to the Early British Periodicals Collection on Microfilm with Title, Subject, Editor, and Reel Number Indexes*** is the print finding aid for this collection. As with *ELP*, an online version of *EBP* is available in ProQuest's *British Periodicals Collection*.

In addition to periodicals, newspapers are often reproduced in microform collections. Because of the transitory nature of their contents, intended to be read upon publication and then most likely discarded, along with the sometimes negligible quality of the paper they have been printed on (especially in the nineteenth century), newspapers are ideal candidates for microform and digitized reproduction. ***Irish Newspapers in Dublin Libraries, 1685–1754*** is an

excellent resource for students who wish to explore the historical backgrounds and intricacies of the issues, events, politics, and social concerns that
may provide context and texture to Irish literary scholarship. The collection
consists of more than 130 titles, most of which were published in Dublin. The
years encompassed by this collection represent a dynamic era during which
the foundations of current discussions about Irish identity and nationhood
were laid. Many titles deal with foreign and domestic concerns, as well as local and municipal matters of general interest. A print finding aid for this collection, by Hayes, is titled ***Irish Newspapers prior to 1750 in Dublin Libraries***. Hayes' reference only covers the first twenty-two reels of the
collection, however. Reels 23 and 24 begin with lists of their respective contents.

Another topical resource relevant to the study of historical contexts for
Irish literature is the ***Act of Union Virtual Library: A Digital Resource for
the Act of Union of 1800***. Though narrowly focused on the legislation that
merged the Irish and English Kingdoms, this resource makes available a
wealth of primary resources relevant to the study of colonialism, Irish history,
English history, parliamentary politics, and the transmission of printed information. This project is the result of collaborative efforts between several cultural institutions in Northern Ireland, among them the Belfast Public Libraries, the Public Record Office of Northern Ireland, and the Ulster
Museum. Currently, researchers can access searchable, high-quality digital
images of pamphlets, parliamentary papers, and statutes. This collection's
website features an elegant search feature that allows users to search the library's contents by keyword, author, title, date, publisher or printer, place of
publication, and holding institution. In addition, researchers can limit their
searches to material type. The *Act of Union Virtual Library* is a model of a
digitized collection that provides high-quality access to rare, fragile, and significant resources selected around a specific topic. Particularly impressive are
the digitized pamphlets, which exceed 250 items published between 1797 and
1800, that document wide-ranging opinion and debate about the Act of Union
and its implications. Sample titles include: "*Union or not? By an Orange-
man*"; "*Dean Tucker's arguments on the propriety of an union between Great
Britain and Ireland written some years since and now first published in this
tract upon the same subject. By the rev. Dr Clarke*"; and "*Short [A] address
to the pretended Catholic Addresser of a Noble Lord. By a citizen, but not a
French one.*"

Related to the *Act of Union Virtual Library* is the **Northern Ireland Political Literature** microfiche collection. This sprawling set currently reproduces
924 titles on 3,179 microfiche, though the microfilming of these resources
continues. The scope of the collection incorporates periodical literature, pri-

marily bulletins, local newspapers, magazines, and newsletters, published since January 1, 1966. Most of these items represent periodicals published in Northern Ireland, primarily in Belfast. The set also includes titles published in England, Ireland, Scotland, and the United States that are relevant to the ongoing documentation of the "Troubles." The finding aid for this considerable collection is titled ***Northern Ireland Political Literature on Microfiche. Catalog and Indexes. Phase 1, Periodicals, 1966–1989*** and is considered an essential resource for negotiating the set. Researchers can also conduct a title search for "*Northern Ireland Political Literature*" in *WorldCat* to locate individual records for titles in the collection, most of which have been cataloged at the title-level.

CONCLUSION

Microform and especially digital collections encompass an infinite variety of reproduced printed materials. In addition to books and serials, researchers have access to broadsides, manuscripts, newspapers, and pamphlets, to name only a few of the types of resources discussed in this chapter. As digitization projects become a standard method of preserving items, it is likely that works reproduced in microforms may become more readily available online. Still, Irish literature scholars currently possess ample tools to help them locate microform and digital collections that are relevant to their research. Reference and subject specialist librarians remain reliable resources for information about microforms and digitized projects. Likewise, browsing union catalogs and subject-specific websites, as well as consulting with other experts of Irish literature and in related fields, can all yield potentially useful leads.

NOTES

1. These subject headings do not necessarily represent the breadth of subjects covered in the collections. The collection *Bernard Shaw diaries, 1885–1897, with earlier and later fragments: facsimile* (30) has been described with headings that do not appear in the *Guide*'s subject index: "Dramatists, Irish—19th century—Diaries" and "Dramatists, Irish—20th century—Diaries." Another useful subject heading not represented in the subject index is "Irish literature—Periodicals" (see *English Literary Periodicals*, 81).

2. Frazier, Patrick, ed. *A Guide to the Microform Collections in the Humanities and Social Sciences Division of the Library of Congress* (Washington, DC: Library of Congress, 1996), 38–39.

Chapter Eight

Manuscripts and Archives

Traditional library research strategies and skills provide solid groundwork upon which to conduct effective manuscript and archival research. However, negotiating manuscript and archival resources is a complex process that demands specialized knowledge and practices. These materials are usually unique, if not irreplaceable, and require careful handling. In addition, institutions house manuscript and archival items in secured, preferably environmentally-controlled areas and facilities in the interest of preservation, while specialists describe and organize these materials according to different cataloging standards and rules. Consequently, a library's catalog may not include bibliographic records for manuscript and archival sources. Whether or not these items appear in the general catalog, published or unpublished guides called "finding aids" are recommended tools specifically designed to help researchers identify special collections records.

Further complicating archival research is the fact that documents originating from a single source, such as an author's manuscripts, are often sold or distributed in pieces. Related works are often geographically scattered, located in archives, libraries, or private collections around the world. Even pieces of single works can be widely distributed. The manuscript of Bernard Shaw's 1881 novel *Love Among the Artists*, for example, survives only in fragments.[1] While Shaw donated the manuscripts of four of his five published novels to the National Library of Ireland in 1945, the manuscript of the aforementioned work was "split up and dispersed among dealers" by bookseller Dan Rider.[2] Currently, extant pieces of this work are housed at the New York Public Library, Princeton University Library, Cornell University Library, and the Humanities Research Center at the University of Texas, Austin.[3]

This chapter covers basic tools and best practices intended to clarify and ease the unique challenges archival research offers scholars. Regardless of one's preparation, using archives and special collections efficiently and effectively requires practice, planning, and patience. Use and handling policies vary between archives and special collections departments. While scholars new to archival research processes may find these policies restrictive, they are designed and implemented in the interests of preservation and security. Researchers who prepare for certain possibilities will be well ahead of the game when the time arrives to use archives and special collections. Pens, notebooks, and other personal items, such as coats, backpacks, or hand-held electronic devices may not be allowed in areas where users consult materials. Laptops may be permissible, while handheld scanners, camera phones, and Personal Digital Assistants (PDAs) may be prohibited. The number of items scholars can consult at one time may be limited, and retrieval of materials from secured areas by staff may require more time than expected. In general, scholars are encouraged to conduct a great deal of preliminary research to identify and locate the materials they seek, including finding the archive and learning the rules for using its facilities and resources. Policies and rules outlining use are often posted on the Web or are available directly from the organization. This chapter first addresses the process of using archives, and follows with an overview of resources and techniques for determining viable sources for archival materials.

GENERAL INFORMATION ABOUT ARCHIVES

The term "archive" refers to a collection of records, created in any format, of enduring historical value. This definition is inclusive and speaks to the idea that, in respect to archives, a "record" can be any number of things: a handwritten letter, a sound recording of a poet reading one of her works, a dramatic performance recorded on film, a typewritten speech, a photograph, a memo created on a word processor, or a contract between a publisher and an author. Everything from personal papers (e.g., an author's diaries, letters, manuscripts, or notebooks) to public records (e.g., governmental correspondence or corporate ledgers), as well as sound and film materials, can comprise an archive. Though seemingly disparate, these materials are commonly designated as unique or rare primary sources and housed in secured areas. In addition, professionals mediate access to them, which is usually limited to scholars researching legitimate projects.

Public record collections are often all-encompassing and may preserve every piece of paper submitted to or generated by an organization: letters written to the government by citizens, meeting minutes of an association or non-profit organization, military records, or shipping records. Vital records detailing births, deaths, marriages, and divorces are also a form of public record. Manuscript collections, on the other hand, are a subset of archives and typically comprise the personal and/or working papers of an individual or family. Traditionally handwritten documents, manuscripts can currently exist in any format, including audio and electronic documents and files. The sheer number and variety of archival materials resist neat categorization, and a single item can represent more than one type of work. Documents such as the original *Magna Carta* or Lincoln's *Gettysburg Address*, for example, are manuscripts and public records. Ultimately, making such fine distinctions distracts from observing that, despite their differences, archival records such as personal papers and public records have more in common with each other than they do with other types of library sources because they require similar techniques for discovery and use.

BEST PRACTICES FOR ARCHIVAL RESEARCH

As indicated earlier in this chapter, the more a researcher knows about her topic before visiting an archive, the more effectively she will use the collection. While it may seem reasonable to start a research project in a collection dedicated to primary sources, starting with a firm grasp of the secondary literature available on a topic and a well-defined research focus before visiting the archive is the recommended course of scholarly action. Having a clear understanding of one's research needs based on knowledge of the existing scholarship on, say, relevant archival and manuscript records, provides a strong foundation for archival research upon which to build.

In addition to knowledge of one's topic, understanding the context within which an archival collection exists improves one's efficient use of the archive, as well as the ability to recognize important threads of information and remain focused. Also, scholars carefully researching secondary sources will begin to discover which archives may be the most useful during their research process by noting that authors of scholarly secondary resources generally specify which institutions they utilized, and acknowledge the individual experts who proved to be the most knowledgeable and helpful within those institutions. Gathering such pieces of information provide both a solid background and clues about valuable archives that will contribute to creating a focused research plan. By carefully defining their projects, researchers can eliminate certain parts of the collections they visit and efficiently spend their time and energy concentrating on the materials most relevant to their work. Finally, well-defined projects make it easier for scholars to apply for funding.

Another factor contributing to the challenges of archival research is time. Depending upon the institution, even prepared users may discover that document retrieval requires several hours, a consequence of archival collections having been gathered and organized differently than items in general access and circulating collections. Namely, archival records are organized according to their relationships to one another as determined by special collections professionals. They are not arranged for browsing or quick retrieval, so researchers may have to review a great deal of material, some irrelevant, to identify needed pieces. A scholar exploring the private opinions of contemporary American writers regarding censorship of Joyce's *Ulysses*, for example, might have to sift through the correspondence, diaries, and notebooks of a few selected literary figures writing during a specific span of years to uncover material addressing this matter.

The physical condition of archival records and materials may also present challenges that add time to the process of working with and interpreting the raw data they contain. Inks on older manuscripts may be faded, and ornate or poor penmanship may be difficult to decipher. Perhaps rare data has been preserved in a format such as negative microfilm that requires highly specialized or antiquated technology to view, and so can not be photocopied or otherwise reproduced. On the other hand, tangential discoveries easily distract from the task at hand, while following promising leads to one dead end after another can be discouraging. Scholars are wise to consider such time-consuming challenges during the planning stages of a project because they will impact the amount of time required to use a collection. This recommendation is especially important for researchers traveling abroad to conduct research for a limited time; the more prepared the scholar, the more she will accomplish.

Patience, flexibility, and preparedness are some of the best practices for archival research. Generally, scholars must travel to other sites for archival materials, so planning ahead is essential. Verifying whether the archive of interest has a website that posts information about access, hours, regulations, and contact names is a good start. Archives are typically open for business fewer hours during the day than public and academic libraries, and may be closed during weekends and at specific times of the year. In addition, archives may require special permission to use the collections and all have rules for the purpose of preserving materials from damage and preventing theft. Scholars are encouraged to correspond with the archivist or librarian prior to their visit to verify that the records they wish to consult are available and to clarify use and handling policies that may pertain to specific materials. The directories below provide addresses of archives without websites and librarians can also provide assistance as needed.

Whether working in an internationally renowned archive or a small special collection in a library, scholars are served well by observing the same rules of etiquette whenever possible even though levels of service may vary from one institution to the next. In a smaller special collection, for instance, an archivist knowledgeable about the collection's contents may give scholars personal attention. In a larger institution, on the other hand, scholars may have to work on their own. To illustrate the process of accessing a manuscript archive, the next section reviews the procedures for using the British Library, which is one of the most restrictive organizations of its kind, as well as one of the greatest repositories of primary and secondary Irish literature sources in the world.

THE BRITISH LIBRARY

Once a researcher has exhausted other library and digital collections in her quest for relevant resources, she may consider, as a last resort, conducting research at a major archival institution such as the British Library. This institution is remarkable in respect to both the scope of its collections as well as its significant holdings in materials relevant to Irish studies, such as its Modern Irish Collections, which feature books, pamphlets, and journals covering a range of subjects in the humanities and social sciences. These collections are particularly rich sources of historical, literary, and Irish language items. Of course, this prospect demands considerable expense both in terms of finances and time. Scholars can review procedures for accessing the manuscripts collections from the British Library website (http://www.bl.uk). Sections covering the steps necessary to prepare for a visit, to apply for a "reader pass," and to use the collections and handle the manuscripts are available from this resource. Acquiring a reader pass requires documented proof that a researcher has exhausted other library collections and has a legitimate research need to use the collections on site. Prospective users can register for a reader pass either in person or in advance by means of email or post. In either case, applicants need to present two pieces of information verifying proof of identity and home address upon arrival at the library. The British Library also recommends bringing supporting documentation, such as a business card, professional membership card, or details of the items one wishes to see, to help establish one's status as a researcher. Scholars could also present a signed letter of support printed on institutional letterhead from a department chair, dean, or academic advisor outlining the project and its desired outcome (e.g., dissertation, article, book), stating the researcher's connection to and status at the institution of affiliation, as well as confirming that the applicant is a student or scholar in good standing.

Once the application has been approved and the reader pass procured, a researcher has access to the Manuscripts division and permission to use the Manuscripts Reading Room and the collection, with potential exceptions in respect to extremely rare, fragile, or significant items. Fragile or important manuscripts may only be accessible as microform reproductions or print fac-similes. Users who wish to use specific manuscripts might circumvent these possible restrictions in advance by sending a request to verify that desired materials are available. Scholars could include a signed letter of recommen-dation from an advisor, chair, or dean stating his or her status and affiliation, explaining the project, and specifying needed manuscripts and related mate-rials to add credibility to their queries. In addition, researchers might consider taking copies of these letters with them in the event that they discover a pre-viously unknown, relevant source; additional documentation will help the cu-rator determine whether the research warrants access to other restricted ma-terials.

The British Library website also posts contact information, including email addresses, for its various departments, rules for using the collections, collec-tion development policies, and copyright issues and regulations. For example, pages listing conditions of use of the Reading Rooms remind visitors that the only writing implements allowed are pencils and that only the person to whom manuscripts have been issued may use them, as well as describe proper handling of materials and the procedures and copyright governing the repro-duction of manuscripts. Prohibited items include "pens, food, drink, sweets (including cough sweets), chewing gum, glue, bottles of ink, correction fluid, cleaning liquids, scissors, knives (including craft knives and razor blades), highlighter pens, scanner pens, adhesive tape and umbrellas," although users can check such items in a cloak room designated for the purpose. The library provides clear plastic bags for carrying approved items into the Reading Rooms, and permits the use of laptops according to certain restrictions in re-gard to accessing and downloading electronic resources.

The conditions of use described above represent only a selection of issues a scholar may encounter in manuscript and archival research. Because every institution is unique, verifying whether an institution of choice has a website and checking it for rules of access and contact information remain a best prac-tice. And while many archives and special libraries require written documen-tation to access their collections, the Web has facilitated faster and more effi-cient communication between researchers and scholarly organizations.

LOCATING RELEVANT ARCHIVES AND MANUSCRIPTS

Ash, Lee, and William G. Miller, comps. *Subject Collections: A Guide to Spe-cial Book Collections and Subject Emphases as Reported by University, College, Public, and Special Libraries and Museums in the United States and Canada*. 2 vols. 7th ed., rev. and enl. New Providence, NJ: R. R. Bowker, 1993.

Dictionary of Literary Biography. Detroit: Gale Research Co. 1978–.

Helferty, Seamus, and Raymond Refaussé, eds. *Directory of Irish Archives*, 4th ed. Dublin: Four Courts, 2003.

Lester, DeeGee, comp. *Irish Research: A Guide to Collections in North America, Ireland, and Great Britain*. Bibliographies and Indexes in World History, no. 9. Westport, CT: Greenwood, 1987.

Location Register of Twentieth-Century English Literary Manuscripts and Letters: A Union List of Papers of Modern English, Irish, Scottish and Welsh Authors in the British Isles. 2 vols. London: British Library; Boston, G. K. Hall & Co., 1988.

Matthew, Henry C. G., and Brian Harrison, eds. *Oxford Dictionary of National Biography: From Earliest Times to the Year 2000*. 61 vols. Rev. ed. New York: Oxford University Press, 2004.

National Library of Ireland. *Manuscript Sources for the History of Irish Civilization*. 11 vols. Ed. by Richard J. Hayes. Boston: G. K. Hall, 1965.

——. *Manuscript Sources for the History of Irish Civilization: Supplement*. 3 vols. Boston: G. K. Hall, 1979.

Sutton, David C., ed. *Location Register of English Literary Manuscripts and Letters: Eighteenth and Nineteenth Centuries*. 2 vols. London: British Library, 1995.

WorldCat. Dublin, OH: OCLC. worldcat.org.

Websites for archives and manuscript collections present a great deal of information for the researcher, including descriptions of collections, finding aids, digitized images of pieces from the collections, and occasionally, as indicated in the previous description of the British Library, an online catalog of the manuscript collection. Online platforms provide archivists with new ways to promote and maintain collections, as well as to communicate with potential visitors. In addition, online archival resources allow scholars to conduct research remotely. Even in this rich research environment, however, questions remain regarding the best techniques for discovering where relevant manuscripts and archives reside. This section describes recommended resources and search strategies for Irish literature scholars and those devoted to British literature in general, as well as others specifically dedicated to Irish Studies.

For locations of personal papers and manuscripts by individual authors, the **Oxford Dictionary of National Biography** (detailed in chapter 2) is an excellent source with which to start. Attempting comprehensive coverage of biographical information on major and minor figures who have left a mark on

British history, including many people with Irish connections, entries feature, when possible, locations of papers and manuscripts. In the case of some authors, however, this information may not be comprehensive, requiring further research. Another useful source of archival and manuscript information is the introductions to or the acknowledgement sections of standard editions or biographies for figures of interest, in which authors or editors often state which collections were consulted and who helped with the research. In addition, scholars can search for facsimile editions of authors' works in local library collections and in **WorldCat** by conducting keyword searches consisting of an author's name and the keyword *facsimile** or *manuscript**, which will return records for monograph or microfilm reproductions of manuscripts. Searching for websites devoted to authors or submitting queries to electronic listservs are other possible strategies. Researchers will also find general information about manuscript and personal paper collections in the **Dictionary of Literary Biography** (outlined in chapter 2).

Ash and Miller's **Subject Collections: A Guide to Special Book Collections and Subject Emphases as Reported by University, College, Public, and Special Libraries and Museums in the United States and Canada** is a two-volume directory of special collections housed in libraries in Canada and the United States. The most recent edition appeared in 1993, so collections developed since then are absent from its contents. Still, these volumes are useful for identifying established collections. The compilers derive their information from questionnaires distributed to libraries, which they supplement with additional research. Consequently, entries correspond in scope and detail to the information provided by participating institutions.

This resource lists special collections covering an expansive list of subjects, from African American cultures to ecology and the environment to feminism and women's rights and ethnic groups, and also contains authors and national literatures such as Irish literature. Entries are arranged by Library of Congress subject heading or name and then subdivided geographically by state, province, and library. Entries typically contain contact information, holdings, a general description of the relevant collection, including whether the collection has been cataloged, if manuscripts and/or images are present, number of volumes, number of linear feet, and notes further clarifying the contents of the collection. *Subject Collections* serves as a valuable supplement to the *Location Registers*, but its considerably broader scope necessarily requires a more general treatment of manuscripts relevant to the study of Irish literary authors, works, and movements. Still, it is a useful tool for identifying pockets of Irish literature collections around the United States and Canada such as those held at Emory University in Atlanta and at Queen's University in Kingston, Ontario, the websites of which researchers may consult to obtain more detailed information about relevant collections.

Though compiled according to a similar methodology, Lester's *Irish Research: A Guide to Collections in North America, Ireland, and Great Britain* stands in marked contrast to *Subject Collections* on account of its specific treatment of Irish-related collections in the United States, Canada, Ireland and Northern Ireland, and Great Britain. Published in 1987, Lester's volume remains a significant and useful guide for scholars researching all matters Irish, from immigrant correspondence to public records about Irish laborers in North America to manuscripts and personal papers and effects of Irish literary and cultural figures, both the widely known and the obscure. Derived from questionnaires distributed to libraries and supplemented by the compiler, this volume's contents are primarily as complete as the information provided by participating institutions. Organized geographically by country and then alphabetically by state, province, county, and institution, a majority of the contents consist of entries describing collections housed in libraries and repositories in the United States. Typical entries present contact information and describe the purpose of the organization, the Irish resources available, special collections, special services (e.g., indexes, catalogs, finding aids), special rules, and recommendations for researchers from librarians working at these locations. In general, entries are extremely thorough and summarize archival collections as well as the extent of an institution's holdings in Irish related materials, including journal subscriptions, audio and visual sources, and strengths of the circulating collections. Two appendixes, one listing book stores and dealers specializing in Irish materials and the other Irish local newspapers, supplement the entries. The volume concludes with a thorough general index to the complete contents.

Manuscript Sources for the History of Irish Civilization and its *Supplement* primarily serve as the union catalog for manuscripts held at the National Library of Ireland (NLI) and cataloged before 1979. Collectively known as the Hayes catalog, these volumes also contain entries describing manuscripts of Irish interest housed in more than thirty countries, though the National Library of Ireland holds copies of many of these manuscripts on microfilm. Entries are generally organized by person, place, subject, and date. While the NLI's website permits researchers to search for its manuscripts cataloged since 1990, *Manuscript Sources for the History of Irish Civilization* provides almost exclusive access to previously described titles and collections. In addition, this reference also lists important manuscripts and collections held in other institutions, information which does not appear in the NLI catalog. Scholars seeking access to entries for manuscripts catalogued from 1979 to 1990 are encouraged to contact the NLI directly since they exist only in an unpublished card catalogue available in its Manuscripts Reading Room.

The fourth edition of Helferty and Refaussé's *Directory of Irish Archives* discusses more than 250 public and private archival institutions and organizations containing resources accessible to scholars and researchers. Entries in this essential resource present contact information for the archives covered, including e-mail and website addresses, opening hours, descriptions of published guides and finding aids, and summaries of collections. Appendixes treat institutions that maintain archival collections and holdings that are not accessible for scholarly research. Other appendixes provide descriptions of and contact information for related organizations that researchers can consult for expert advice.

Both the *Location Register of English Literary Manuscripts and Letters: Eighteenth and Nineteenth Centuries* and the *Location Register of Twentieth-Century English Literary Manuscripts and Letters: A Union List of Papers of Modern English, Irish, Scottish and Welsh Authors in the British Isles* are two-volume directories of locations for manuscripts based on information collected by teams of researchers that surveyed British institutions maintaining literary manuscript collections. The data gathered in this process has been loaded into searchable databases, and the volumes devoted to eighteenth- and nineteenth-century collections are, essentially, print-outs of these portions of the database. The *Location Register of Twentieth-Century English Literary Manuscripts and Letters* also covers photographs, proofs, sound recordings, and electronic documents. Volumes are arranged alphabetically by author and list the literary manuscripts and letters held in hundreds of selected archival repositories and libraries in England, Scotland, Ireland, and Wales. Because coverage is limited only to those institutions and organizations surveyed and visited by the works' compilers, holdings for repositories outside Britain and Ireland or in private collections are not listed. Entries include the title or a brief description of an item, location, manuscript number, date, and physical description (e.g., autograph, microfilm, or photocopy), if known, as well as the date the manuscript was added to the database. Some entries may lack certain details, such as physical description, as a result of the compilers' occasional reliance on finding aids. In addition to English, Irish, Scottish, and Welsh authors writing in the English language, these volumes also address work by immigrants, refugees, and others who lived considerable spans of their lives in the British Isles and Ireland. This last point may be of particular interest to scholars of Irish literature interested in literary output from immigrants and exiles.

Marcuse's chapter on "Archives and Manuscripts," in *A Reference Guide for English Studies* (see chapter 2), lists additional sources. Although coverage only includes directories and guides published before 1990, the lists of printed guides and the guides to manuscript collections contain evaluative annotations and succinct descriptions of collections held in individual repositories. Some entries provide information about several printed sources for a single repository. Chapter sections that may be especially relevant to the scholar of Irish literature are: "General Guides to the Location, Study, and Use of Archives and Manuscripts," "British Repositories," "American Repositories," "English Studies—Manuscripts," and "British Archives."

WEBSITES FOR LOCATING ARCHIVES
AND MANUSCRIPT COLLECTIONS

Abraham, Terry, comp. *Repositories of Primary Sources*, January 2007, at www.uidaho.edu/special-collections/Other.Repositories.html (accessed 31 March 2008).

Archives Ireland, at www.archives.ie/ (accessed 31 March 2008).

ARCHON, at www.nationalarchives.gov.uk/archon/ (accessed 31 March 2008).

British Library Manuscript Catalogues, at www.bl.uk/catalogues/manuscripts .html (accessed 31 March 2008).

DocumentsOnline, at www.nationalarchives.gov.uk/documentsonline/ (accessed 31 March 2008).

Guide to the Contents of the Public Record Office. London: H. M. Stationary Office, 1963–1968.

Index of Manuscripts in the British Library. 10 vols. Teaneck, NJ: Chadwyck-Healey, 1984–1986.

Irish Literary Collections Portal, at irishliterature.library.emory.edu/ (accessed 31 March 2008).

The National Archives, at www.nationalarchives.gov.uk/ (accessed 31 March 2008).

The National Archives Catalogue, at www.nationalarchives.gov.uk/catalogue/ (accessed 31 March 2008).

The National Archives of Ireland, at www.nationalarchives.ie/ (accessed 31 March 2008).

National Library of Ireland, at www.nli.ie/ (accessed 31 March 2008).

National Register of Archives. London: The National Archives.www.national archives.gov.uk/nra/ (accessed 31 March 2008).

Nickson, Margaret A. E. *The British Library: Guide to the Catalogues and Indexes of the Department of Manuscripts*. 3rd rev. ed. London: British Library, 1998.

Once a researcher has identified an archive or collection she wants to consult, she can use an institutional website, if available, to learn how to search the archive. While some organizations, such as the British Library and National

Library of Ireland, maintain tools for searching the contents of their collections, traditional library catalogs may not include records describing manuscripts and other archival materials partly due to the specialized standards required for cataloging unique items. Many archive and repository websites indicate which parts, if any, of a special collection are in the online catalog, as well as provide finding aids to browse some contents. Either way, searching print guides or online databases is far different than searching conventional library catalogs. This section explores Web-based resources designed and suited for researching archives and manuscripts.

The British Library offers scholars print catalogs and a separate catalog for the Western "manuscript acquisitions of the British Museum and British Library from 1753 onwards," called the *British Library Manuscript Catalogues*. Currently, the British Library is in the process of scanning the published catalogs to create the online catalog. Records are based on the library's traditional cataloging practices, which consist of two parts: *indexes* (personal names, place names, subject terms) and *descriptions* (a narrative detailing content, date, physical details, bibliography, and provenance). The British Library offers separate search engines that permit users to search either indexes by name or selected subject, or descriptions by manuscript reference or keyword, since the description field is often used to describe an author's occupation, rank, or relationship with another individual. If looking for references to the Abbey Theatre, for example, information recorded in the descriptive field may reveal to the researcher a letter on the topic, while data recorded in an indexing field will not. An extensive "Search tips" webpage and an online, printable "User Guide" outline how to conduct each type of search effectively, including why certain searches fail. Both are worth consulting. While the conversion of print catalogs to searchable online resources is an ongoing project, the website posts the current status of the project for researchers. In addition, the ten-volume *Index of Manuscripts in the British Library* provides name and title level access to the collections through 1950, and M. A. E. Nickson's *The British Library: Guide to the Catalogues and Indexes of the Department of Manuscripts* outlines the various catalogs for the parts of the manuscript collections. Though scholars can remotely search online catalogs to identify manuscript records, they may still not be able to request or access these items online. Once a researcher knows what sources she needs, she can review access requirements outlined on the website to verify whether or not the documents and collections are available for her use.

The largest governmental archive in the United Kingdom is *The National Archives*, headquartered in Kew, near London. Formerly the Public Records Office, this institution houses and maintains British state and central court documents from the eleventh century to the present, including a massive archive of items documenting colonial rule of Ireland and Irish migration to Britain, many of which complement holdings at comparable Irish institutions. The website features pages listing recommended steps to help potential users prepare for visits, including: verifying that the National Archives has the materials sought; checking opening hours; planning the day around the provisions that only three items may be requested at a time and that requests must be placed by 4:15 p.m. at the latest; registering online; and ordering up to three documents in advance. Visitors must bring proof of identity to obtain a "Reader's Ticket," which is valid for three years and must be presented at every visit. Researchers who bring background information on their research topics enable staff to provide even better assistance. The National Archives permits users to bring only graphite pencils, "no more than one spiral-bound, stapled or sewn (not glued) notepad," and up to twenty loose sheets of paper stapled together at the security desk into the Reading or Reference Rooms. Scholars intending to write a lot might consider bringing a laptop. Other advice posted on these pages outlines securing valuables, paying for copies of documents, the availability of food and drink, and clothing appropriate to a climate-controlled environment.

The National Archives Catalogue, formerly called *PROCAT*, currently contains more than ten million records arranged "under the different government departments that originated them." While help and search tips screens describe the structure of the catalog and how to search it effectively, researchers possessing a solid knowledge of their projects are more likely to have success searching this unique archive. In addition, the three-volume set *Guide to the Contents of the Public Record Office* describes National Archives records up to the mid-1960s. Organized by class, it provides a breakdown of the numbering system that may clarify how to interpret retrieved records. The Catalogue also features links to research guides designed to facilitate the retrieval of records pertinent to the study of a specific topic, such as the Easter Rising of 1916 and the history of the Royal Irish Constabulary from 1786 to 1922. In addition, scholars have the option of conducting "Places, Prominent People and Subject" searches, which point users to prepared searches for frequently explored topics, including the Irish Famine, 1846–1850, and the records of the Irish Deportee Tribunal (1923–1924).

Generally, users must consult the documents at The National Archives onsite, either in paper or microform, depending on the restrictions for use. However, scholars working remotely who identify in the online catalog the records they want may order and purchase them as photocopies or digital reproductions from *DocumentsOnline*, a document delivery service that allows researchers from abroad to use these collections without visiting the holding institution. In addition to fulfilling individual requests, The National Archives has in the works several digitizing projects designed to allow broader access to important and popular parts of its collections, such as the wills of famous people, including several significant British literary figures, Shakespeare, Edmund Burke, and Dr. Johnson among them. This collection is a subset of a larger digitization project which provides images, available for purchase from *DocumentsOnline*, to all Prerogative Court of Canterbury wills from 1384 to 1858 in The National Archives.

The *Historical Manuscripts Commission* (HMC) serves as the advisory agency regarding archives and manuscripts to the British government. In April 2003, the HMC and the Public Records Office merged to form The National Archives. The HMC maintains the **National Register of Archives** (NRA), the central resource for researchers who need to identify and locate relevant records. Unlike The National Archives, the HMC does not itself hold any manuscripts or historical records. Instead, the NRA "consists of over 44,000 unpublished lists and catalogues that describe archival holdings in the United Kingdom and overseas." The NRA's online database permits searches by corporate, personal, family, or place name. A personal name search for *wilde, oscar* returns a single entry with sixteen records attached, including brief references to the *Location Register of 20th Century English Literary Manuscripts* and correspondence, letters, and literary manuscripts held at the University of California Library, Los Angeles, the Library of Congress, and Oxford University's Bodleian Library.

Also under the jurisdiction of the HMC, **ARCHON** is an electronic directory of repositories in the United Kingdom and abroad as well as the portal to information regarding archival initiatives and projects such as digitization initiatives, online finding aids, and archival descriptive and conservation standards. The *ARCHON* directory lists repositories by institution name or region, and items returned from the NRA database link to *ARCHON* for directory information, including contact information, e-mail addresses, and links to websites for collections. The website presents users with a hyperlinked map of England, Wales, Scotland, Northern Ireland, the Republic of Ireland, the Channel Islands, and the Isle of Man that points to directories of repositories in these respective areas. ARCHON lists seventy-seven records for institutions in the Republic of Ireland and twenty-four in Northern Ireland.

The National Archives of Ireland (NAI) website outlines institutional use policies and permits users to conduct keyword searches of electronic finding aids. Primarily suited for onsite research, the *NAI* maintains a limited online presence. Researchers who wish to visit its Reading Rooms are encouraged to apply in advance for a Reader's Ticket, which can be downloaded and filled out in advance, but can only be processed upon arrival. Reader's Tickets require photographic identification for validation and are valid for three years. As with most manuscript and archival agencies, only pencils, paper, and a laptop are allowed in the Reading Rooms, though taping devices, electronic, and photographic equipment may be allowed with special permission. While the website's search feature permits scholars to run simple or advanced searches across nineteen finding aid databases, records themselves are not viewable online. In addition, online finding aids may not cover collections in their entirety; print guides housed in the Reading Rooms are required to discern a collection's full coverage. By and large, the *NAI* contains "records of the modern Irish state which document its historical evolution and the creation of its national identity," primarily generated by government departments and agencies. The contents of most of these collections are well suited to local history and genealogy research, though literature scholars will discover several records possibly relevant to the study of relations between the Irish state and cultural figures, such as Nobel Prize proposals and reports on the enforcement of obscenity laws, as well as correspondence from private citizens to the government.

The website for the ***National Library of Ireland*** (NLI) makes available online catalogs to several principal collections. While not a lending institution, the *NLI* is not strictly an archive, either. Rather, it is a cultural repository devoted to the collection, preservation, and use of "books, manuscripts and illustrative material of Irish interest." The contents of some collections have been described in chapter 3, "Library Catalogs," many of which are particularly relevant to Irish literary scholarship. Unlike many of the other organizations discussed here, the *NLI* is not as restrictive in its use policies. Users must gain admittance to Reading Rooms by means of Readers Tickets valid only in specific areas, and the Library maintains separate facilities for general collections and manuscripts. The website alludes to "rules for readers" posted within the Library, but they are not available on the website itself. Though access to electronic reproductions of documents and images is limited, users can search separate online catalogs dedicated to the main collections, newspapers, new Irish books, photographic databases, and lists of manuscripts and special collections. Lists of manuscripts available in the online catalog are selective, and users who seek access to all manuscript holdings will have to contact the *NLI* directly or use the onsite print references.

Several online directories of archives exist on the Web. Compiled by Terry Abraham at the University of Idaho, ***Repositories of Primary Sources*** is an extensive example of such a directory. It lists URLs for archives, manuscripts, rare books, photographs, and other primary sources held at institutions around the world. Arranged geographically by continent and then country, links to websites are organized alphabetically by institution. A section devoted to "Additional Lists" lists other directory websites by country, such as *ARCHON*,

Archives Ireland, and Eneclann's *Record Repositories in Ireland*. While these additional links may be duplicated in other website directories, each possesses a unique archival focus and any may lead to new sites of interest.

Sponsored by the Heritage Council of Ireland, *Archives Ireland* points visitors to repositories of archives in Ireland, as well as contact information and summaries of their holdings. In addition, this website aims to treat "all aspects of Records Management, File Management, Imaging, Offsite Storage and Legislation including the Freedom of Information Act." Organized into four sections, "Archives and Record Management," "Professional Resources," "Consultants," and "Irish Archives," *Archives Ireland* serves as an online forum for archive users, researchers, and professionals to share information on all aspects of archives creation, administration, and best practices. This resource is especially rich in material covering electronic records, microfilm and reproduction, and the scanning and digitizing of records. For Irish literature, the "Irish Archives" section is an especially rich source of descriptions of and links to websites for archival repositories.

Finally, the *Irish Literary Collections Portal*, maintained at Emory University's Manuscripts, Archives and Rare Book Library (MARBL) is an indispensable Irish literary studies resource. Of all the resources discussed in this chapter, this portal is the only one exclusively concerned with Irish literature. It provides access to more than one hundred digitized finding aids for Irish literary manuscript collections housed in North America. Represented collections range in date from the late nineteenth century to the present and contain a wide variety of materials including correspondence, photographs, printed documents, and typescripts and manuscripts of literary works. The portal makes available finding aids from several participating institutions in a single searchable database, the contents of which researchers can browse or search. The browse function allows users to view an alphabetical listing of all the collections in the portal, while the search function permits researchers to conduct keyword searches within finding aids and to limit searches by creator and/or repository. Participating organizations hold significant Irish literature collections, and the portal links to websites posting general information regarding hours, location, and access to the collections at these institutions.

CONCLUSION

Libraries and other information organizations are currently in a dynamic, and sometimes volatile, transition period. Manuscript and archival repositories are no exception, and in many ways, these types of institutions are at the vanguard of utilizing new technologies such as the Web and digitization tools to impact the scholar's ability to locate, contact, and access relevant archives. In addition to facilitating easier and faster communications by means of websites and e-mail, digitization projects and document delivery services, such as The National Archives' *DocumentsOnline*, continue to change how users access archival materials, as well as how these materials are distributed. Despite these changes, print directories, standard editions, and bibliographies continue to play a crucial part in the research process because a great deal of information about authors' manuscripts and personal papers remains centralized in a few locations. Over time, however, these resources become dated, and the Web is poised to play an increasingly pivotal role in archival scholarship. Despite technological advances, the nature of archival materials themselves will not change; a literary manuscript will always be a manuscript. Therefore, whether finding aids, research guides, or documents are available in print, microform, or digital formats, working with manuscript and archival materials will still require scholars to possess the patience and skills to create and carry out deliberate, knowledgeable research plans. The best practices recommended in this chapter provide researchers with the tools to navigate primary source materials.

NOTES

1. Grene, Nicholas. "Some Principal Shaw Research Sources: V. The National Library of Ireland." *SHAW: The Annual of Bernard Shaw Studies* 20 (2000): 152.

2. Peters, Margot. "Bernard F. Burgunder: Collector of Genius." *SHAW: The Annual of Bernard Shaw Studies* 15 (1995) 171–72.

3. Laurence, Dan H. *Bernard Shaw: A Bibliography* (Oxford; New York: Clarendon Press; Oxford University Press, 1983), 894.

Chapter Nine

Web Resources

Many sites devoted to Irish literature exist on the Web and serve the needs of researchers possessing various levels of knowledge and expertise. Students new to the study of Irish literature, for example, will find numerous sites that present introductory materials to the field, including: biographical information about canonical and non-canonical authors; full-text editions of Irish drama, fiction, poetry, and prose; and sources that provide cultural, historical, and political contexts. Graduate students, on the other hand, have access to electronic scholarly journals, online bibliographies of Irish literature resources, and discussion lists where subscribers can monitor current scholarly debate and trends. As pointed out in chapter 8, "Microforms and Digital Collections," the Web has facilitated unprecedented access to texts previously only available on microfilm or in special collections as libraries and other cultural institutions reproduce published and unpublished texts and make them available online. Some of these electronic texts are searchable by keyword. In addition to textual resources, Web-based reference tools such as Irish, British, and North American union library catalogs and general Irish literature and author-specific bibliographies and chronologies are becoming more widely available to scholars and students.

Because the Web is a dynamic, relatively inexpensive, and increasingly accessible publishing platform, online resources can be posted by individuals or groups, and maintained by inexperienced enthusiasts working alone or well-funded and organized specialists and agencies. As a result, quality varies widely between Web resources, and many sites created in earnest are abandoned or deleted. Still, untold numbers of websites requiring maintenance or upkeep remain accessible to users seeking viable information for their research needs, and the experience of locating authoritative, up-to-date online resources can be frustrating for scholars. Web-based information sources, though increasingly sophisticated and credible research tools, do not replace other scholarly resources. They can, however, complement traditional reference tools. This chapter will describe a representative selection of Irish literature websites of varying scope, functionality, and quality for the purpose of illustrating the wide range of online resources available. Some of the sites discussed here have been mentioned in other chapters. The present summaries expand on information previously presented. On the other hand, Web-based scholarly journals, newspapers, and other periodicals are outlined elsewhere in the present volume, in chapters treating specific types of resources.

The Web is a search environment distinct from an online library catalog or a database such as the *MLA International Bibliography*. While controlled vocabularies and authoritative entities influence how users search and use databases and catalogs, their overall importance for website searching is minimal. In contrast to literature databases that solely index scholarly materials, the Web contains a vast selection of resources, most of which are not relevant to academic research. So not only does searching for scholarly resources on the Web yield very different outcomes than searching in a controlled database environment, but the number of irrelevant hits from a general Web search is significantly greater than the number of irrelevant results returned from a database. The following criteria are designed to help users evaluate whether or not resources identified by general search engines for research projects fulfill their scholarly needs:

Authority. Who is responsible for the site's content and upkeep? Is it produced and maintained at an academic institution or government agency? Is it authored or edited by an expert in the field?

Currency. When was the site last updated and how frequently is it maintained? Does it post time-sensitive information?

Scope. What is the subject matter and range of coverage? Who is the intended audience (undergraduates, scholars, general readers)?

Objectivity. What, if any, bias does the site creator possess? How does that affect the site's content?

Accuracy. How accurate is the material presented? Can it be verified in other sources?

As suggested in chapter 1, "Basics of Online Searching," scholars can use these same criteria to evaluate any potential print or electronic resource they may be considering for research.

SCHOLARLY GATEWAYS

Ireland: Language and Literature, 4 May 2006, at www.loc.gov/rr/international/main/ireland/langlit.html (accessed 31 March 2008).

Liu, Alan. *Voice of the Shuttle: Gaelic & Celtic*, at vos.ucsb.edu/ browse.asp?id=982 (accessed 31 March 2008).

———. *Voice of the Shuttle: Ireland*, at vos.ucsb.edu/browse.asp?id=1437 (accessed 31 March 2008).

Schreibman, Susan. *IRITH: Irish Resources in the Humanities*, at irith.org/ index.jsp (accessed 31 March 2008).

Teeter, Brian. *British and Irish Literature*, at www.interleaves.org/~rteeter/ litukire.html (accessed 31 March 2008).

Scholarly gateways consist of links to a selection of recommended resources. Typically, subject specialists create and maintain these websites. They are convenient starting points during the research process because they eliminate the guesswork of sorting through lists of results retrieved from a search of the entire World Wide Web. Scholarly gateways do not share a common template or scope. Instead, they often represent the work of individuals who possess some expertise as scholarly researchers. As the products of individual endeavor, however, links in scholarly gateways sometimes require updating. The resources discussed in this section permit users to notify site owners of broken links as well as suggestions for new citations. In a sense, then, scholarly gateways also serve as platforms for scholarly interaction and the development of communities based on shared interests.

One of the Library of Congress's "Portals to the World" websites, *Ireland: Language and Literature* is a useful starting point for Irish literary scholars seeking a list of viable Irish literature websites. Currently, the site features links to approximately ten standard Irish literature online resources. Selected by Library of Congress subject specialists, these online resources treat specific aspects of Irish literary study, including drama, folklore and mythology, and philology. In general, the resources selected are themselves portals providing links to other sites and online documents.

Cited on the *Ireland: Language and Literature* portal, literature professor Alan Liu's *Voice of the Shuttle* (*VoS*) is a highly regarded scholarly gateway that has existed in various versions since 1994. Originally a collection of static websites, the current version of *VoS* is a database serving dynamic content to the Web. It organizes links to websites and online sources relevant to a number of disciplines, including architecture, gender and sexuality studies, literature, and religious studies. Scholarly areas are organized on individual webpages, and links are cross-indexed between different disciplines when appropriate. Currently, *VoS* features several pages of potential use to Irish literary scholars, notably *Voice of the Shuttle: Ireland* and *Voice of the Shuttle: Gaelic & Celtic*. Both introduce a range of scholarly resources available for the study of Gaelic language and literature and Irish literature in English. Irish literary scholars may also identify relevant resources on the *VoS: History:*

Ireland page. *VoS: Ireland* consists of seven sections, over half of which are devoted to Irish authors: general resources in Irish literature; Samuel Beckett; James Joyce; Sean O'Casey; George Bernard Shaw; William Butler Yeats; and Irish literature courses. *VoS: Gaelic & Celtic* is organized into five sections: general Gaelic and Celtic resources; Irish; Manx; Scottish; and Welsh. Brief descriptions, including mention of creators and/or place of origin, accompany some of the resources listed. In the main, sources listed in *VoS* possess scholarly value, although some links require updating.

Similar in design and functionality to *Voice of the Shuttle*, though more modest in scope, librarian Brian Teeter's **British and Irish Literature** consists of an organized list of links to websites and online resources relevant to British and Irish literary study. Teeter's gateway is highly selective in scope and generally corresponds to his personal scholarly and cultural interests. Broadly categorized into general literary resources, period resources, genre resources, and resources devoted to individual authors, links point to selected websites and databases. Although some of the Irish literature websites listed in this gateway overlap with sources listed in *VoS*, many others provide extensive links to useful sources for Irish author biographical information and texts of Irish literary works, such as an online directory to "British and Irish Authors on the Web," an electronic reproduction of Padraic Colum's *Anthology of Irish Verse*, and the website "A Gallery of Bloomsday Cards." Comparing *British and Irish Literature* with *VoS* illustrates the idea that the contents of scholarly gateways devoted to the same subject can diverge significantly in terms of coverage.

In addition to being a premier site for Irish literary study, **IRITH: Irish Resources in the Humanities** serves as a microcosm of Irish Studies resources available on the Web. It exclusively covers Irish resources and, as its titles indicates, this website's scope exceeds literary studies and points to sources pertinent to Irish archaeology, architecture, art, biography, film, geography, grants and fellowships, history, language, and music, though commercial sites are not linked. The main page directs scholars to the most recent entries added to the gateway and permits users to conduct keyword searches of database contents. The literature section alphabetically lists one hundred links to websites and online resources covering bibliographies, digitized texts, individual authors, literary genres, scholarly journals, academic organizations and societies, and significant publishers and presses. Resources devoted to Irish women literary figures are particularly well represented on *IRITH*. Thorough summaries outlining the coverage, creator(s), history, and scope accompany each resource citation. Developed in 1999 at Trinity College Dublin by Dr. Susan Schreibman, the earliest version of this site consisted of a list of links to "substantial content in the various disciplines of the humanities in the area of Irish Studies" and has since evolved into a searchable database now resid-ing at the University of Maryland, College Park. Its extensive breadth and depth of coverage make *IRITH* an indispensable component for all stages of the online research process.

ELECTRONIC TEXT ARCHIVES

Bartleby.com, at www.bartleby.com (accessed 31 March 2008).

Bear, Risa Stephanie. *Renascence Editions: An Online Repository of Works Printed in English Between the Years 1477 and 1799*, at darkwing.uoregon .edu/~rbear/ren.htm (accessed 31 March 2008).

Bibliomania, at www.bibliomania.com/ (accessed 31 March 2008).

CELT: Corpus of Electronic Texts, 13 July 2007, at www.ucc.ie/celt/ (ac-cessed 10 February 2008).

Cuala Press Broadside Collection, at digital.library.villanova.edu/ Cuala%20Press%20Broadside%20Collection/ (accessed 31 March 2008).

Information about Ireland. *Irish Literature*, at www.ireland-information.com/ irishliterature.htm (accessed 31 March 2008).

Irish Script on Screen, at www.isos.dias.ie/ (accessed 31 March 2008).

Oxford Text Archive, 11 August 2006, at ota.ahds.ac.uk/ (accessed 31 March 2008).

Sundermeier, Michael. *Irish Literary Sources and Resources*, at mockingbird .creighton.edu/english/micsun/IrishResources/irishres.htm (accessed 31 March 2008).

The most common types of literary resources published on the Web are elec-tronic versions of literary texts, whether transcribed in word processing pro-grams and mark-up languages or digitized reproductions. Works in the public domain or otherwise unrestricted by copyright, in particular, are frequently available on the Web. In respect to Irish literature, several online archives provide access to full-text editions of works by authors writing and publish-ing through the mid-twentieth century, while sites devoted to the lives and works of individual writers may also feature links to full-text novels, poems, and prose. As with other research resources, canonical Irish literary figures and texts are well represented on the Web. Yet, online publishing has also fa-cilitated the transmission of information about and texts by artists tradition-ally not as well known or regarded as others. For example, several electronic text archives covering women writers of different literary periods exist on the Web. While scholars can access more and more online texts from a wide va-riety of authors, quality may vary between different versions of electronic texts available in a range of formats, including ASCII plain text, marked-up HTML and SGML versions, and digitally scanned reproductions of manuscripts and print editions of books, correspondence, and illustrations. Given the variety of electronic text choices offered to the researcher, confirming the scholarly credibility of an online edition becomes a crucial concern. To determine an online text's authority, it is necessary to note the source, publication date, and the publisher of the selected edition. In addition, verifying the authority of the text's editors and hosting institution (e.g., a university, an academic library, or a commercial organization), as well as establishing whether or not texts are subject to editorial review as suggested by the inclusion of critical apparatuses (e.g., introductions, notes, glossaries), can help scholars choose an online edition that matches their needs.

A notable example of a scholarly credible electronic text archive is the *Oxford Text Archive* (*OTA*). Founded in 1976, the *OTA* has been a collaborative project from its inception. Partnering with scholars in arts and humanities disciplines who deposit texts for distribution, the *OTA* collects, catalogs, and preserves "high-quality electronic texts for research and teaching," and "currently distributes more than 2000 resources in over 20 different languages." Holdings are almost exclusively available in the public domain, though scholars may discover that access to certain texts requires permission from the depositing individual, institution, or organization. Despite being an online depository of downloadable digitized information, the *OTA* requires researchers requesting access to restricted titles to mail order forms in hard copy. Irish literature holdings include texts by Burke, Joyce, Shaw, Wilde, and Yeats, among others, as well as a couple of Irish language texts. The site permits users to browse by author, title, or language, or to search by means of various fields. Most texts in this archive are published in a variety of digital text formats, and the *OTA* recommends using Microsoft Internet Explorer to view its contents. For a fee, versions of texts are also available in physical media such as diskettes, data and DAT cartridges, and CD-ROMs.

Bibliomania is another site that has emerged from the collaboration between academics and new media experts. Similar in scope and purpose to the *OTA*, this archive offers free, unrestricted access to more than two thousand literary texts from a variety of genres, including criticism, drama, fiction, interviews, non-fiction, and poetry. Irish literature scholars will find full-text access to works by Hearn, Joyce, Sheridan, Synge, Wilde, and Yeats. In addition, *Bibliomania* also provides full-text access to a selection of study guides and reference works to supplement critical appreciation and understanding of available literary works. Titles in this archive consist of HTML reproductions of public domain works, which are searchable by section and subject. The site also permits basic keyword searching of its contents, although this feature sometimes returns inconsistent results. Currently maintained on a voluntary basis by former employees of the site, *Bibliomania* remains a useful source of free, full-text canonical works. Extensively supported by commercial sponsors, some scholars may find the ad banners appearing on the site distracting. Still, *Bibliomania* may serve as a viable back-up for texts either not available or restricted on other electronic text archives, such as *OTA*.

More current and diverse in its coverage of primary texts and reference materials, **Bartleby.com** is a commercial site offering access primarily to nineteenth- and early twentieth-century writers and works available in the public domain. Contents are indexed and searchable by author, subject, and title. Organized into four sections, *Bartleby.com* makes available reference, verse, fiction, and non-fiction works. Of the electronic text archives so far discussed, this site offers an excellent selection of relevant materials to Irish literary scholars, including Padraic Colum's *Anthology of Irish Verse* (1922) and the complete *Collected Poems of A.E.* (1913), as well as significant volumes by Burke, Shaw, Yeats, and Wilde. Anthology holdings in all genres are particularly strong on this site, and entries are judiciously cited, documented, and easy to navigate. Despite its status as a commercial resource, *Bartleby.com* offers credible scholarly content to the researcher and casual reader alike, as well as stable data and functionality.

Renascence Editions aims to "make available online works printed in English between the years 1477 (when Caxton began printing) and 1799, the date of the first edition of Wordsworth and Coleridge's collaboration on a new kind of poetry." Texts are electronic transcriptions of authoritative print resources. Though the site's publisher and editor, Risa Stephanie Bear, insists that the works included in *Renascence Editions* are not "represented as scholarly editions," entries are prefaced by scholarly notes detailing sources and by whom, when, and where texts were transcribed for inclusion in the archive. Sorted by author, users may search contents by keyword or conduct selected narrower searches by significant Renaissance figures such as Montaigne, Shakespeare, and Spenser, as well as by major works such as *The Faerie Queene*. Primary texts receive principal emphasis here, and Irish literature scholars researching early modern views of Ireland and the Irish, especially from a British perspective, are well served by the documents reproduced at *Renascence Editions*. Relevant titles include Spenser's *A View of the Present State of Ireland*, John Norden's *Vicissitudo Rerum*, and Thomas Nashe's *Pierce Penilesse, His Supplication to the Divell*, among others. This database offers works in all genres, including official and government documents and declarations from the fifteenth through the eighteenth century.

Another high-quality repository of transcribed and scanned primary resources, ***CELT: Corpus of Electronic Texts*** has been discussed in chapter 8, "Microforms and Digital Collections," as an example of a digital collection. As an electronic text archive, *CELT* offers users a wealth of texts representing numerous genres, in several languages, and from over seven centuries of Irish literary history, as well as supplementary scholarly information. Organized by language, genre, and time period, the site allows users to conduct either free-text *Google* searches of texts in the database or a traditional, customizable keyword search. *CELT* is an evolving site, so texts are available in a variety of formats, including HTML, SGML, and downloadable scanned documents (i.e., PDF files). In addition to full-text resources, this database also features a substantial reference section offering researchers links to: bibliographies; chronologies and biographies of significant Celtic scholars; libraries, archives, and other cultural repositories and organizations; listservs; maps; online textual projects and sites; and tables of contents from Irish Studies journals. Another previously outlined electronic text archive is ***Irish Script on Screen***, which seeks to provide digitized copies of Irish manuscripts to a wide range of students and scholars while preserving these rare and irreplaceable resources. Aside from making available high-quality versions of archival texts, *Irish Script on Screen* also offers researchers credible scholarly support in the form of documentation, notes, and bibliographical criticism.

The ***Cuala Press Broadside Collection*** is an important online archive of digitized issues of *A Broadside*, a monthly of contemporary Irish poetry and popular balladry published between 1908 and 1915. Produced and maintained by the Villanova University Digital Library initiative, this collection consists of high-quality, scanned images that users can search by keyword, title, subject, date, or author, as well as freely view, download, and syndicate by means of RSS feeds. This title holds enormous cultural potential for Irish literary scholars on several levels. Published by Elizabeth Cabot Yeats, W. B. Yeats' sister, and illustrated by their brother, J. B. Yeats, each issue of *A Broadside* features either a brief sampling of work from prominent writers publishing at the time, versions of Irish ballads, popular songs, and sea shanties, translations from the Irish, or poems from past authors such as Sir Walter Raleigh and James Clarence Mangan. Contemporary authors frequently published in its pages include Padraic Colum, James Guthrie, Wolfe T. MacGowan, Seumas O'Sullivan, and James Stephens. The ballads and songs printed in *A Broadside* offer scholars a rich store of popular stories and themes that persist to the current era. Familiar titles include "Blow Bullies Blow," "The Cowboy's Lament" (versions of which the American country and western singer Marty Robbins recorded as "The Streets of Loredo" and the Irish poet Paul Muldoon adapted into song as "Blackwatertown"), "Granuaile," "The

Green Linnet," "The Love-Sick Maid," and "Jesse James." Scholars interested in identifying literary sources and traditions underlying the music of the Clancy Brothers, the Dubliners, the Pogues, and the Tossers will find this resource invaluable, as will those researching the history of Irish small presses, the role of women publishers in the twentieth century, or the development of Irish identity in popular print media.

In contrast to the expansive breadth and searching capabilities of the websites covered above, Professor Michael Sundermeier's ***Irish Literary Sources and Resources*** is a highly selective and comparatively static electronic text archive. Possibly emerging from course reading lists, this modest site offers students and scholars of Irish literature classic treatments of Irish folklore, drama, and fiction primarily from the Literary Revival. Translations by Lady Gregory of ancient Irish myths about the children of Lir and the legend of Oisin and Patrick, as well as full texts of Synge's *Riders to the Sea* and Maria Edgeworth's *Castle Rackrent*, are notable works available here. Sundermeier provides scholarly commentary and notes to explain his selection and editing processes, though he generally does not cite the editions from which he has transcribed his electronic versions of public domain texts. Though limited in its coverage and scholarly documentation, this site serves researchers seeking online versions of texts not readily available on other forums. The ***Irish Literature*** page available on the *Information about Ireland* site is similar to *Irish Literary Sources and Resources* in respect to scope and usability. Ostensibly a commercial concern, *Information about Ireland* provides visitors with a small selection of freely accessible electronic versions of Irish fiction, both novels and short-stories. While the choice of texts is very limited, the site's owners encourage users to download resources. Researchers can also subscribe to a newsletter announcing when new texts (and Irish-themed products) have been added to the website. The short-story section includes brief summaries of available texts, while longer works can be downloaded in either RTF or TXT formats.

AUTHOR SITES

The Belfast Group, at chaucer.library.emory.edu/irishpoet/index.html (accessed 10 February 2008).

Casey, Philip. *Irish Writers Online*, 22 July 2007, at www.irishwriters-online.com/ (accessed 31 March 2008).

Muldoon, Paul. *Paul Muldoon*, at www.paulmuldoon.net/ (accessed 31 March 2008).

The Oscholars, at www.oscholars.com/ (accessed 31 March 2008).

Sites devoted exclusively to Irish authors abound on the Web. As suggested in other chapters, canonical Irish writers, especially Beckett, Joyce, Shaw, Wilde, and Yeats, are often subjects of author-specific print resources. This trend persists in regard to Web-based resources. Conducting a simple *Google* or *Yahoo!* search for any of these writers yields multiple results. Of course, artist-specific material covered in individual websites diverges widely, and contents may consist of biographical data, primary texts and secondary resources available in various formats, bibliographic citations, chronologies, images, newsletters, directories to other websites, or personal opinions. Generally, the scholarly authority and credibility of sites dedicated to literary authors and figures depends upon the party responsible for publishing the resource. Associations, organizations, and societies formed to study the life and work of particular writers often sponsor online forums for the purpose of publishing announcements, newsletters, and proceedings of official functions and meetings. On the other hand, individual or small groups of enthusiasts may publish lists of resources, images, or excerpts relevant to the appreciation of certain literary figures. The following selection of sites, with one exception, emphasizes resources that cover more than one author in order to provide a contrast to other author-specific resources discussed in other chapters.

Philip Casey's ***Irish Writers Online*** is an electronic directory currently offering users bio-bibliographical information on more than five hundred Irish authors. Contents are updated and revised on a continuing basis, and coverage extends to all literary periods and genres with an emphasis on twentieth-century and contemporary writers. Casey's criteria require only that authors recommended for inclusion have published at least "one poetry or short story collection, novel, play or script published by a bona fide publisher or produced professionally." The editor welcomes suggestions for additions to the directory, so long as they fulfill the criteria quoted above. Organized into sections outlining news about the site and updated entries, as well as links to writers' websites and resources, online booksellers, Irish publishers, and reference resources, users can search this site by means of keyword or an alphabetical list of personal names. Entries typically consist of biographical descriptions of varying length that emphasize bibliographical information (e.g., titles of significant works, publishers, and dates), and a brief selection of links to sites and resources of potential interest to readers, such as images, texts of speeches, audio files of readings or portions of interviews, and *Wikipedia* articles. Entries also feature internal links to booksellers and online resources providing additional context for subjects. This website is a viable tool for scholars seeking basic biographical and bibliographical information about specific writers.

Based on documents housed in the Special Collections Department of the Robert W. Woodruff Library of Emory University and in the Irish Collection of the Queen's University Library, *The Belfast Group* website collects substantial documentary information on the history of a famous writing workshop based at Queen's University, Belfast in the 1960s and early 1970s. Members of the Group, as it has come to be known, included influential Northern Irish poets Seamus Heaney, Michael Longley, James Simmons, and later, Ciaran Carson, and Paul Muldoon. The archive includes "biographical notes on the participants (well-known and obscure), a catalog of all known Group sheets, and fully searchable electronic texts of Group sheets" by the authors mentioned. This author site is noteworthy for its contextual coverage of a historical era during which several Irish poets, many of whom have become seminal writers on an international level, interacted with and directly influenced one another. This site is particularly useful as a source of comparison between early versions of poems and the texts eventually published by these authors, as a well as a credible resource for exploring the profound influence creative writing produced in Northern Ireland continues to have on the development of Irish literature and its impact on other literary traditions.

Paul Muldoon is the official website of this utterly unique former member of the Belfast Group, Pulitzer Prize-winning poet, and Oxford Professor of Poetry. Seldom are author-specific websites created, maintained, or sanctioned by writers themselves. Yet in the case of Muldoon, it seems fitting that an author with a critical and popular reputation for literary sleights-of-hand, rigorously intelligent linguistic, conceptual, and thematic play, and an uncanny facility for turning poetic conventions, traditions, and expectations inside-out should have his own website. Links direct users to biographical information, a current schedule of upcoming readings, audio files of the poet reading his work, news concerning his latest volume, other relevant websites, a bibliography, information about musical compositions to which Muldoon has contributed libretti, and the homepage for the poet's garage-rock combo, Rackett (which also has its own MySpace page complete with audio tracks). Primarily a promotional tool for Muldoon and his work, this site still offers scholarly utility, especially in respect to the complete bibliographical information it provides. Muldoon's bibliography lists each of his publications, whether produced in limited numbers or for a mass market, and provides data on dual imprints, audio-visual productions of readings, lectures, commentary, and interviews, and work in other genres. Also, this site is a potential resource for scholars researching images of artists in the popular imagination, writers as celebrities, and new forums for literary self-promotion and the crafting of a cultural identity or persona.

Like the Belfast Group site, *Oscholars* covers multiple authors who share a connection. Originally an electronic publication devoted to scholarship of Oscar Wilde and his contemporaries, this site now serves as an online hub to a handful of related publications: *Oscholars*, concerning Wilde's work and milieu, as well as its French sister-publication *Rue des Beaux Arts*; *Shavings*, a survey of Shaw's life and work during Wilde's lifetime; and *Moorings*, a "bulletin of all things George Moore." Two additional titles cover non-Irish figures (James McNeill Whistler and Vernon Lee/Violet Paget, respectively) to complete this suite of publications centered on Wilde. Initially, *Shavings* was published as a section in *Oscholars*, while *Moorings* is a new publication intended to supplement the original title. All three titles, however, review and exchange information on current research, publications, productions, and society and association activity relevant to the scholarly consideration of these authors. In addition, contents typically feature bibliographies, conference announcements and reports, calls for papers, exhibit notices, and critical notes. The site also permits interested users to register for access to discussion and notification forums. Unlike other resources devoted to individual authors, these publications share a similar theme that provides the editorial and contextual scope of each title. They also share a website. As a result, these electronic journals present researchers with a concentrated, inherently comparative view of these authors and their works, as well as a sense of the intensive critical and scholarly work currently devoted to them.

CURRENT AWARENESS RESOURCES

American Conference for Irish Studies (ACIS), at www.acisweb.com/ index.php (accessed 31 March 2008).
British Association for Irish Studies (BAIS), at www.bais.ac.uk/ (accessed 31 March 2008).
International Association for the Study of Irish Literature (IASIL), 22 June 2007, at www.iasil.org/ (accessed 31 March 2008).

The World Wide Web can be, among other things, an excellent platform for current awareness in specific fields and areas of scholarly interest. Online bibliographies, scholarly electronic journals, online tables of contents and abstracts of journals, and society and association discussion lists enable scholars to keep abreast of current developments in Irish literary study. Some of these types of resources have been addressed in other chapters. This section focuses on the presence of Irish Studies and Irish literature on the Web and the information available on sites covering these disciplines. Included in this discussion is an example of a subscription-based online community devoted to fostering current awareness of Irish literature trends.

Many academic associations, organizations, and societies dedicated to Irish literary study exist. Most of them maintain an electronic presence on the Web for the purposes of outlining their charters and goals, publishing announcements, news, and calls for papers, and providing resource support to members as well as site visitors. Some content on these sites may be restricted and available only to members, though most forums contain valuable unrestricted information. Founded in 1969 and originally called the *International Association for the Study of Anglo-Irish Literature* (IASAIL), the ***International Association for the Study of Irish Literature*** (IASIL) changed its name in 1990 to reflect more accurately the diversity of its members' interests, which transcend Irish literature in English. The IASIL aims to: promote the world-wide teaching and study of Irish literature; facilitate international contact between Irish Studies scholars; and serve as a vehicle for bringing Irish writing to a world-wide audience. The IASIL website supports the stated goals of this charter by offering users access to an online archive of association newsletters (1997–present), solicitations for contributions to the bibliography published annually in the scholarly journal *Irish University Review*, and information concerning upcoming and past annual association conferences. The online version of the *IASIL Newsletter* is updated once a week and publishes: conference details and calls for papers; general news; lists of new publications by members; employment, fellowship, and publication opportunities; and new links added to the website. Organized by subject, links pages point scholars to websites for Irish Studies groups, libraries, listservs and electronic discussion boards, newspapers, publishers, booksellers, archives and databases, universities, individual authors, theaters, and Irish language.

The website for the ***British Association for Irish Studies*** (BAIS) serves as the online platform for this group's official business and member support. Established in 1985, the *BAIS* seeks "to encourage and support Irish cultural activities, and the study of Ireland and Irish culture, in Britain." Links on the homepage direct users to sections concerning: *BAIS* news and newsletters; information about the association's scholarly journal, *Irish Studies Review*; announcements and summaries of events and conferences; opportunities for postgraduate funding; and Irish Studies resources. The Irish Studies resources portion of the site offers a comprehensive and up-to-date list of online publications and journals, Irish language links, Irish Studies libraries, Irish Studies organizations, and institutes and centers devoted to Irish Studies. Providing similar information from a North American angle, the ***American Conference for Irish Studies*** (ACIS) site also points users to information about prizes, announcements of upcoming conferences, calls for papers, summaries of past meetings, a directory of Irish Studies programs and courses offered in the United States, and an *ACIS* archive, which consists of a former version of the website. Founded in 1960 as the American Committee for Irish Studies, the *ACIS* is a multidisciplinary scholarly organization that sponsors national and regional annual conferences in the United States. It also co-sponsors joint sessions at the annual meetings of the Modern Language Association and American Historical Association. Scholars interested in keeping abreast of this group's news, events, and publications can subscribe to RSS feeds. In addition, this resource also lists external links to a wide selection of sites relevant to the study of Irish literature and related disciplines.

REFERENCE TOOLS

ARCHON, at www.archon.nationalarchives.gov.uk/archon (accessed 31 March 2008).

British Library Integrated Catalogue, at catalogue.bl.uk (accessed 31 March 2008).

Copac, at www.copac.ac.uk (accessed 31 March 2008).

Library of Congress Online Catalog, at catalog.loc.gov (accessed 31 March 2008).

National Archives, at www.nationalarchives.gov.uk (accessed 31 March 2008).

National Library of Ireland Online Catalogue, at www.nli.ie/en/online-catalogue.aspx (accessed 31 March 2008).

National Register of Archives, at www.nra.nationalarchives.gov.uk/nra/ (accessed 10 February 2008).

National Union Catalog of Manuscript Collections (NUCMC), 19 April 2007, at www.loc.gov/coll/nucmc/ (accessed 31 March 2008).

Queen's University Belfast Library, at www.qub.ac.uk/directorates/Information Services/TheLibrary/ (accessed 31 March 2008).

Trinity College Library Dublin Online Catalog, at www.tcd.ie/Library/ (accessed 10 February 2008).

Traditional print reference tools, such as bibliographies, biographical material, chronologies, concordances, dictionaries, and library and archive catalogs, are widely available on the Web, including sources designed specifically for Irish literary research. Although chapters 3 and 9 cover library catalogs and archival resources, respectively, this section again explores these resources and some of their unique scholarly features and functions. However, more detailed descriptions and comprehensive coverage of these and other resources appear in the chapters on catalogs and manuscripts and archives.

Copac provides unified access to twenty-six British and Irish library online catalogs, including the British Library, Cambridge University, Oxford University, and University of Edinburgh, as well as the ***Trinity College Library***

Dublin Online Catalog. Patrons can search the database by author/title, periodical, or keyword subject search. Users can also limit searches by publication date and/or library. The *British Library Integrated Catalogue* and the *Library of Congress Online Catalog* websites also feature freely accessible online catalogs of their considerable collections.

The *National Archives* website combines the resources held in the Public Record Office, the Historical Manuscripts Commission, the Office of Public Sector Information, and Her Majesty's Stationery Office Historical Manuscripts Commission to form an impressive document collection relating to British history, including past and ongoing relations with Northern Ireland and the Irish Republic. The catalog, formally known as PROCAT, "contains 10 million descriptions of documents from central government, courts of law and other UK national bodies, including records on family history, medieval tax, criminal trials, UFO sightings." From the "Search the Archives" section of the site, users can search the *National Register of Archives* indexes to more than 44,000 unpublished lists, as well as published catalogs and finding aids describing archival collections, including a tremendous selection of materials relevant to Irish Studies, such as corporate records, genealogical data, and local history organized by town and county, held in the United Kingdom and other countries. From this section scholars can also access *ARCHON*, an online directory of participating record repositories; twenty-four organizations in Northern Ireland and seventy-seven in the Republic of Ireland participate in this partnership.

A gateway maintained by the Library of Congress, the *National Union Catalog of Manuscript Collections (NUCMC)* permits researchers to search records in OCLC databases describing literary and historical documents, public records, and primary source materials cataloged after 1986. Participating archives primarily include institutions in the United States and its territories, though the *NUCMC* website provides directories of repositories of primary sources throughout the world, including links to approximately fifty Irish organizations.

Users of the *National Library of Ireland Online Catalogues* can limit searches by format (e.g., books and periodicals, manuscripts, photographs, prints and drawings) or database (e.g., newspapers, photographs, manuscripts). Currently, thirty-two downloadable finding aids to literary manuscript collections held at this institution are available. Collections feature materials by, about, or related to Austin Clarke, Eilis Dillon, Brian Friel, Michael Hartnett, Rosamond Jacob, Sean O'Casey, Una Troy, and other Irish literary figures, of both major and minor status. In addition, electronic finding aids concerning Irish literary periodicals and presses are also available. Likewise, the *Queen's University Belfast Library* website offers scholars several ways to search various holdings, including materials housed in Special Collections (e.g., books, manuscripts, maps, images) and the Seamus Heaney Library, a facility and collection designed specifically to meet student needs. The "Special Collections" section of the site lists and describes a majority of over forty manuscript collections. Users can also access electronic finding aids for collections, some of which hold potential literary interest, such as Heaney manuscripts, a Somerville and Ross collection, and notebooks, drafts, and translations by scholar and critic Helen Waddell.

CULTURAL AND HISTORICAL RESOURCES

Culture Ireland, 28 July 2007, at www.cultureireland.com/ (accessed 31 March 2008).
Irishdiaspora.net, 29 July 2007, at www.irishdiaspora.net/ (accessed 31 March 2008).
Rolston, Bill. *Literature of the 'Troubles,'* 4 January 2007, at cain.ulst.ac.uk/bibdbs/chrnovel.htm (accessed 31 March 2008).
Wright, Julia M. *Bibliography of Nineteenth-Century Irish Literature*, 2 June 2007, at irish-literature.english.dal.ca/ (accessed 31 March 2008).

Scholars can avail themselves of many cultural and historical websites to place Irish literary studies in broader artistic, economic, political, social, and religious contexts. Many of the sites already mentioned in this chapter also incorporate historical and cultural dimensions in their respective treatments of Irish literature. Several subject indexes (e.g., history, religious studies, politics) on the scholarly gateway *Voice of the Shuttle*, for example, include links to sites addressing the suppression of Catholics in Ireland during the Renaissance, the nineteenth-century famine, and the creation of the Republic of Ireland during the first half of the twentieth century. The websites covered in this section represent a selection of online cultural and historical resources suggesting a range of contextual Irish literature research tools.

A not-for-profit site sponsored by the Irish government agency Culture Ireland/Cultúr Na hÉireann, ***Culture Ireland*** serves basic information needs regarding Irish culture and history, including facts, statistics, outlines, and detailed summaries of significant people, events, landmarks, and lore relevant to the development of modern Ireland, both the Republic and Northern Ireland. Extensive photo galleries and maps accompany narratives, and individual sections (e.g., Ireland facts, artists, history) contain links to external supplementary sources. While Irish literature is not directly covered, exhaustive directories pointing users to resources devoted to Irish local history, heraldry, street slang, and thematic information resources and services offer literary scholars a wide selection of intriguing, if not unorthodox, research options.

Irishdiaspora.net provides both a directory of resources devoted to the study of the experience of the Irish abroad and an online forum and community for scholars of this compelling subject. The website's editor describes Irish Diaspora Studies as the "world-wide, scholarly, inter-disciplinary study of the Irish Diaspora, and its social, linguistic, economic, cultural and political causes and consequences." Links allow researchers to navigate through an eclectic mix of topics, including teaching resources, the Irish in Mexico, and representations of the Irish in television and film productions. This site functions like a wiki, with approved editors posting topic-specific folders as appropriate. Folders contain announcements, calls for papers, research prospectuses, works in progress, book reviews, criticism, and commentary. Literature scholars have full-text access to excellent bulletins such as *Books Irlandais*, "a monthly digest of the coverage of Irish literature in a very broad sense in the French press," and *Leabhar*, which covers academic and popular interest in Irish literature in Great Britain and the United States. Both titles are freely available to interested readers by means of email subscription. In addition, individual submissions entered into *Irishdiaspora.net* are automatically date-stamped, thus indicating when specific files were last updated.

Julia M. Wright's ***Bibliography of Nineteenth-Century Irish Literature*** is an online version of a traditional reference resource. It consists of alphabetically arranged lists of writers and texts, and users can browse its contents by means of author or title indexes, including a brief index of Irish language authors. Some entries feature brief descriptions of authors' lives and works, while others link to full-text, electronic reproductions of brief works. What distinguishes Wright's work from many other bibliographies is the addition of a selection of nineteenth-century texts that provide historical and cultural context for the literature of the period. Selections feature contemporary responses to the enactment of the Act of Union between Great Britain and Ireland (1800) and the repeal of the Act (1840s), as well as contemporary commentary on colonialism. In general, this site serves as a solid introduction to the literary output of nineteenth-century Irish writers and some of the cultural and historical forces that shaped their lives and work.

Like the *Bibliography of Nineteenth-Century Irish Literature*, Bill Rolston's ***Literature of the 'Troubles'*** consists of citations to works organized around a specific theme. In this instance, titles listed refer to novels published between approximately 1969 and 2002 that address in some way the ongoing political and social struggles in Northern Ireland. The site permits users to browse lists arranged chronologically by date of publication, alphabetically by author, or alphabetically by title. While not very dynamic in terms of functionality, this bibliography does provide valuable access points to a provocative subject. Furthermore, it is only one example of several research resources accessible from the University of Ulster-based CAIN Web Service, which "contains information and source material on 'the Troubles' and politics in Northern Ireland from 1968 to the present." This portal is a thorough online source of background information and descriptions of key events and issues relevant to critical considerations of Northern Ireland, including literary responses to these cultural and historical matters. The CAIN site also directs users to other online bibliographies, databases, and electronic resources that cover diverse subjects relevant to Northern Irish Studies, such as symbols, facsimiles of public records, and photographic archives documenting the "Troubles."

CONCLUSION

This chapter presents a representative sampling of Web-based resources relevant to Irish literary study. Though organized into discrete sections, some readers may contend that a few of the websites discussed here could have been included in multiple categories. While distinctions between different types of Web sources may seem arbitrary at times, a factor that remains consistent is the scholarly authority of these sites. The increasing availability of the Web to experts and knowledgeable individuals has shifted the balance regarding who produces and publishes credible references and research tools. In addition, the Web facilitates ready access to works previously available only on microforms or in special collections, and provides a forum fostering scholarly communities through online bibliographies, journals, and association sites. Even with the greater distribution of expertise on the Internet, however, scholars must still carefully scrutinize websites to determine their reliability and relevance, and primarily consult them as sources that complement traditional print materials and online databases.

Chapter Ten

Researching a Thorny Problem

The preceding chapters present best practices and resources for researching Irish literary authors, works, subjects, and issues. While these tools and approaches yield results in many research situations, some questions do not have clear answers, and scholars may have to try several approaches to solve a problem. In such instances, researchers might consider gathering a range of information for the purpose of surveying the existing scholarship (or lack of it) on the subject, or making a solid case about a compelling literary matter rather than providing a conclusive answer to a scholarly question.

Identifying authors who published in a specific periodical is not always as straightforward a project as it seems, especially in respect to titles that are not widely held or indexed. For example, a scholar who wishes to identify authors who published in the Irish periodical *The Bell* (1940–1954) can approach this issue from several angles depending upon how much scholarship exists on authors of interest. Sean O'Faolain, who both edited and contributed to this journal, serves as a good example of an author who has received considerable critical attention. O'Faolain's comparatively high literary profile eases the task of finding citations to his works and where he published them. When researching such a well-known figure, a scholar can attempt to compile a complete list of citations to O'Faolain's total contributions to this periodical, as both editor and author. Searching a local library catalog for bibliographies and critical works pertaining to this author, for example, Richard Bonaccorso's *Sean O'Faolain's Irish Vision*, which contains an extensive bibliography of O'Faolain's writings, is a logical first step. Likewise, researchers may use these same resources to identify secondary materials such as scholarly monographs, essays, and articles that may contain information relevant to the topic.

As the O'Faolain example suggests, finding information on widely studied writers can be a relatively straightforward process. Identifying less-documented authors who published in *The Bell*, however, requires different search strategies. One option is reversing the search process described above, which focuses on a single author, and beginning with a review of the periodical itself for the purpose of compiling a list of contributors. Consulting print and online reference sources, such as union catalogs and periodical indexes and databases, to verify which institutions hold *The Bell* as well as which databases and publications, if any, index this periodical might be one way to start such an investigation. If issues of *The Bell* prove difficult to locate or access, scholars may need to turn to secondary or reference sources to identify relevant data. Print and electronic archival resources such as finding aids, special collections inventories, and digitized works may also yield useful insights regarding this periodical's publication history and contributors.

In the absence of works directly related to *The Bell*, material by scholars and historians of Irish periodical publishing may be more readily available and provides researchers with other approaches to verifying author contributions to this periodical. Secondary resources treating an author's life and work, the history of *The Bell*'s publication and impact, or twentieth-century Irish publishing history in general all offer potential avenues of study.[1] Searching catalogs and other databases for books, dissertations, scholarly essays, and magazine articles on these and related topics present the researcher with citations to other relevant primary and secondary resources, including unpublished indexes and finding aids, that may not appear in other sources.

Despite being one of the most influential serials devoted to Irish literary culture published during the twentieth century, along with *Samhain* (1901–1908), *Ireland Today* (1936–1938), *Irish Writing* (1947–1957), *The Honest Ulsterman* (1968–), and *The Crane Bag* (1977–1985), *The Bell* is neither widely held nor indexed. *WorldCat* currently contains three records for this title, each representing a different publication format (print, microfiche, and microfilm) and indicates that fewer than one hundred institutions have attached holdings to these records. In addition, *The Bell* is not indexed in the *MLA International Bibliography*, *ABELL*, or *Subject Index to Periodicals* (published in London, 1915–1962), and it does not appear in archival journal databases such as *JSTOR*. As a result, identifying an individual writer's contributions to this serial is a challenging task and offers the interested scholar a compelling research project. While general reference resources and catalogs yield few leads for identifying author submissions to *The Bell*, the enterprising researcher can slightly alter her focus and use these same resources to identify secondary materials that may contain crucial information.

The Northern Irish novelist, short story writer, and children's book author Mary Beckett serves as a solid example of a literary figure whose work appeared in *The Bell* but whose contributions to it may be difficult to verify. Though she published several pieces in later issues of this periodical during the early 1950s, she only began to publish her own books in the 1980s. Hypothetically, a student enrolled in a course devoted to Irish women writers researching Beckett's life and work may discover this hiatus in publishing, as well as mention of early contributions to *The Bell*. In an effort to compile a list of these efforts, this researcher could try to locate print and online bibliographies of Beckett's works. Another strategy is utilizing an author's name to perform a subject search in an academic library catalog to locate secondary sources. While such a search returns little if any information about Beckett, whose work enjoys critical acclaim but has not yet received much scholarly attention, these exercises can be very useful. A subject search for "O'Donnell, Donat," for example, the author of the influential literary study *Maria Cross: Imaginative Patterns in a Group of Modern Catholic Writers* (first published by Chatto & Windus in 1952) who frequently contributed to later issues of the *The Bell*, reveals that this name is a pseudonym used by the prolific Irish writer and scholar Conor Cruise O'Brien, whose full subject and author heading is "O'Brien, Conor Cruise, 1917–." Noting the controlled terms employed by library catalogs to index subjects of interest at this point in the research process eases the subsequent task of searching for relevant primary and secondary resources addressing this elusive topic in other forums such as cooperative, union, and national library catalogs.

In addition to paying attention to catalog search terms, it is important for scholars to recall that indexing is not consistent from one resource to another. As a result, they may need to look for variations among the controlled headings used in citation and full-text databases. By way of illustration, conducting a keyword search in the Web-based version of *WorldCat* for *bell dublin ireland* retrieves a list of several records, including a few describing multiple editions of Seán McMahon's anthology *Great Irish Writing: The Best from "The Bell,"* which collects a broad selection of representative pieces published in this seminal periodical. It includes early contributions from an impressive list of thirty-nine contemporary Irish authors, including Mary Beckett, Denis Johnston, Robert Greacen, Mary Lavin, and Michael McLaverty, as well as useful biographical notes on each.

Perusing the detailed versions of these records in WorldCat reveals useful information for researchers. First, they indicate that "Bell (Dublin, Ireland)" is a controlled subject heading in this database that the scholar can use as a search term in subsequent searches. Likewise, conducting a keyword search for *the bell* in the *MLAIB* returns citations to a number of scholarly articles, some of which utilize the subject term "The Bell (Dublin)" while others use the variant term "The Bell (periodical)." While these differences seem slight, scholars possessing a thorough knowledge of a range of headings indexed in multiple databases and catalogs stand better chances of conducting successful searches for a wide selection of materials relevant to their research topics. Second, the detailed view of a record describing this title lists the names of the authors and the titles of the works gathered in this volume. For the student researching Mary Beckett, this data confirms that she contributed a piece entitled "Millstones" to *The Bell*. Next, the researcher may try to find this title at a local library or submit an interlibrary loan request for the purpose of reviewing the volume for more information, including the date of this piece, in which issue it appeared, and citations to other primary or secondary sources.

As described in chapters 3 and 4, catalogs and databases contain information about sources that have been described for purposes of identifying, locating, and accessing materials. Yet some libraries and archives may hold potentially useful resources that have not been cataloged, including finding aids or inventories created for local use. Researchers may learn of the existence of these kinds of resources through citation analysis of notes and bibliographies in secondary sources or by searching the online catalogs and finding aids of libraries and archives holding materials pertinent to the topic. For example, initiating a title search for "bell" in Trinity College Library Dublin's online periodicals index retrieves a list featuring two records for the title "The Bell: a survey of Irish life," one of which describes a copy of this periodical in print, the other a reproduction of the same on microfilm. The full display for the print record of *The Bell* shows that the Early Printed Books Reading Room contains an "index to the Bell, compiled by Rudi Holzapfel." This note does not give the researcher much to work with other than an author's name and a description of the resource. In addition, conducting an author search for "holzapfel, rudi" in the Trinity College Library Dublin main catalog does not retrieve a separate record for this potentially valuable tool, but rather links searchers to the original record for the print version of *The Bell*. At this point, a scholar may wish to search for Holzapfel's index in other catalogs, databases, and archival websites to discover whether it has been published and has been cataloged and is held elsewhere. For example, *WorldCat* contains a record for Hozapfel's *An Index of Contributors to* The Bell, which features the subject heading "Bell (Dublin)—Indexes." In addition, *WorldCat* indicates that several (17) libraries in the United States own this title. With this additional information, a researcher can use the subject heading to search for other indexes to this publication or use the holdings information to submit an ILL request for this particular book. Even with Holzapfel's index in hand, however, the scholarly task remains to compare the contents of this index with the contents of *The Bell* itself in order to verify an author's contributions to this publication.

In the instances of Beckett and O'Brien, explored above, this prospect is further complicated by the fact that many writers published in *The Bell* anonymously or under a pen-name. The possibilities exist, for example, that both authors submitted anonymous contributions or employed multiple literary personas. How does a scholar find the answers to these questions? Biographical works, whether book-length studies devoted to individual authors or entries in biographical reference tools, such as the *Dictionary of Literary Biography* or the *Oxford Dictionary of National Biography*, are potential sources for such information. A close reading of Holzapfel's introduction to and notes in his index may also yield some clues, especially if he describes his methodology for creating this research tool. Did he simply look at issues of *The Bell* to compile a list of authors, titles, bibliographic information (e.g., volumes, issues, dates), and page numbers, or did he conduct research in archives containing documents pertinent to the publication of this title (e.g., correspondence between editors and contributors, publishing contracts and agreements)? If the latter, does he point readers to repositories of primary sources that may be of use to other researchers? On the other hand, if Holzapfel does not supply this information, the scholar may take further steps to identify these resources on her own. In the course of such researches, she may also seek other archival sources relevant to, say, individual writers such as Mary Beckett, in order to uncover more information about the possibility of anonymous publications, the use of pen-names, or contexts for her publishing hiatus. Ultimately, it is the researcher's responsibility to set the parameters of a research project and to deploy the most relevant strategies and sources to fulfill it.

CONCLUSION

Research projects typically begin as seemingly simple quests for answers to questions. As this chapter illustrates, however, researching some literary topics demands complex deductive work that may raise additional questions and may even point up significant inconsistencies and knowledge gaps about previous scholarship on the topic itself. In such situations, scholars may need to utilize an array of sources, as well as adapt and repeat numerous strategies in order to identify, locate, and access the newest and most relevant materials available. Reference librarians spend a great deal of time keeping informed of new developments. Researchers can consult and collaborate with them as they progress in their research to gain additional insights and training to fulfill their research needs, as well as to remain current on developments impacting important collections and resources.

This volume has discussed some of the best sources and most effective processes for researching Irish literary topics. Even so, existing print sources and webpages will continue to be updated, database and search engine interfaces improved, and digital projects will continue to appear. Still, the basic skills needed for conducting research efficiently and effectively remain relevant to most research sources and scenarios. Undoubtedly, new resources will be available by the time this book is printed that would have been included here if published at the time. Information is produced at a rapid pace, so scholars must be flexible and willing to deal with changes. Many of these changes offer positive results, such as increasing access to materials online and fleshing out the scholarly record. By honing their research skills and considering the best practices for literary research discussed in this volume, scholars of Irish literature can confidently and ably address any research problem and effectively utilize the resources available to solve it.

NOTE

1. See Arther Sherbo's "More Periodical Grubbings: Sean O'Faolain's Contributions to *The Bell*" (*Notes and Queries*, 43 (241), 1996, p. 59–60) for a brief discussion of the selective citation of O'Faolain's work in the bibliographies appearing in the latest edition of Maurice Harmon's standard critical biography (London: Constable, 1994). Harmon specifies in his work that his bibliography is not complete, a point that challenges Sherbo's argument. Still, Sherbo admirably describes some of the logistical difficulties of verifying an author's contributions to *The Bell*. (Sherbo does not mention Holzapfel's bibliography.)

Appendix

Resources in Related Disciplines

Interdisciplinary research is an almost inevitable consequence of scholarship in any field. Literary study is particularly amenable to interdisciplinary research because literary works, fiction and non-fiction, poetry and drama, address every conceivable aspect of human existence. What follows is a highly selective list of sources for Irish literature scholars to consult as they consider researching within other disciplines. These recommendations represent good places to start exploring other fields. In some cases, such as *Women Playwrights in England, Ireland, and Scotland, 1660–1823*, a source is included because it specifically addresses Irish literature and serves as an example of the many specialized and potentially useful resources available.

This section aims to convey the idea that unique and conventional reference and research tools (e.g., bibliographies, dictionaries, encyclopedias, indexes) exist for other academic disciplines. In addition, scholars can also browse library reference shelves within a discipline of interest to identify other titles and types of sources that may prove valuable in their research. Conveniently, the same skills and practices discussed throughout this volume apply to the use of most reference works, and searching the library catalog for books on a topic is a tried-and-true way to begin research projects in any discipline.

Resources discussed in other chapters, especially the general references addressed in chapter 2, remain reliable sources for bibliographies of further reading within different fields of study. Scholars can consult both Harner and Marcuse, also described in chapter 2, for citations to additional research tools relevant to other disciplines as well as recommended background reading. The "Guides" section that follows also highlights sources that list important and specialized research tools in disciplines outside literature.

GENERAL

Guides

Balay, Robert, ed. *Guide to Reference Books*. 11th ed. Chicago: American Library Association, 1996.

This title remains the standard guide to general and specialized reference sources across various disciplines. While unique guides to research sources exist for individual disciplines and branches of study exist (as evinced by works cited in the "Guides" sections listed throughout this appendix), the Balay and Walford guides included here are essential tools consulted by reference librarians for guidance.

Blazek, Ron, and Elizabeth Aversa. *The Humanities: A Selective Guide to Information Resources*. 5th ed. Englewood, CO: Libraries Unlimited, 2000.

Lists major print and electronic resources covering the general humanities, languages and literatures, performing arts, philosophy, religion, and visual arts. Entries feature evaluative annotations.

Lester, Ray, and A. J. Walford. *The New Walford Guide to Reference Sources*. London: Facet, 2005–.

The standard British equivalent to Balay's *Guide*. Currently, only the first two volumes covering *Science, Technology, and Medicine* and *Social Sciences*, respectively, have been published. Volume 3: *Arts, Humanities, and General Reference* is forthcoming.

Indexes and Bibliographies

Academic Search Premier. Ipswich, MA: Ebsco. search.epnet.com/.

An article database indexing more than 8,000 scholarly and general interdisciplinary journals. Full-text articles are included when available.

Dissertations and Theses A&I. Ann Arbor, MI: ProQuest-CSA LLC, 2004. www.umi.com/products_umi/dissertations/.

Though both *MLAIB* and *ABELL* (see chapter 4) index dissertations on literary topics, records for these materials do not contain abstracts. Appearing in print as the standard reference tool *Dissertation Abstracts International*, this database supplements *MLAIB* and *ABELL* as a source for abstracts as well as citations to dissertations from other disciplines.

Expanded Academic ASAP. Farmington Hills, MI: Thomson Gale. infotrac .galegroup.com/.

Interdisciplinary in scope, this resource indexes both scholarly and general periodicals and provides full text to articles when available. Its coverage and full-text coverage differs significantly from *Academic Search Premier*'s, however, so it is a valuable complement to this and other tools.

ART

Dictionaries, Encyclopedias, and Handbooks

Brigstocke, Hugh, ed. *The Oxford Companion to Western Art*. New York: Oxford University Press, 2001.

Entries provide biographical sketches of individuals, as well as definitions and histories of terms significant in Western art, excluding architecture. Some entries are expanded to detail background and context for selected artists, art movements, and patronage and collecting.

Chilvers, Ian, ed. *The Oxford Dictionary of Art*. 3rd ed. New York: Oxford University Press, 2004.

Primarily defines concepts, practices, and movements important in Western European art, including drawing, painting, printmaking, and sculpture from antiquity through the present. Includes biographical information when appropriate.

Turner, Jane, ed. *The Dictionary of Art*. New York: Grove, 1996. Reprinted, with minor corrections, 2002. Available online at www.groveart.com/.

This work is the standard, scholarly dictionary for research in art and art history. Lengthy entries are signed and include bibliographies. Several collections of articles extracted from this work and organized by time period, such as *The Grove Dictionary of Art: From Renaissance to Impression* and *The Grove Dictionary of Art: From Expressionism to Post Modernism*, are also available to scholars who do not have access to the print or electronic versions of the reference set.

Guides

Arntzen, Etta, and Robert Rainwater. *Guide to the Literature of Art History*. Chicago: American Library Association, 1980.

Marmor, Max, and Alex Ross, eds. *Guide to the Literature of Art History 2*. Chicago: American Library Association, 2005.

GLAH and *GLAH2* offer annotated citations to reference works for art history research, including bibliographies, dictionaries, encyclopedias, as well as handbooks and histories. Subjects covered include architecture, decorative and applied arts, drawings, paintings, photography, prints, and sculpture. Entries are subdivided by medium and geographic location, including Great Britain and Ireland. Though international in scope, Western-language resources receive special attention.

Jones, Lois Swan. *Art Information: Research Methods and Resources*. 3rd ed. Dubuque, IA: Kendall/Hunt, 1990.

A guide to art and art history research methods, including an annotated bibliography of research tools.

Jones, Lois Swan. *Art Information and the Internet: How to Find It, How to Use It*. Phoenix, AZ: Oryx Press, 1999.

A guide describing how to search for art information on the Internet as well as valuable art and art history research websites.

Indexes and Bibliographies

Art Index. New York: H. W. Wilson. Available online from multiple vendors.

Indexes over 450 periodicals from around the world devoted to art, art history, architectural history, decorative arts, painting, and sculpture. Three versions of this index exist: *Art Index* (1984–present), *Art Abstracts* (1984–present), and *Art Index Retrospective* (1929–1983). Different libraries may hold one or more of these titles.

BHA: Bibliography of the History of Art. Santa Monica, CA: J. Paul Getty Trust, Getty Art History Program. Available online from multiple vendors.

More international and varied in scope than *Art Index*, this database indexes and summarizes books, dissertations, exhibition catalogs, and more than 4,000 periodicals covering European and American visual arts from antiquity to the present. This title continues *RILA: International Repertory of the Literature of Art* (1975–1989), and the online version provides access to both resources.

HISTORICAL ATLASES

Cunliffe, Barry, Robert Bartlett, John Morrill, Asa Briggs, and Joanna
  Bourke, eds. *The Penguin Atlas of British and Irish History: From Earliest
  Times to the Present Day*. New York: Penguin, 2002.

By means of overview and small-scale maps, photographs, illustrations, and
essays, this atlas chronologically examines five periods of British and Irish
history: ancient, medieval, early modern, nineteenth century, and modern.
Within each period, thematic sections focus on narrower topics, such as the
Anglo-Irish and Irish Civil wars of the 1920s. A detailed chronological table,
a list of rulers of Britain and Ireland, and a bibliography complete this volume.

Edwards, Ruth Dudley, and Bridget Hourican. *An Atlas of Irish History*. 3rd
  ed. London: Routledge, 2005.

Organized into twelve sections, including a prefatory reference section and a
concluding chapter devoted to modern Irish literature, this atlas covers two
thousand years of Irish history. More than 100 maps, charts, and graphs accompanied by scholarly narrative detail the major political, military, economic, religious and social changes that have occurred in Ireland and among
Irish living abroad. Contains a selected bibliography.

HISTORY

Dictionaries, Encyclopedias, and Companions

Arnold-Baker, Charles. *The Companion to British History*. 2nd ed. New
  York: Routledge, 2001.

This work contains entries on all aspects of English, Scottish, Welsh, and
Irish history from 55 B.C. to 2000. Contents emphasize relationships between
nations. Three appendixes are included: "English Regnal Years"; "Selected
Warlike Events"; and "Genealogies and Diagrams."

Cannon, John, ed. *The Oxford Companion to British History*. Rev. ed. New
  York: Oxford University Press, 2002.

Entries in this companion cover people, places, events, institutions, and concepts relevant to the development and study of English, Scottish, Welsh, and

Irish history. Some entries describe places and events of local interest. Also contains maps, genealogies, and a subject index

Connolly, S. J., ed. *The Oxford Companion to Irish History*. 2nd ed. New York: Oxford University Press, 2007.

This source presents more than 1,800 brief, descriptive entries describing cultural and political figures, organizations, and events relevant to the study of Irish history. In addition, entries covering local and daily matters, such as clothing, diet, music, and recreation add depth to the more obvious contents. Features historical maps and a subject index.

Gillespie, Gordon. *Historical Dictionary of the Northern Ireland Conflict*. Lanham, MD: Scarecrow Press, 2008.

Entries are cross-referenced and describe main events, individuals, and organizations significant in the thirty-year history of "the Troubles" in Northern Ireland. Includes a useful chronology and bibliography.

Thomas, Colin, and Avril Thomas. *Historical Dictionary of Ireland*. Lanham, MD: Scarecrow Press, 1997.

Contains more than 400 entries addressing significant Irish people, places, institutions, and trends. Coverage is comprehensive and treats the nation's pre- and post-independence history. Appendixes list lord lieutenants and chief secretaries of Ireland who served as British subjects; the presidents, prime ministers, and deputy prime ministers of the Republic of Ireland; and influential religious leaders.

Mellersh, H. E. L., and Neville Williams. *Chronology of World History*. 4 vols. Santa Barbara, CA: ABC-CLIO, 1999.

A useful general chronology, this work consists of brief entries on annual political events, government, economics, science, technology, medicine, the arts, education, culture, religion, sports, and births and deaths. Volume 1: *The Ancient and Medieval World, Prehistory–AD 1491*, Volume 2: *The Expanding World, 1492–1775*, Volume 3: *The Changing World, 1776–1900*, and Volume 4: *The Modern World, 1901–1998*.

Guides

Fritze, Ronald H., Brian E. Coutts, and Louis A. Vyhnanek. *Reference Sources in History: An Introductory Guide*. 2nd ed. Santa Barbara, CA: ABC-CLIO, 2004.

Arranged by type of resource into fourteen chapters, 930 annotations describe print and electronic historical reference works covering all time periods and geographical areas. This guide discusses standard resources (e.g., bibliographies, dissertations, guides, periodical guides and core journals, periodical indexes and abstracts) as well as geographical and cartographic materials, historical statistical sources, archives, and microforms. Annotations for works covering Irish history appear throughout the guide in appropriate categories.

Indexes and Bibliographies

Historical Abstracts Online. 1954–present. Santa Barbara, CA: ABC-CLIO. serials.abc-clio.com/.

This resource is the primary bibliographic database for historical research. It indexes books, journal articles, and dissertations on the history of the world after 1449 and published from 1954 to the present. Works covering United States and Canadian history are excluded here, but treated in another database, *America: History and Life*. This database includes coverage of key historical journals from all over the world, as well as selected social sciences and humanities journals. Advanced searching options permit researchers to limit by decade(s) or century (e.g., 1920, 1700–1799) and subject terms (e.g., nationalism, Abbey Theatre). This source is useful for interdisciplinary research exploring a wide range of subjects such as popular culture, science, and medicine within a historical period.

National University of Ireland, Maynooth. *Irish History Online.* Maynooth: Department of Modern History, National University of Ireland, Maynooth, 2004. www.irishhistoryonline.ie/.

International in scope, this online bibliography permits scholars to search by subject, place, and personal name for citations to monographs and book and journal articles relevant to Irish historical study. Local history receives particular attention. Currently, this database contains more than 61,000 records for items published from 1936 to 2003.

Webb, R. K. "Britain and Ireland since 1760," in *The American Historical Association's Guide to Historical Literature*. 3rd ed., gen. editor Mary Beth Norton. New York: Oxford University Press, 1995.

A selective annotated bibliography citing scholarly articles and books published primarily from 1961 to 1992. This source covers a broad range of historical areas, including general, politics, law, government, urban and regional, economic, social, labor and working class, religious, intellectual and cultural,

scientific and medical, and diplomatic and military, as well as regional histories of the British Empire and commonwealth, Scotland, Wales, and Ireland.

MUSIC

Dictionaries, Encyclopedias, Companions, and Handbooks

Keogan, Gillian, ed. *Irish Music Handbook*. 2nd ed. Dublin: Arts Council,
   2000.

This unique handbook emphasizes contemporary music performance in Ireland and Northern Ireland. More than 2,000 entries cover music festivals, in-
strument makers, and musicians. While all types of music are referenced,
classical, traditional Irish music, and jazz receive primary focus.

Latham, Alison, ed. *The Oxford Companion to Music*. New York: Oxford
   University Press, 2002.

A good introductory reference work addressing current scholarship and including entries on individuals, instruments, movements, and definitions of
musical terms. Western classical music is strongly represented.

Randel, Don Michael, ed. *New Harvard Dictionary of Music*. Cambridge,
   MA: Belknap Press of Harvard University Press, 1986.

This basic reference presents international coverage of all styles and forms of
music.

Sadie, Stanley, ed. *The New Grove Dictionary of Music and Musicians*. 2nd
   ed. 29 vols. New York: Grove, 2001. Available online at www.grove
   music.com.

This dictionary is a core reference resource containing authoritative, scholarly
entries covering all aspects of music history, composition, performance, and
ideas. Entries describe composers, performers, genres, movements, and theories.

Vallely, Fintan, ed. *The Companion to Irish Traditional Music*. New York:
   New York University Press, 1999.

Richly illustrated with explanatory diagrams, maps, and music transcription,
entries in this work address topics relevant to Irish traditional music from the

Bronze Age to the present. Contents emphasize twentieth-century music and musicians. Biographies of notable figures and essays on musical instruments and playing styles are particularly compelling. The volume includes a useful chronology of significant events in the history and development of traditional Irish music.

Guides

Duckles, Vincent H., Ida Reed, and Michael A. Keller, eds. *Music Reference and Research Materials: An Annotated Bibliography*. 5th ed. New York: Schirmer Books, 1997.

A core guide of music scholarship and research materials published through 1995. It includes selected bibliographies, catalogs, chronologies, companions, dictionaries, indexes, websites, and other types of reference sources.

Indexes and Bibliographies

The Music Index: A Subject-Author Guide to Music Periodical Literature. Warren, MI: Harmonie Park Press. Available online at www .harmonieparkpress.com/.

Indexes approximately 850 popular and classical music periodicals published worldwide. The print version covers 1949 to the present, and the online version 1973 to the present.

RILM Abstracts of Music Literature. New York: RILM. Available online at www.rilm.org/.

This international resource provides abstracts to articles, books, dissertations, reviews, films and videos, online databases, and electronic resources from 1967 to the present. It covers all aspects of music literature.

Sources and History

Grout, Donald Jay, J. Peter Burkholder, and Claude V. Palisca. *A History of Western Music*. 7th ed. New York: Norton, c. 2006.

This standard survey addresses music history from antiquity through the twentieth century. Classical music receives primary emphasis.

PHILOSOPHY

Dictionaries, Encyclopedias, and Handbooks

Audi, Robert. *The Cambridge Dictionary of Philosophy*. 2nd ed. New York: Cambridge University Press, 1999.

Featuring lengthy, scholarly entries defining philosophical terms, movements, and concepts, as well as biographical information on individual philosophers, this dictionary addresses all time periods. The second edition expands coverage of non-Western philosophies and living philosophers.

Craig, Edward, ed. *Routledge Encyclopedia of Philosophy*. New York: Routledge, 1998. Available online at www.rep.routledge.com/.

Standard encyclopedia characterized by substantial signed entries and bibliographies. The detailed index in volume 10 is a recommended source for subjects.

Honderich, Ted, ed. *The Oxford Companion to Philosophy*. New ed. New York: Oxford University Press, 2005. Available online at www .oxfordreference.com/.

Contains brief, signed entries and bibliographic references for ideas, individuals, movements, and theories.

Horowitz, Maryanne Cline, ed. *New Dictionary of the History of Ideas*. 6 vols. New York: Charles Scribner's Sons, 2005.

A classic reference tool featuring detailed, lengthy, signed essays providing overviews concerning all aspects of intellectual history. Concepts are varied and examples potentially relevant to Irish studies include aesthetics, revolution, and political protest.

Zalta, Edward N., principal ed. *The Stanford Encyclopedia of Philosophy*, 1995. Online at plato.stanford.edu (accessed 5 February 2008).

Experts contribute and review entries submitted to this free, online scholarly encyclopedia. Though available for over a decade, some entries are still in process and can be updated by authors as new research is published.

Guides

Bynagle, Hans E. *Philosophy: A Guide to the Reference Literature*. 3rd ed. Englewood, CO: Libraries Unlimited, 2006.

This essential annotated bibliographic guide to reference tools devoted to scholarly research in philosophy includes citations to and descriptions of more than 700 sources, including bibliographies, companions, dictionaries, encyclopedias, indexes, websites, and others. English-language works are emphasized, but not to the exclusion of important non-English materials.

Indexes and Bibliographies

The Philosopher's Index: An International Index to Philosophical Periodicals and Books. Bowling Green, OH: Philosopher's Information Center. Available online through various vendors.

Offers international coverage of books, book reviews, and over 550 journals from 1940 to the present. Updated quarterly.

RELIGION

Dictionary, Encyclopedias, and Handbooks

Jones, Lindsay, ed. *Encyclopedia of Religion*. 2nd ed. 15 vols. Detroit: Macmillan Reference USA, 2005.

Substantially revises and updates the first edition of this standard, core reference for world religions. Volume 15 contains an appendix, index, and an outline of contents which lists entries by related topics.

Guides

Blazek's volume (see "General" category above), *The Humanities: A Selective Guide to Information Resources*, serves as a helpful supplementary source for religion and other humanities.

Johnson, William M. *Recent Reference Books in Religion: A Guide for Students, Scholars, Researchers, Buyers, and Readers*. Rev. ed. Chicago: Fitzroy Dearborn, 1998.

This guide evaluates more than 300 reference resources published between 1970 and 1997. Print references covering Christianity, Judaism, Asian religions, Buddhism, and other religions worldwide receive primary focus, though mythology, the social sciences of religion, and philosophy of religion are also addressed.

Indexes and Bibliographies

MLAIB and *ABELL* cover religion and literature, while *Historical Abstracts* addresses the history of religion.

ATLA Religion. Chicago: American Theological Library Association. Available online via various vendors.

Indexes religious and theological journal articles, book reviews, and collections of essays from 1948 to the present. An ongoing retrospective indexing project provides indexing for journals prior to 1948.

SCIENCES AND MEDICINE

Dictionaries, Encyclopedias, and Handbooks

Bynum, William F., E. Janet Browne, and Roy Porter. *Dictionary of the History of Science*. Princeton, NJ: Princeton University Press, 1981.

Defines and describes scientific ideas throughout the history of Western science. This volume begins with a useful bibliography arranged by broad subject categories.

Bynum, W. F., and Roy Porter. *Companion Encyclopedia of the History of Medicine*. 2 vols. New York: Routledge, 1993.

This seminal reference work includes seventy-two essays covering all aspects of the history of medicine. Includes an informative chapter, "Medicine and Literature."

Rosner, Lisa, ed. *Chronology of Science from Stonehenge to the Human Genome Project*. Santa Barbara, CA: ABC-CLIO, 2002.

Chronicles scientific advances and discoveries in various scientific fields, astronomy, biology, chemistry, earth sciences, ecology, mathematics, and physics among them.

Trautmann, Joan, and Carol Pollard. *Literature and Medicine: An Annotated Bibliography*. Rev. ed. Pittsburgh: University of Pittsburgh Press, 1982.

Annotated bibliography citing and describing literary works exploring medical themes and issues. Chapters are arranged by specific centuries and an index provides access to topics such as abortion, medical ethics, and suicide.

Indexes and Bibliographies

Historical Abstracts is a reliable resource for finding articles on the history of social sciences, the sciences, and medicine. *Academic Search Premier* and *Expanded Academic ASAP* are good starting points for interdisciplinary sources.

Web of Science. Philadelphia, PA: Institute for Scientific Information. isi10.isiknowledge.com/.

This interdisciplinary databases indexes articles from more than 8,000 international science and social sciences journals. Generally, years of coverage vary depending on the library's subscription.

Sources and History

Hessenbruch, Arne, ed. *Reader's Guide to the History of Science.* Chicago: Fitzroy Dearborn, 2000.

Entries review and compare recommended and important works about individuals, disciplines and institutions, and themes relevant to the history of science, technology, and medicine.

Kiple, Kenneth F., ed. *The Cambridge World History of Human Disease.* New York: Cambridge University Press, 1993.

This volume consists of essays and statistical data providing historical overviews of medical practices, public health issues, and major diseases from around the world and throughout the ages. Particularly fascinating are the tables, figures, and maps illustrating various trends and developments, such as infant morality rates, annual cigarette consumption, and distribution of specific diseases.

SOCIAL SCIENCES

Guides

Herron, Nancy L., ed. *The Social Sciences: A Cross-Disciplinary Guide to Selected Sources.* 3rd ed. Greenwood Village, CO: Libraries Unlimited, 2002.

Lists and annotates citations to print and electronic sources for research in the general social sciences, as well as political science, economics, business, history, law, anthropology, sociology, education, psychology, geography, and communication.

Indexes and Bibliographies

Historical Abstracts is a reliable resource for finding articles on the history of social sciences, the sciences, and medicine. *Academic Search Premier* and *Expanded Academic ASAP* are good starting points for interdisciplinary sources.

Web of Science. Philadelphia, PA: Institute for Scientific Information. isi10.isiknowledge.com/.

This interdisciplinary database indexes articles from more than 8,000 international science and social sciences journals. Generally, years of coverage vary depending on the library's subscription.

Sources and History

Lindberg, David C., and Ronald L. Numbers. *The Cambridge History of Science*. New York: Cambridge University Press, 2003–.

Volume 7 of this series, *Modern Social Sciences*, contains useful scholarly essays addressing the history of various social sciences, including economic theory, education, ethnography, political science, and psychology. Issues relevant to Irish studies, such as class, race, and travel, are covered.

THEATER

As indicated in previous chapters, literary research tools often devote pages to drama and dramatists. This situation is especially evident in resources about Irish literature, which presents a robust tradition of dramatic writing and performance. The following works are examples of some conventional and some unique references that supplement sources discussed in this guide.

Dictionaries, Encyclopedias, and Handbooks

Hartnoll, Phyllis, ed. *The Oxford Companion to the Theatre*. 4th ed. New York: Oxford University Press, 1993.

A basic reference useful for finding condensed overviews of actors, directors, dramatists, theaters, and definitions of terms.

Mann, David, and Susan Garland Mann. *Women Playwrights in England, Ireland, and Scotland, 1660–1823*. Bloomington: Indiana University Press, 1996.

Brief biographical entries cover approximately 600 women playwrights and descriptive entries treat the individual plays they wrote. Entries for plays contain references to available modern print and microform versions. Scholars can check library and union catalogs to verify if modern editions of desired plays have been published since this work appeared. A chronology concludes this volume.

Guides

Simons, Linda Keir. *The Performing Arts: A Guide to the Reference Literature*. Englewood, CO: Libraries Unlimited, 1994.

This title is an annotated bibliography covering theatrical research materials, including dance. Citations describe bibliographies, biographical sources, catalogs, companions, dictionaries, encyclopedias, indexes, and libraries and archives.

Indexes and Bibliographies

MLAIB and *ABELL* are both excellent indexes for scholarly research on theater and dramatic literature.

Statman, Carl J. *A Bibliography of British Dramatic Periodicals, 1720–1960*. New York: New York Public Library, 1962.

Presents a chronologically arranged list of English, Scottish, and Irish periodicals by initial dates of publication. Periodicals selected for inclusion focus on drama, while those that simply feature columns devoted to drama have been excluded.

Sources and History

Morash, Christopher. *A History of Irish Theatre, 1601–2000*. New York: Cambridge University Press, 2004.

A chronological survey of modern Irish theater focusing on the cultural influences of this rich tradition. Brief "A Night at the Theatre" sections evoking the intellectual, social, and political atmospheres and production details of specific performances follow main chapters. Concludes with a biographical glossary and a useful and informative bibliographical essay.

Bibliography

Altick, Richard D., and John J. Fenstermaker. *The Art of Literary Research*. 4th ed. New York: W. W. Norton, 1993.

Bonaccorso, Richard. *Sean O'Faolain's Irish Vision*. Albany: State University of New York Press, 1987.

Corcoran, Neil. *Seamus Heaney*. London: Faber & Faber, 1986.

Doyle, Peter A. *Sean O'Faolain*. Twayne's English Authors Series, 70. New York: Twayne Publishers, 1968.

Harmon, Maurice. *Seán O'Faoláin*. London: Constable, 1994.

———. *Seán O'Faoláin, a Critical Introduction*. Dublin: Wolfhound Press, 1984.

———. *Seán O'Faoláin: A Critical Introduction*. Notre Dame: University of Notre Dame Press, 1966.

Harner, James L. *Literary Research Guide: An Annotated Listing of Reference Sources in English Literary Studies*. 4th ed. New York: Modern Language Association of America, 2002.

Hayley, Barbara, and Edna McKay, eds. *300 Years of Irish Periodicals*. Dublin: Association of Irish Learned Journals, 1987.

Holzapfel, Rudi. *An Index of Contributors to "The Bell."* Dublin: Carraig Books, 1970.

Keeran, Peggy, and Jennifer Bowers. *Literary Research and the British Romantic Era: Strategies and Sources*. Literary Research: Strategies and Sources, no. 1. Lanham, MD: Scarecrow Press, 2005.

Madden, Richard Robert. *The History of the Irish Periodical*. 2 vols. New York: Johnson Reprint Corporation, 1968. Original edition published London: T. C. Newby, 1867.

Mann, Thomas. *The Oxford Guide to Library Research*. New York: Oxford University Press, 2005.

McMahon, Sean. *The Best from "The Bell."* Totowa, NJ: Rowman and Littlefield, 1979.

Munter, Robert. *The History of the Irish Newspaper, 1685–1760*. Cambridge, UK: Cambridge University Press, 1967.

Pierce, David, ed. *Irish Writing in the Twentieth Century: A Reader*. Cork, Ireland: Cork University Press, 2000.

Sher, Richard B. *The Enlightenment and the Book: Scottish Authors and Their Publishers in Eighteenth-Century Britain, Ireland, and America*. Chicago, IL: University of Chicago Press, 2006.

Sherbo, Arthur. "More Periodical Grubbings: Sean O'Faolain's Contributions to *The Bell*." *Notes and Queries*, 43, no. 1 (March 1996): 59–60.

Shovlin, Frank. *The Irish Literary Periodical, 1923–1958*. Oxford, UK: Oxford University Press, 2003.

Sweeney, Elizabeth, and Kathleen Williams. "Irish Studies Research Guides." Irish Studies Program, Boston College. 7 November 2007. http://www.bc.edu/centers/irish/studies/research.html.

Index

AACR2R (Anglo-American Cataloging
  Rules), 42
*ABEIJ (ABEI Journal: The Brazilian
  Journal of Irish Studies),* 88, 95
*ABEI Journal: The Brazilian Journal of
  Irish Studies. See ABEIJ*
*ABELL (Annual Bibliography of English
  Language and Literature),* 176;
  bibliographies relating to, 62–63, 65,
  68–71, *70,* 82; general literary
  reference resources relating to, 24;
  periodicals, newspapers, reviews
  relating to, 109; scholarly journals
  relating to, 86–87, 101, 106
academic journals, 85
Academic Search Premier, 64, 87
*Accessing English Literary Periodicals:
  A Guide to the Microfilm, Collection
  with Title, Subject, Editor, and Reel
  Number Indexes* (Puravs, Kavanagh,
  and Smith), 131, 132
*ACIS (American Conference for Irish
  Studies),* 168, 169
Ackerly, Chris, 38
ACTFL (American Council on the
  Teaching of Foreign Languages), 66
*Act of Union Virtual Library: A Digital
  Resource for the Act of Union of
  1800,* 131, 136

Adam Matthews, 127
Adams, Elsie Bonita, 81
*American Conference for Irish Studies.
  See ACIS*
American Council on the Teaching of
  Foreign Languages. *See ACTFL*
American Historical Association, 170
Anglo-American Cataloging Rules. *See*
  AACR2R
*Anglo-Irish Literature: A Bibliography
  of Dissertations* (O'Malley), 76, 77
*Anglo-Irish Literature: A Review of
  Research* (Finneran), 81
*An Annotated Bibliography of Modern
  Anglo-Irish Drama* (Mikhail), 76, 79
*Annual Bibliography of English
  Language and Literature. See ABELL*
Anthology of Irish Verse (Colum), 160,
  163
archival retrieval, best practices for,
  141–43
archives: electronic text, on Web,
  161–65; manuscripts and, xi, 139–56
Archives Ireland, 149, 154
ARCHON, 149, 152, 153, 170, 171
articles
articles, reviews and, finding of, 115–21
art resources: dictionaries,
  encyclopedias, and handbooks, 183;

204 *Index*

guides, 191; indexes and bibliographies, 192

Renascence Editions: An Online Repository of Works Printed in English Between the Years 1477 and 1799 (Bear), 161, 163

Repositories of Primary Sources, 149, 153

RES (Review of English Studies: A Quarterly Journal of English Literature and the English Language), 101, 105

research guides, xi, 21–24

research, Irish literary, xi

Research Library Group. *See* RLG

research methodology, xi

research question, written as topic sentence, 1–2

research resources: bibliographies, print and online, xi; contemporary and current reviews, xi; electronic texts, journals, and Web resources, xi; manuscripts and archives, xi; microfilm and digitization projects, xi; research guides, general, xi; scholarly journals, periodicals, and newspapers, xi; union library catalogs, xi

resources. *See* general literary reference resources; research resources; Web resources

resources, in related disciplines: art, 183–84; general, 182–83; historical atlases, 185; history, 185–88; music, 188–89; philosophy, 190–91; religion, 191–92; sciences and medicine, 192–93; social sciences, 193–94; theater, 194–95

Review of English Studies: A Quarterly Journal of English Literature and the English Language. See RES

reviews: annual, bibliographies, indexes, and, 61–84; contemporary and current, xi; periodicals, newspapers, and, 107–22. *See also* scholarly journals

Richards, Shaun, 28

Riders to the Sea (Synge), 165

RLG (Research Library Group), 53–54

Rolston, Bill, 172, 173

Rue des Beaux Arts, 168

Saenger, Erwin, 110

Samhain, 176

scholarly gateways, on Web, 158–61

scholarly journals, xi, 85–106; author specific journals, 97–100; general literature journals, 100–106; Irish literature journals, 88–97

The Scholarly Journal Archive. See JSTOR

Schrank, Bernice, 28

Schreibman, Susan, 159, 160

sciences and medicine resources: dictionaries, encyclopedias, and handbooks, 192; indexes and bibliographies, 193; sources and history, 193

Seamus Heaney: A Reference Guide (Durkan and Brandes), 62, 81, 83

Sean O'Faolain's Irish Vision (Bonaccorso), 175

search engines, database v., *16,* 16–17

searches. *See* library catalogs

searching online. *See* online searching

search strategies, creation of: Boolean searches, 6–8, *7–10,* 16–19; field searching, 5–6; limiting/modifying searches, 15–16; nesting, 10–11; phrase searching/proximity operators, 11–13; relevancy searching, 15; subject v. keyword searches, 13–15, 48; truncation/wildcards, 9–10

Select Bibliography for the Study of Anglo-Irish Literature and Its Background: An Irish Studies Handbook (Harmon), 76, 77–78

"Selective Index to 'A Supplement to Bernard Shaw: A Bibliography'" (Lawrence), 81

About the Author

Greg Matthews is a cataloging librarian at the Washington State University Libraries, where he has also been active in library instruction and reference programs and services. He earned a B.A. in English from Whitman College, an M.A. in English literature from the University of Idaho, and an M.L.S. from Indiana University, Bloomington. He regularly reviews critical studies and contemporary Irish and Welsh literary works for several scholarly and trade publications, and is a fan of the tenor banjo playing of The Dubliners' Barney McKenna and the late Tom "The Beast" MacManamon of Dingle Spike and The Popes.